# HOW to Program MICROSOFT JScript Scripting Interface

# HOW to Program MICROSOFT JScript Scripting Interface

MARK · STONE

Ziff-Davis Press
An imprint of Macmillan Computer Publishing USA
Emeryville, California

| | |
|---|---|
| Publisher | Stacy Hiquet |
| Acquisitions Editor | Simon Hayes |
| Development Editor | Kelly Green |
| Copy Editor | Mitzi Waltz |
| Technical Reviewer | Selim Tuvi |
| Project Coordinator | Edith Rex |
| Proofreader | Jeff Barash |
| Cover Illustration and Design | Megan Gandt |
| Book Design and Layout | Bruce Lundquist |
| Technical Illustration | Sarah Ishida |
| Indexer | Valerie Robbins |



Ziff-Davis Press imprint books are produced on a Macintosh computer system with the following applications: FrameMaker®, Microsoft® Word, QuarkXPress®, Adobe Illustrator®, Adobe Photoshop®, Adobe Streamline™, MacLink®Plus, Aldus® FreeHand™, Collage Plus™.

Ziff-Davis Press, an imprint of
Macmillan Computer Publishing USA
5903 Christie Avenue
Emeryville, CA 94608



PART OF A CONTINUING SERIES



ISBN 1-56276-484-5

Manufactured in the United States of America
10 9 8 7 6 5 4 3 2 1

**This book is dedicated to**

**Alexander**

# Table of Contents

# Acknowledgments

All of us who work with books have seen the rapid pace of change on the Internet push the engine of publishing to its limit. Writing a book on such a tight schedule, particularly on a new programming language, is not a task for the fainthearted. Completing this project has only been possible because of the tremendous support I have received.

Only my family can really say if it has all been worth it, for they are the ones who have suffered the most during this process. I also want to thank Mitzi Waltz and Selim Tuvi, who have done their best to catch my hurried mistakes. Any errors that remain are of course mine alone. Finally, I want to thank two people at Ziff-Davis Press without whom this project would not have been possible. Simon Hayes talked me into all this in the first place and then vigorously championed this project through all adversity. Kelly Green has shepherded this book through every obstacle with grace and humor; no author could ask for a better editor to lend a guiding hand.

# Introduction

Once in a great while a change in technology occurs that truly empowers people. The gates are thrown open on what had been the domain of a few technical specialists. The PC revolution brought one such change, giving ordinary people unprecedented computing power on their desktops. The advent of the World Wide Web revolutionizes the PC industry further. New occupations have emerged; suddenly the Internet is populated not just with computer scientists and academics, but with content providers and Web developers, people who are bringing news, information, and even art to the networked PC.

Content providers don't necessarily have a strong computing background. They know HTML and computer graphics, but often their programming experience is limited to implementing a few simple CGI packages. Content providers and Web developers need an alternative to learning a full-blown language like Java or C in order to bring interactivity to the Web.

Client-side scripting languages provide an alternative. While scripting languages are a bit more complex than HTML, anyone comfortable with HTML and a few basic programming concepts should be able to master a scripting language. Indeed, many of the elements of a scripting language will look like familiar HTML components in a new guise.

Until now, content providers have had two choices: JavaScript, a client-side implementation that runs on Netscape Navigator as the client; or Visual Basic Scripting Edition (VBScript), a client-side implementation intended to run with the new release of Microsoft's Internet Explorer (3.0). Content providers are understandably reluctant to develop content that is platform-specific.

Now Microsoft has introduced a third alternative: JScript. JScript is an open implementation of JavaScript incorporated into the new version of Internet Explorer. Because JScript is an implementation of JavaScript, Explorer works with JavaScript pages, and a JavaScript-capable browser can work with JScript pages. Because Microsoft has chosen to make JScript an open implementation, it can be freely licensed and the source code is available.

JScript promises the best of both worlds: an implementation of JavaScript in the familiar environs of the Microsoft Windows desktop.

## JScript and Navigating the Web with Internet Explorer

For many of us the Web has become so quickly integrated into our lives that it's hard to imagine what we did without it, or to remember that the Web as a popular medium has only been around for a couple of years. JScript arrives as one of many advances that promises to make the Web a much more dynamic, exciting, and useful place in the future. If you are browsing the Web you will notice more pages that come alive rather than simply serving as flat document displays; you will notice faster response times to your interaction with objects on Web pages; and you will notice more features appearing on Web pages. If you develop content for the Web, you will find that JScript puts a powerful new tool in your hands for creating content.

Getting the most out of JScript assumes some background on your part. You should have some familiarity with both navigating the Web and publishing on the Web. You should have some familiarity with the Windows 95 operating system. You should have some familiarity with Internet Explorer as a Web browser.

### Web Basics

The Internet has been transformed from a medium that allows us to transport documents, using services like e-mail and FTP, to one that allows us to view, and, to some extent, interact with documents. The new protocol that makes this all possible is HTTP, the Hypertext Transfer Protocol. HTTP allows a Web server to be added to the suite of services an Internet host can provide (the *transfer* part of the protocol), and allows documents served to have links to other documents embedded within them (the *hypertext* part of the protocol).

HTTP is only one innovation that makes the Web possible. HTML, the Hypertext Markup Language, is the glue that holds hyperlinked documents together. This formatting language provides the design elements that determine how a Web document looks within a Web browser, and provides the address links that tell a browser where to ask for other documents and images.

We assume here that you are familiar with the addressing scheme used on the World Wide Web, and understand the function of links that tie documents together. We assume also that you are comfortable enough with HTML to have put a few HTML documents on the Web, even if nothing more than a home page.

## Windows 95

The Internet is becoming a medium in which not only documents but applications may be distributed across the network. JScript is one of a new family of tools that make distributed applications possible, and Windows 95 is the first PC operating system that attempts to have the needed level of network awareness built right into it.

JavaScript—and hence any JScript program you write—will run on Netscape Navigator 2.0 or higher. Navigator is supported on a range of operating systems: Windows 3.1, Unix, MacOS. Internet Explorer 3.0 should be available on other operating systems by the end of 1996, most likely Windows 3.1 and Unix. This book, however, will focus on Windows 95.

Windows 95 differs dramatically from Window 3.1. This is a true graphical user interface, supporting icons as well as the familiar program group windows. These icons can represent not just applications, but shortcuts that launch particular documents within those applications. The desktop is drag and drop, allowing you to move icons and windows around to customize appearance. The desktop includes a taskbar that can be customized, and which updates automatically to reflect session activity.

While the Windows 95 interface is a refreshing improvement, the most important enhancements are under the hood. Now a 32-bit operating system, Windows 95 supports multitasking. In a network environment, this enables features like downloading files in the background while you work within other applications.

Network capability is now fundamental to Windows 95. Peer to peer networking and enabling file and application sharing between Windows 95 computers are both built-in. A TCP/IP stack is also built-in, eliminating the need to install and configure a separate Winsock just to use network applications. E-mail, telnet, and FTP are all standard applications. We assume here that you know how to use these under Windows 95, and that you have been able to successfully establish your Internet connection with Windows 95.

In the long run Windows 95's most exciting feature may be the support for ActiveX, enabling applications that can serve as ActiveX hosts to be installed. ActiveX technology brings network awareness to applications, not just the operating system. Internet Explorer 3.0 is an ActiveX host.

## Internet Explorer

With the release of Internet Explorer 3.0 Microsoft now offers a Web browser competitive with any other. At first glance Internet Explorer 3.0 looks similar to 2.0. The buttons and menus will look familiar to anyone who has used a graphical

Web browser from Mosaic to Netscape. Explorer does include some helpful enhancements. Explorer has its own list of bookmarks you can build, called favorites, but it also allows the easy integration of bookmarks from other browsers under "Imported Bookmarks." Explorer's own bookmarks are stored as files within a folder, rather than one unwieldy file. This enables you to make a shortcut out of any bookmark, and drag it to wherever would be useful on the desktop. Explorer's toolbars can be resized simply by dragging, rather than using menu options.

The real changes to the new Internet Explorer begin when you load Web pages. Explorer supports all of the latest HTML features, such as frames, and has improved support for recent HTML features such as tables. Most importantly for our purposes, Explorer supports Microsoft's implementation of JavaScript: JScript. Internet Explorer will be your primary program development platform as you learn JScript. You should be completely familiar with how to use it.

## Who Should Read this Book

The excitement surrounding the World Wide Web has drawn an unprecedented number of people to contribute to this new medium. From an individual posting a simple home page to a Webmaster for a small business putting up its virtual storefront to a member of a design team for a large commercial site, the Web is now populated by people who are comfortable with new technology but don't necessarily have a strong computer background.

Indeed a computer background is no longer enough. A dazzling Web site that will draw visitors to it again and again requires the design skills of a production editor and the choreography skills of a movie director. So the denizens of the Web really fall into two groups: those who provide content for Web sites and those who provide maintenance for Web sites.

If you have strong views about the relative merits of C and C++, or if the sight of a Unix shell prompt fills you with a deep sense of contentment, then you may well have the talent to be a system administrator, but this book probably is not for you.

If, on the other hand, you want to know how to harness JScript to improve the design of your Web pages, then read on. This book assumes that whatever programming experience you have is largely self taught. While not intended as a full introduction to the art of programming, the material presented here should be sufficient to get you up and running with a few simple JScript programs.

Those of you who have run up against the limits of what a Web site host can offer will also benefit from this book. If your system administrator, either because of security concerns or server load concerns, will not give you access to a CGI directory in which to run executable programs, then JScript gives you an alternative to add interactivity to your Web pages. Even on a site where you can run executables, you may find your server straining under its load. JScript provides a means of pushing some of that processing load onto the client side, freeing up your server to handle more visitors.

Those already familiar with JavaScript will see the language in a new light after reading this book. Microsoft has a history of bringing the power of programming to the nonprogrammer, with languages like Visual Basic and an impressive array of software development tools designed to make the task of coding invisible to the developer. Microsoft has a unique vision of the future of Web applications, and offers some unique tools to make this vision a reality.

In the Internet's rapidly changing world of distributed computing, the distinction between a Web site and an application is not always clear. This distinction will blur further in the future. Today's Web designers may find themselves being called tomorrow's software developers.

Tomorrow's developers will only be limited by the design and layout controls to which they have access. HTML provides a useful but limited range of such controls: input boxes, radio buttons, check boxes, the familiar elements of an HTML form. Computer users are familiar with a much broader range of controls from the applications they have run on Microsoft Windows desktop applications. These are the controls shared by popular applications like Word, Excel, and Access. In other words, these are the controls made possible by OLE objects.

With Internet Explorer 3.0 Microsoft holds out the prospect of bringing OLE (Object Linking and Embedding) to the Internet with its ActiveX technology. ActiveX is the glue that makes object sharing possible, so that whether we are talking about OLE objects, Java objects, or object libraries yet to be developed by independent software vendors, all in principle can be accessible through any application that acts as an ActiveX host.

Internet Explorer is one of the first applications to act as an ActiveX host. Thus the scripting languages it supports, VBScript and JScript, have the potential to access a broad and open-ended range of ActiveX controls. Nor is this potential limited to the Web. In theory JScript can serve as an interface to customize not just the behavior of Internet Explorer, but any standalone application that utilizes ActiveX technology.

While this technology is in its infancy now, the potential is enormous. Those who can tap into that potential today will be empowered to bring us the Web sites and applications that will dazzle us tomorrow.

## Conventions Used in this Book

JScript is a true object-oriented language. This object structure makes JScript programs powerful and portable for a simple scripting language. However, JScript's object hierarchy can be a little bewildering to the beginner. The following conventions are used to help clarify the program listings.

Program listings and HTML listings are set off from the rest of the text like this:

```
<A HREF="mypage.htm">Home</A>
if (a == b ) { a++ }
```

Some elements of JScript are *objects*. Objects in a listing will be listed in blue, as with the location object here:

```
location = "mypage.htm";
```

Objects in JScript typically have *properties*. Properties of an object will be listed in green, as with the value property of the document object here:

```
val = document.value;
```

Objects in JScript typically have *methods* that apply to them as well. Methods of an object will be listed in red, as with the open() method of the window object here:

```
if (a == true) then { window.open() }
```

Various means of user interaction with a Web page are referred to as *events*, and the functions in JScript that are triggered by those events are referred to as event handlers. Events and event handlers will be listed in magenta, as with the processForm function here:

```
<INPUT TYPE="BUTTON" VALUE="SUBMIT" onClick="processForm()">
```

These classifications are not completely rigid. How an element of a JScript program gets classified depends on context. An element that is a property in one context, for example, might be treated as an object in another context, or something that is merely a variable at one point in a program might have an object assigned to it as the value of the variable. So as you view the color coding in the program listings, keep in mind that these are not based on rigid rules, but based on an interpretation of how elements are being used in that context.

## JScript Resources

The starting point for JScript resources is the Microsoft Web site. The latest version of Internet Explorer can always be found at http://www.microsoft.com/ie. JScript will require either Netscape Navigator 2.0 or higher, or Internet Explorer 3.0 or higher. Information on JScript itself can be found at the Microsoft Web site at http://www.microsoft.com/jscript. Other useful resources from Microsoft can be found by looking for information on ActiveX. A list of ActiveX resources is included in Appendix C.

Apart from Microsoft, another fine source of information is the comp.lang.javascript newsgroup. This is always a lively discussion group, fielding queries on both JavaScript and JScript. A lot of experienced scripters—and several authors—frequent this newsgroup, and are generally helpful to those just starting out.

The CD-ROM included with this book contains a copy of Internet Explorer 3.0, all of the scripts discussed in this book, and other useful tools and documentation. The book also has a Web site at http://www.kudonet.com/~markst/jscript, which will include live versions of all the scripts, including any current bug fixes.

## Recent Developments

As this book goes to press Microsoft has just released Internet Explorer 3.0 in beta for Windows 3.1. This can be downloaded from the Microsoft Web site at http://www.microsoft.com, or from one of the mirror sites listed there.

This beta release allows both VBScript and JScript to run under Windows 3.1. Since the majority of Windows machines are still running Windows 3.1 rather than Windows 95 or Windows NT, this release broadens the appeal of JScript tremendously. Apart from the Macintosh and UNIX markets, JScript will now run on all the platforms that support JavaScript. Microsoft has promised a UNIX version of Internet Explorer in the next few months.

Internet Explorer 3.0 for Windows 3.1 is not identical to Internet Explorer 3.0 for Windows 95/NT. Microsoft appears to have used a very different development path to create this version. For Windows 95/NT, Internet Explorer is built out of ActiveX technology (see Chapter 2). This means that the object model for the browser uses objects that are ActiveX controls, and that those objects we think of as HTML elements are just a special case of the broader set of ActiveX controls. However, ActiveX is a 32-bit technology that cannot easily be ported to a 16-bit operating system such as Windows 3.1. Therefore the implementation of Internet Explorer 3.0 for Windows 3.1 does not use ActiveX technology.

This means that in the beta testing period there are likely to be a few commands in JScript that behave differently under Windows 3.1 than they do under Windows 95/NT. More importantly, it means that there is no support for ActiveX controls. Thus the script developed in Chapter 12 will not be fully functional under Windows 3.1.

Still the implementation of Internet Explorer 3.0 in Windows 3.1 is an important addition to the JScript market. With care you can develop scripts that will work equally well under Internet Explorer 3.0 or Netscape Navigator, and equally under Windows 3.1, Windows 95, or Windows NT. Among client side scripting languages, only JScript opens the door to such a large share of the Web browser market.

HTML Standards and Browser Competition

JScript or JavaScript?

What Is Client-Side Scripting?

Scripting Limitations

# Chapter 1
# Client-Side Scripting

Active content has become the holy grail of World Wide Web development. Today's Web demands pages that update in real time, pages that interact, pages that make the Web experience dynamic. The content developers who have mastered HTML must update their skills or face obsolescence. Yet Web developers also want tools for bringing active content to their sites, tools that do not require a programmer's expertise to master.

Scripting languages provide a tool that is more sophisticated than simple HTML, but not as demanding as a full programming language. While a script must be programmed, writing a script is a natural extension of writing HTML. With Netscape's JavaScript and now with Microsoft's JScript, active content is within the grasp of anyone who can master HTML.

What is JScript? What is JavaScript? Are they the same, or are they different? To understand the answer, we must look back into the dim reaches of Internet antiquity. For those of you not used to measuring time in the online world, antiquity would be about three years ago.

On Saturday, January 23, 1993 Netscape cofounder Marc Andreessen posted a message to the WWW-Talk mailing list with the subject line "NCSA X Mosaic 0.5 released." This message announced the first release of a new UNIX-based browser for the World Wide Web, a region of the Internet that very few people outside of the WWW-Talk mailing group had heard of at that time. Tim Berners-Lee, the architect of the World Wide Web, gave an immediate and enthusiastic response, calling Andreessen's program "brilliant." If anything, that response has proved to be an understatement. Mosaic was only one of several browser projects under development at the time; no one in the mailing group could see just how completely it would revolutionize the Web. About a month later, Andreessen posted another message to the group, with the innocuous subject line, "proposed new tag: IMG." In the body of the message, he said "I'd like to propose a new, optional HTML tag: IMG. Required argument is SRC='url'. This names a bitmap or pixmap file for the browser to attempt to pull over the network and interpret as an image, to be embedded in the text at the point of the tag's occurrence."

This was not a new idea—everyone wanted to bring multimedia capabilities to the Web, although they had not yet agreed how to do this. The real bombshell in Andreessen's message was an aside about inline images toward the end: "This is required functionality for X Mosaic; we have this working, and we'll at least be using it internally."

In other words, Mosaic already had graphical capability: the question was, would others follow along? The rest, as they say, is history. Andreessen left the NCSA to help Jim Clark found Netscape, and pioneered the Web browser we know today as Navigator.

Yet Andreessen's stunning achievement already contains a hint of controversy to come. He did not propose the IMG tag, and then wait for agreement from the group on how to implement it. Indeed, several members of the group had serious reservations about his suggestion. Instead he implemented the tag first, and then proposed it. This impatience with standards has become a hallmark of Netscape (and Web) development. The evolution of the Web exhibits constant tension between the need for rapid development and the need to develop to an open standard.

## HTML Standards and Browser Competition

The Internet grows exponentially. Not only is the population exploding, but its composition has changed dramatically. When Andreessen posted his first Mosaic announcement early in 1993, commercial activity on the Internet was almost nonexistent. The most common way to connect to the Internet was through a university account. The Internet backbone was maintained by the National Science Foundation (NSF). Contrast this with the Internet of today, where the number of host computers with .com extensions exceeds the number with .edu extensions, where dial-up PPP accounts are common, and where NSF has handed over curatorship of the backbone to six telecommunications companies.

Standards bodies like the Internet Engineering Task Force (IETF) established their procedures in the earlier environment. While they have tried to adjust to the sudden changes in size and composition of the Internet, the results have been mixed. This is understandable, as the process is akin to trying to surf a tidal wave.

The response of companies like Netscape is understandable as well. They have an urgent commercial need to respond to the rapid changes, a need that cannot wait for standards bodies to catch up. The result, however, has been considerable confusion for Web users, and some hard choices for Web designers.

The Web most people are familiar with has gone through three evolutions in HTML standards: HTML 2.0, HTML 3.0 (referred to at one time as HTML+), and HTML 3.2. HTML 3.0 was never an adopted standard; it was a draft standard from March to September of 1995, but was never officially revised after that. The May 1996 release of the HTML 3.2 draft provides the first concrete step toward standardization in over a year. Standards committees should pick up the pace from here; look for an HTML 3.3 draft by early 1997.

In the midst of this confusion, browser technology has forged ahead. Netscape, with its control of about 70 percent of the browser market, has assumed that its choices will become the de facto standard. Let's review some of the highlights of these changes:

- **HTML 2.0**: Compared to the slick pages of today, pages written to this standard seem crude: gray backgrounds, blue borders around every clickable image, and no text flow around images.
- **HTML 3.0**: Many Web designers jumped ship from strict adherence to standards when Netscape began supporting a number of extensions, often called "Netscapisms," that were not a part of the HTML standard. These included background colors and images, tables, customizations for fonts and horizontal rules, and added elements for format control like the <CENTER> tag and the ALIGN attribute. The Web saw a proliferation of warnings on Web pages such as "These pages best viewed with Netscape." It's actually a bit of a Web myth that Netscape started all of this. Tables, for example, were first supported by Mosaic.
- **HTML 3.2**: Most of the major features introduced during the 3.0 period are now part of the 3.2 draft. Some notable additions include tags to enable client-side processing of image maps, and the <APPLET> tag to enable Java applets to run.

Notably absent from 3.2 are frames and client-side scripts. While the controversy over the ideal behavior for frames is likely to continue for some time, look for style sheets and client-side scripting to be included in the next draft standard.

Microsoft has found itself in the unusual position of playing catch-up. When Windows 95 went into beta testing, the World Wide Web revolution had not yet gripped the Internet. Then suddenly, in the midst of preparations for the official launch of Windows 95, Microsoft had to devise a plan to develop and market a browser for the Web. To their credit, the folks at Microsoft rose to the challenge. They did release a serviceable browser in 1995, although it lagged behind

Navigator in features. They also adapted to the open, nonproprietary nature of the Internet and made their browser freely available.

The release of Internet Explorer 2.0 in spring of 1996 represented a major step forward for Microsoft's browser. Many of the HTML 3.0 features were supported, including background colors and images, and tables. Still, Internet Explorer 2.0 lagged behind Navigator 2.0 in features; Explorer lacked support for frames, Java applets, and JavaScript, all features Navigator supported.

With the release of Internet Explorer 3.0, Microsoft now has a top-of-the-line Web browser. Explorer supports the HTML 3.2 draft. Explorer supports Netscape-specific tags. Explorer supports Java applets and supports JavaScript through its JScript implementation. In some areas Explorer's capabilities exceed those of Navigator. As of this writing Explorer is the only browser besides Arena to support style sheets and is the only browser to directly support ActiveX controls and VBScript. ActiveX and its scripting interfaces, VBScript and JScript, form the heart of Microsoft's whole desktop programming strategy, not just its Internet strategy. We'll look more at ActiveX in the next chapter.

Microsoft has also taken the approach of encouraging standards, rather than setting them. Internet Explorer is freely available, not just for 30 days, and not just for evaluation or educational use only. JScript, including source code, can be freely licensed from Microsoft. Management of ActiveX will be handed over from Microsoft to an independent standards body.

## JScript or JavaScript?

The dizzying changes of the last two years reveal several trends. First, Web designers have more and more tools at their disposal to control the content of Web pages. From formatting text and graphics to including sound and animation, to enabling user interaction, Web pages today have become documents with a much richer texture than the pages of a couple of years ago, and the overall appearance of this complex presentation can be more tightly controlled.

Second, as the capabilities of browsers expand, more of an effort has been made to push processing from the server to the browser. Client-side image maps and client-side scripting languages have also helped the Web better fit the strictures of the client-server computing model.

Finally, and most importantly, we are seeing a real contest shape up for the future of operating system technology. Browsers now have greater power to process and display a richer variety of information. Browsers can handle an array of network protocols, and our conception of the PC has changed from desktop machine to network machine. As operating systems adapt to these changes, the Web browser stands as the single most important application to which the operating system must adapt.

Netscape seems to envision its browser as a sort of network operating system. Navigator can handle e-mail, Usenet newsgroups, Telnet, and downloading files. Internet telephony and conferencing are enhancements that can be added to Navigator. In general Navigator's plug-in facility allows it to launch applications to handle file types that it cannot handle natively. The trend is to make the browser the one application that orchestrates your use of all the others, so that other applications need not be network-aware: in short, to conceive of the browser as a network operating system.

Although Internet Explorer has essentially the same capabilities as Netscape Navigator, Microsoft's approach is different. Internet Explorer is only one facet of an evolving network strategy. Microsoft aims to make all of its popular desktop applications, such as Word and Excel, "network-aware" so that documents may be linked and embedded across a network much as they can be on the desktop now. The result will be not so much a network operating system as an operating system that makes the network transparent to the user.

We can see hints of this in Windows 95 already. "My Network Neighborhood," for example, is just another node on the Windows 95 file system. As another example, you can take a URL saved under Internet Explorer's list of Favorite Places and make a shortcut out of it by dragging the icon to the desktop or a folder. Clicking on the icon will launch Internet Explorer and load that URL (see Figure 1.1). Loading a Web page becomes as easy as loading a Word document.

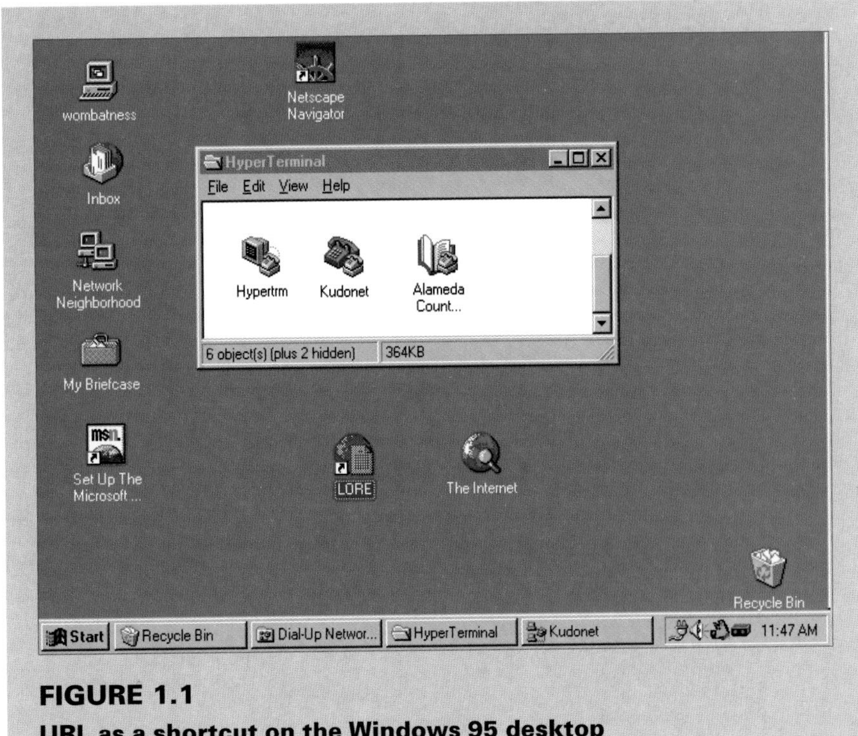


**FIGURE 1.1**
**URL as a shortcut on the Windows 95 desktop**

These enhancements will be extended as Microsoft moves forward with the project code-named Nashville.

The key technology that makes it all possible is ActiveX, Microsoft's extension of OLE (Object Linking and Embedding.) We will look at ActiveX more closely in the next chapter. The point here is that an application can be made network-aware by making that application an ActiveX host. Internet Explorer is an ActiveX host, but it need not be the only ActiveX host on the desktop.

As browsers become more complex, and as their integration into the operating system becomes more complete, Web-page development threatens to become dramatically more difficult. Everyone has heard, for example, of the capabilities the Java programming language brings to the Web. Java can put animation on Web pages, Java can put real-time updates on Web pages, Java allows executable content to be downloaded. Yet Java pages on the Web are few and far between. Java, after all, is a full object-oriented programming language, and the cost of mastering both the Web and object-oriented programming is just too high for the average developer, and particularly for the unpaid developers who have created so much of today's Web environment.

What's needed is a simpler language, one in which program length can be measured in dozens of lines, not thousands—one that, while object-oriented, grounds its objects in the familiar Web-page objects of HTML. Netscape introduced just such a simplified scripting language, called JavaScript, and included it with the release of Navigator 2.0.

Netscape kept JavaScript proprietary. They did not release the source code, and indeed JavaScript is a registered Netscape trademark. Microsoft has continued its open-standards Internet strategy by creating JScript, an open implementation of JavaScript, and making it freely available with source code.

As a Web designer you face a tough choice: should you program using JavaScript or JScript? At one level, the obvious answer is both: after all, JScript is just an implementation of JavaScript; programming one is the same as programming the other. But at a more conceptual level, there is a choice to be made here. Netscape's vision of the future differs considerably from Microsoft's, and design decisions you make today could be affected by which vision is realized on the Internet of tomorrow.

For example, an ActiveX host has a programmable interface of ActiveX controls. While in theory any programming language could be used to manipulate these controls, VBScript and JScript are designed specifically to provide a simple, though limited, means of programming ActiveX controls. When you write a JScript program that runs in Internet Explorer, you may not see yourself as an ActiveX programmer, but you are.

Thus while JavaScript is limited to the confines of a Web browser, JScript will broaden its range as the range of ActiveX applications broadens. JScript can even be used to write standalone desktop applications. The Web designer really can evolve into an applications developer using Web design tools already available.

## What Is Client-Side Scripting?

Programming languages can be divided into two general categories: compiled languages and interpreted languages. For any program to run, it must be translated into the sequences of 0's and 1's, the bytes, that the computer understands as instructions. Compiled and interpreted languages differ in how they perform this translation.

A compiled program is translated in its entirety in one step; the program cannot be executed until it has been compiled. The program in its original form, intelligible to humans, is called the source code. The program in its binary form, intelligible only to your computer, is called the executable. That's what all those .exe files on your hard drive are: compiled binary executables.

An interpreted program is translated one line at a time, and no translation occurs until the program is actually run. No separate executable file is ever generated; your computer decides how to run each instruction on the fly.

Programming in a compiled language is an involved process. You must have a separate program—the compiler—on your computer to do the translation. The program will fail to compile if your source code has any syntax errors in it. Thus you must go through a preliminary debugging stage just to get the program to compile. This debugging stage can be difficult. You have no output to look at to tell you how far the program got, only line numbers and error messages. Once the program compiles successfully, you must run it to see if it behaves as expected. At this stage, the real debugging challenge begins. The file you are running is now in binary; you can't just examine it to find a problem. You must be able to track breakdowns back to the original source code. This is often an insurmountable task without additional tools like debuggers and tracers. Once a problem is identified and source code changed, the whole program must be recompiled and rerun to see if the change really solves the problem.

Programming in an interpreted language is much easier. Because the computer translates and executes each line one at a time, it is much easier to identify where a problem arises. Changes and possible solutions can also be tested much more quickly, because there is no extra step of compiling to binary. Change the source code, and you can rerun the program immediately.

Why, then, would anyone go to the trouble of working with a compiled language? Because compiling is a much more efficient translation process. An interpreter is blind to the future; because it handles lines one at a time, it has no way of knowing that a particular command or sequence of commands will be used repeatedly, and thus must do a completely new translation each time. A compiler, on the other hand, looks at the entire program before performing any translation and thus can identify code fragments that, though used repeatedly, need to be translated and stored only once. The resulting binary takes up less disk space and uses less RAM when running. Compiled programs easily run 10 to 100 times faster than equivalent interpreted programs.

Thus, for applications where speed and processing power are essential, only a compiled language will do. If rapid development time is vital and the speed requirements of the final program are not an issue, then an interpreted language offers the best choice.

You should be aware that the programming community constantly struggles to find a middle ground between these two extremes. As a result, there are languages that fit neither of these models. Java, for example, is a compiled language, but not a pure compiled language. Rather than compiling all the way to binary, it compiles into something called *byte code*. Byte code is not quite as fast, but it is much more portable, enabling the same Java program to run on a Mac, PC, or UNIX machine. TCL, to use a different example, is an interpreted language, but it is also an embeddable language. This means that a TCL program can be included in the source code of, say, a C program, and the whole can be compiled. The TCL code will still only run at interpreted speed, but if the processing-intensive portions of the program are written in C, the result will still be reasonably fast and often easier to program and debug.

Scripting languages like JScript are interpreted languages. JScript is intended to enhance the control you have over the design and look of your Web pages. JScript is also intended to add a degree of interactivity to those Web pages without relying on the usual server-side mechanism, the Common Gateway Interface (CGI). Because the entire JScript program is downloaded to the browser as part of a Web page, a JScript program must be kept brief enough to download within a reasonably short period of time. For these goals, and within these constraints, there is no need for a compiled language.

JScript is not just an interpreted language, it is an *object-oriented* language. Rather than following a linear structure, JScript is event-driven. User interaction with objects initiates the events that drive program actions. While the object-oriented approach can seem like a large hurdle to cross to learn a programming language, JScript has a small object set, and these objects are just the familiar objects of an HTML page: text windows, radio buttons, checkboxes, frames, and the like.

JScript is really nothing more than a tool for turning an HTML page from a formattable document into a programmable document. Instead of just using HTML tags to tell a browser how to lay out HTML objects, you can use JScript to program the behavior of those objects. For the Web designer, JScript should feel like a natural extension of the Web development you are already doing with HTML.

Because JScript is a simple language, and its object orientation mirrors the objects of HTML, it offers an easy introduction to object-oriented programming. Because it is an interpreted language, it should be relatively easy to develop and debug programs. Because it runs within a Web browser, you can use JScript to really make your Web pages come alive.

## Scripting Limitations

Any time that you add a new executable program to your computer system you face a security risk. Running a new program can reveal problems ranging from mismanagement of RAM to alteration of files, causing anything from a system crash to a loss of data on your hard drive.

When we decide to purchase or download a piece of software, we are making a conscious decision, and part of that decision is based on the trustworthiness of the software source. Client-side executable content downloaded as part of a Web document constitutes an entirely different situation. These programs are specifically designed to be transparent to the user. Thus the user may not see an immediate difference between a document of simple HTML, one containing Java applets, one containing VBScript, and one containing JScript.

A client-side scripting language like JScript raises serious security questions. Client-side security on the Web can be improved in two general ways; Microsoft uses both approaches to some extent. On the one hand, a program source can be certified. This would mean that verifiable information is passed to your computer about the author and/or source of the program. Your computer could be configured to prompt you before accepting a new program, or to accept new programs automatically only from certain sources. ActiveX controls, which we will learn more about in the next chapter, use this approach to security.

Alternatively, a program's capabilities can be limited. JScript uses this approach to security. JScript cannot read files from your hard drive. JScript cannot create or alter files on your hard drive. Any information contained in a JScript program will be lost the moment you leave behind the document containing the program and load a different document. JScript is a programming language with no storage capabilities.

This places some significant limitations on JScript's capabilities. JScript cannot be a complete solution to orchestrating every interactive element you might want to add to your Web pages. JScript will excel at certain tasks, such as customizing a user's view of information or performing small database queries. Other tasks, such as adding to or modifying a database, JScript alone cannot do. It will have to be used in conjunction with other approaches to interactivity, like CGI.

Still, JScript has a lot of power. As we will see in later chapters, it can dramatically enhance your Web pages. JScript has a bright future, and much of that future, both on the Web and in other contexts, will depend on Microsoft's ActiveX technology.

OLE

From OLE to ActiveX

ActiveX on the Web

Scripting for ActiveX

# Chapter 2
# ActiveX

Developing a major new operating system release like Windows 95 takes years. When the people at Microsoft began working on Windows 95, they knew that providing a platform that could enable Microsoft to compete in the online marketplace would be vital. However, the online world looked very different then. Even as late as the beta-testing period for Windows 95—a point when the operating system's basic functionality could not be significantly changed—online commerce did not yet mean the Internet and the World Wide Web.

As 1994 drew to a close, Microsoft's chief competition appeared to be Compuserve and America Online. Microsoft planned to compete by founding its own commercial online service: MSN, the Microsoft Network. Microsoft's strategy at the time was considered to be so perfectly in tune with trends in the online market that other online services, led by America Online, threatened legal action to block the release of Windows 95 because it would include an automatic startup icon for MSN right on the Windows 95 desktop. News stories were filled with speculation about which magazines and newspapers might become content providers for MSN, and who might defect from Compuserve and America Online.

With hindsight, all of this seems a little comical. Even a few months into 1995, it became obvious that Microsoft had made a serious strategic miscalculation. All the talk, all the hype, was not about the forthcoming release of Windows 95, but about the Internet. Commercial interest in the online world was not focused on Compuserve, America Online, and the forthcoming Microsoft Network, but instead focused on the World Wide Web. As if from nowhere a new medium had been born, and most in the computer industry, including Microsoft, were taken by surprise.

The great irony of this turn of events is that Microsoft, as much as any company in the world, had the technology and the resources already in place to capitalize on the World Wide Web. That technology was called *OLE* (Object Linking and Embedding.)

# OLE

Imagine that two years ago you were working with a technology that let you link documents together, that would let you embed one file within another for display; including graphics; and that would let you enter changes or input to one file from within another. The technology just described is not the HTTP protocol that is the basis for the World Wide Web, but Microsoft's OLE.

Most Windows applications have a similar look and feel. They use buttons in the same way, their scrollbars function in the same way, the mouse operates in the same way. Many of these similarities occur because these different applications use the same programming code. To facilitate reusable code, Microsoft has developed a standard called the Common Object Model (COM.) COM provides a specification for developing a module of code that has these characteristics:

- **It is self-contained**. The code is a binary module that will run on its own when called by another program, and will also terminate itself and remove itself from active memory when no longer needed.
- **It is uniformly accessible**. The code presents a standard set of interfaces, enabling other programs to pass input to and receive output from the module without having to know how the module actually works.
- **It is updatable**. The code presents a different interface for each version of the module, enabling programs that require an older version to simply link to the associated interface.

Thus COM provides the blueprint for making program building blocks. These building blocks are called *objects*. They can be combined and integrated into larger modules, or objects. It is the portability and reusability of objects that allows such a variety of programming resources to be utilized in the same way within different Windows applications.

This glimpse at COM shows us several features we will see echoed in JScript. JScript also employs the idea of making programs modular, so that they can be used in a variety of circumstances. JScript, too, is object-oriented; this means, in part, that objects can be arranged hierarchically, with one object containing other objects.

Component objects can be built up into more complex objects until they form recognizable application elements on screen. These elements are called *OLE controls*. An OLE control is an object built on a hierarchy of objects, hence the *O* in *OLE*. Because OLE controls are all built to the COM standard, one OLE control can easily send input to and receive output from another OLE control (see Figure 2.1.)

This is the feature that allows an Excel spreadsheet to be embedded in a Word document, for example, and that enables the two to be linked in such a way that updates to the spreadsheet are reflected in the Word document—hence the *L* and *E* in *OLE*.

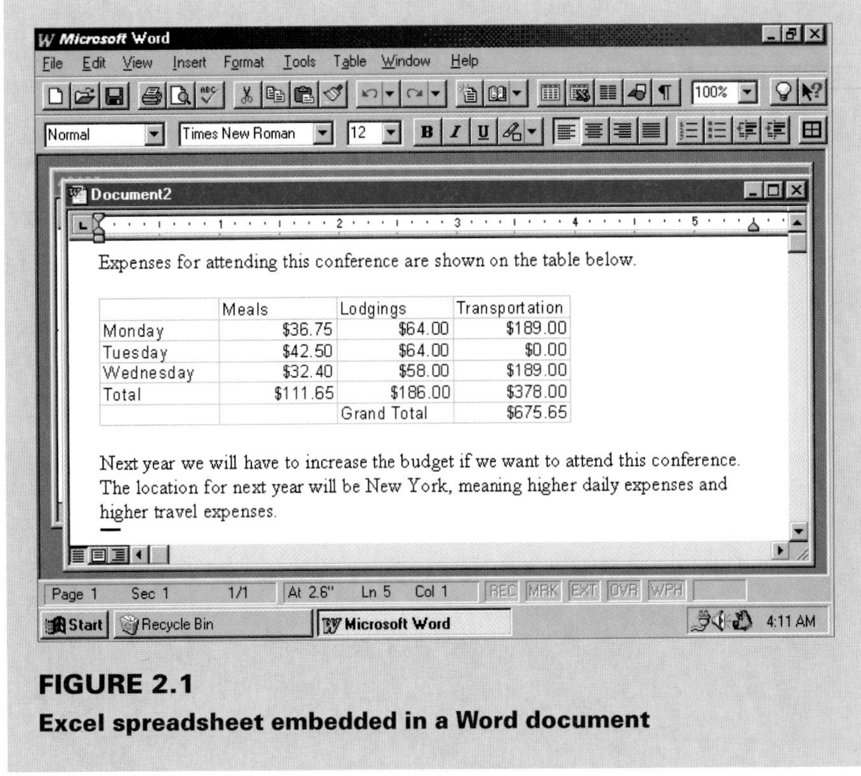


**FIGURE 2.1**
**Excel spreadsheet embedded in a Word document**

What OLE makes possible on the desktop is a suite of files and applications that have most of the raw ingredients we associate with HTML and the World Wide Web. Microsoft Help is an excellent example of a document delivered in hypertext style, and it predates HTML. OLE documents communicate with each other and link to each other easily. Furthermore, this technology is not entirely desktop-bound. On a local-area network, a document on one desktop machine could be linked to a file on the network file server.

Leading up to the release of Windows 95 in August of 1995, what OLE lacked was true network awareness. Yet network capabilities are an inherent part of the Windows 95 operating system. Peer-to-peer networking can easily be established between two Windows 95 machines. No separate winsock utility need be installed, because a TCP/IP stack is built into Windows 95. In other words, all the ingredients were in place to extend OLE controls to work with other OLE controls not just anywhere on the desktop, but anywhere on a network, even anywhere on the Internet.

This latest extension of OLE technology is *ActiveX*.

## From OLE to ActiveX

Internet Explorer 3.0 was released less than 18 months after the point when Microsoft's entire announced online strategy was the Microsoft Network, and nine months after Bill Gates called a press conference to present his vision of Microsoft's Internet strategy. The speed with which Microsoft has changed strategies and released products to support its new strategy has stunned the computer industry. Microsoft's Internet Information Server (IIS) is competitive with any Web server running on Windows NT. Internet Explorer is a state-of-the-art browser for Windows NT and Windows 95. Enterprises once destined as content for MSN have been reborn as Web publications like www.slate.com. Microsoft is an active member of the W3 Consortium panel that sets new standards for HTML. Suddenly Microsoft stands shoulder to shoulder with companies like Netscape and Sun in charting the future of Internet technology.

Yet anyone who looked closely at COM, OLE, and the networking capabilities of Windows 95 should not be surprised by this sudden turnaround. Microsoft had only to pull these elements together, and ActiveX is the technology that does exactly that.

Those software objects that used to be called OLE controls are now called ActiveX controls. An application that utilizes ActiveX controls and can contain an ActiveX document is called an ActiveX host. On the Windows 95 desktop, two ActiveX hosts are typically present, although neither comes with Windows 95 yet: the Office 95 Binder and Internet Explorer 3.0. Because these applications serve as ActiveX hosts, the documents they contain can be handled as ActiveX documents.

Documents can be shared between ActiveX hosts live. Netscape Navigator's plug-in viewers only let you view a document from another application, but do not let you interact with it; ActiveX documents can be both viewed and manipulated in a process Microsoft calls *visual editing.* Look carefully at the illustrations in Figures 2.2, 2.3, and 2.4. Figure 2.2 shows a Word 95 document viewed in Word on the desktop. This document was subsequently uploaded to a

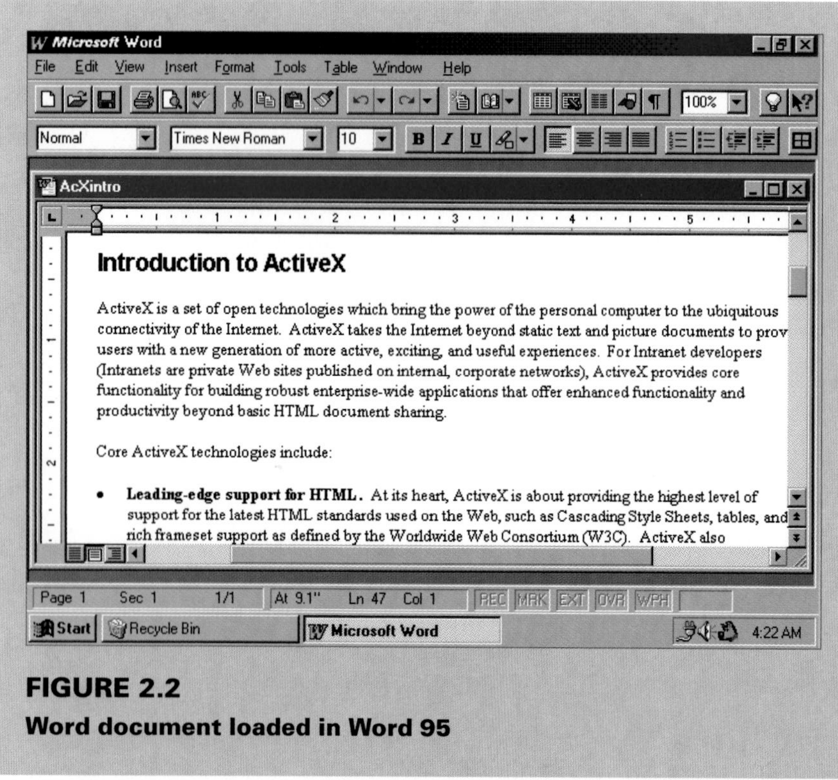


**FIGURE 2.2**
**Word document loaded in Word 95**

Web site, still in Word format, and an HTML page was created with a link to that document; this HTML page is shown in Figure 2.3. When that link is followed, the display shown in Figure 2.4 results.

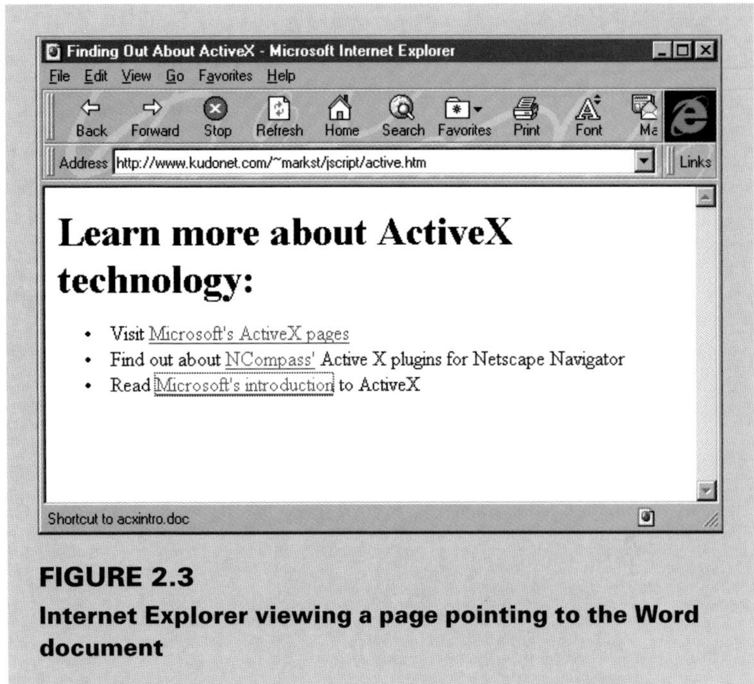


**FIGURE 2.3**

**Internet Explorer viewing a page pointing to the Word document**

Look carefully at how the toolbar has changed from Figure 2.3 to Figure 2.4. The result is a merge of Word and Internet Explorer. The document has not only been downloaded and displayed in Word format, but it can now be edited and changed using the familiar Word editing routines, and the edited version can be saved locally in Word format. Continuing to further URLs returns Internet Explorer to its normal browser mode. The only thing missing from this picture is the ability to upload the edited file back to the server, but that capability is one small programming step away. This is the technology that others envision for the future available today from Microsoft.

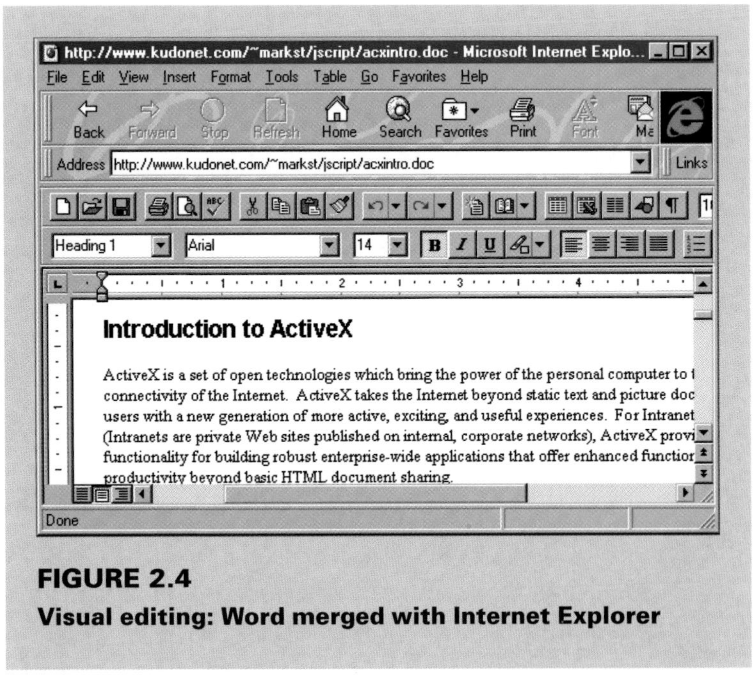


**FIGURE 2.4**

**Visual editing: Word merged with Internet Explorer**

By adding network awareness to OLE controls to make them ActiveX controls, Microsoft has been able to leverage years of programming work that went into OLE development. Microsoft need not program an entire new library of objects for the Internet; it simply needs to add network awareness to the library of objects it already has. Microsoft need not program an entire new groupware application for sharing and editing documents and applications over the Internet; it simply needs to add network awareness to the applications it already has.

## ActiveX on the Web

ActiveX controls provide a way to enhance your Web pages with active content, and a way to extend your Web browser with new capabilities. ActiveX documents can enable the interactivity and real-time response that static Web pages lack. They can also enable new features in your Web browser, such as Internet telephony and videoconferencing. Because ActiveX controls are programmable, their capabilities are limited only by what a programmer can devise. Furthermore, the set of ActiveX controls is extensible. Microsoft and independent software vendors will continually be adding new controls to the library of available ActiveX controls.

Should your browser encounter a document requiring a control that it lacks, the browser can be instructed where to find the control on the Internet. The browser will then retrieve, download, and execute the required control. ActiveX documents and hosts become dynamic entities, changing to meet the needs of the current application.

All of this may sound a little like the capabilities touted for Sun Microsystems's Java. In fact, Java and ActiveX are complimentary technologies, not competing technologies. Both enable executable content to be downloaded and run on a client machine, and both thus enable active content as part of a Web page. Neither can function alone, however. Java is a language that can do nothing without a set of objects on which to operate. The Java Virtual Machine provides a full set of these objects, and certain browsers provide a limited set of objects enabling Java applets to run. ActiveX is precisely the opposite: a set of objects that can do nothing unless programmed by a language. As we will see, ActiveX is not tied to a specific programming language.

One choice with ActiveX would be to write a Java interpreter using ActiveX controls. Any ActiveX host that deployed this interpreter could then run Java applets. In fact, this is exactly what Microsoft has done with Internet Explorer 3.0 (see Figure 2.5.) So, not only are ActiveX and Java complimentary, but ActiveX enables the use of Java applets with Internet Explorer.

ActiveX and Java differ significantly in how they implement security. Any new executable downloaded to a client computer poses a security risk, and on the Web such downloads can happen in the background. Java prohibits applets from accessing the client computer's hard drive. This substantially limits what Java applets can do. In the future Java will likely have limited access to a "container" on the hard drive, perhaps a secure directory of limited size. This has proven difficult to implement in a crossplatform manner, and still places significant limits on Java's capabilities.

ActiveX follows an entirely different approach to security. Microsoft is providing a way for ActiveX controls to be registered so that every ActiveX control will come with a digital signature indicating who the control's author is, what version number it is, and where it has been registered in order that the authenticity of its signature may be verified. Client computers can make use of this security mechanism at different levels. You can ask to be prompted each time your computer wants to download a new ActiveX control, so that you can decide whether to download and authenticate each control on a case by case basis. Alternatively, you can configure a list of trusted sources, so that ActiveX controls from those sources will be downloaded transparently in the background. Any control from outside a source you have designated as trusted would still initiate a prompt before downloading. You can, of course, designate all sources as trusted, but this approach is not recommended.

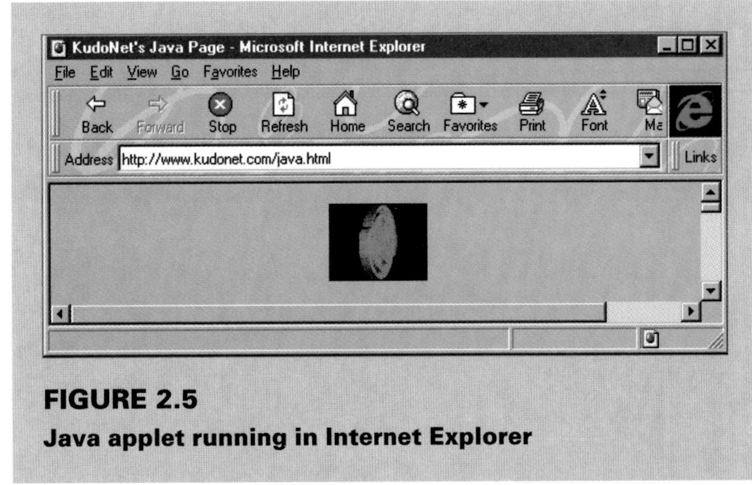


**FIGURE 2.5**
**Java applet running in Internet Explorer**

## Scripting for ActiveX

You may find yourself thinking at this point, "But I don't want to have to program ActiveX controls just to get active content on my Web pages." While the prospect of running Java over ActiveX or using C++ to create new ActiveX controls is daunting, you can relax. As soon as you load a page of conventional HTML in Internet Explorer, you are "programming" ActiveX controls.

A Web browser is not created out of a vacuum. It is an application that must be programmed to understand HTML and the HTTP protocol, and it must be programmed out of some programming environment. Internet Explorer 3.0 is programmed out of ActiveX components. Thus while Explorer understands HTML, it understands HTML as a set of ActiveX controls. So what you think of as telling the browser what to do with HTML, the browser understands as being told what to do with ActiveX controls. In other words, you have already been programming ActiveX without knowing it.

In fact, ActiveX supports several layers of programming. At the lowest level you can simply code pages with HTML. You are then making use of a limited subset of ActiveX controls, specifically those that correspond to HTML elements, and you are only using the default behaviors of those controls. At the highest end, you can program using a full programming language like C++ or Visual Basic to create new controls or fully customize the behavior of existing controls. Neither of these approaches is really satisfying. HTML is too limited on the one hand, but the costs in time and expertise to fully master ActiveX programming are too high on the other hand.

To help you navigate between these extremes, Microsoft has created the ActiveX Scripting Interface. The Scripting Interface is a specification detailing how to embed scripts within ActiveX documents that will be interpreted and run when the document is loaded by an ActiveX host. Currently Internet Explorer supports two scripting languages: Visual Basic Scripting Edition, also known as VBScript, and Microsoft's JavaScript implementation, known as JScript. However, the Scripting Interface is not specific to these two languages. It is an open specification, permitting any interpreted language to be ported to ActiveX using the guidelines of the interface. Both TCL and Perl are being ported and may be available as ActiveX scripting languages by the time you read this.

Seen in this context, JScript takes on enormous importance. Unlike JavaScript, when you learn JScript you are mastering not just a Web-browser scripting language, but an ActiveX scripting language as well. Whatever you do with JScript can be applied to any ActiveX host, not just Internet Explorer. Thus JScript gives you entry to many scripting environments, not just the Web. At the same time, Internet Explorer, unlike Netscape Navigator, currently supports more than one scripting language and will continue to support a growing list of scripting languages. Thus unlike JavaScript, when you learn JScript you are learning the first of a family of languages. JScript is relatively easy as a first programming language, particularly if you are comfortable with HTML. If, however, you find after using it for a while that you are not satisfied with its capabilities, then you can use JScript as a stepping stone to another language, such as VBScript. Finally, remember that Microsoft and its associated independent software vendors have a history of producing software tools that ease the task of programming. While the tools available at present for ActiveX are limited, this will change. If you invest the time to learn JScript, then very likely in the short time it will take you to get comfortable with JScript new tools will already be on the market. With your newfound programming expertise and some new tools, you will find that Web programming feats that once seemed unimaginable are within your grasp.

Much of this is talk about the future. We'll finish off this chapter with a look at what is available now. We'll briefly contrast JScript and VBScript, and we'll look quickly at Microsoft's first programming tool, the ActiveX control pad.

## VBScript and JScript

Microsoft's first product was a BASIC interpreter for the Altair computer. The language has gone through many changes to reach its present incarnation as Visual Basic, but some traits endure. While Visual Basic lacks the power of languages like C and C++ that can make use of low-level programming techniques like pointers, it is nonetheless a full, structured programming language. The language has always used a syntax closer to that of ordinary language, and it can be used in conjunction with a variety of programming tools. For these reasons, Visual Basic has remained a popular choice with software developers.

Visual Basic Scripting Edition retains much of the syntax and control structure of Visual Basic. Many of the input/output functions are missing; in particular, VBScript cannot read or write to files. Still, those who are more familiar with programming than simply HTML will find that VBScript is easy to learn, and that it provides a good introduction to the workings of the Web.

On the other hand, VBScript is not compatible with Netscape Navigator. If you write your Web page scripts in VBScript, currently you are excluding about 70 percent of the browser market. If your background is Web development, and your target audience is the Web audience at large, JScript is a more appealing choice. Further, Visual Basic is a structured language with some object-oriented features grafted on, while JScript was designed with an object-oriented approach from the beginning. We will look more at this distinction in programming styles in Chapter 4. For Web developers though, JScript offers the more enticing choice for a scripting language. It reaches the widest audience, provides a good introduction to object-oriented programming, and shares enough features with VBScript to make if feasible to extend your knowledge to VBScript as needed.

JScript and VBScript work almost entirely with the same set of objects. For the most part these objects are the familiar components of HTML: forms, text-entry areas, radio buttons, and so on. JScript's shortcoming is its limited interaction with ActiveX controls beyond this basic set of HTML features. One extra HTML tag recognized by Internet Explorer is the <OBJECT> tag. The <OBJECT> tag is really just a specification for including new ActiveX controls on a Web page. By matching attributes and parameters of the <OBJECT> tag to the interface of an ActiveX control, you can make any ActiveX control a programmable feature of VBScript. JScript has some <OBJECT> interaction capabilities. It can set a value for a parameter, or have an event handler called from an <OBJECT> event.

Most of the dilemmas the Web developer currently faces will dissolve soon. One company, NCompass, has already made an ActiveX plug-in for Navigator that supports scripting with VBScript. Navigator may well have built-in support for VBScript in a future version. Future versions of JScript will likely include greater support for the <OBJECT> tag. At that point, the difference between VBScript and JScript will be a difference in style rather than a difference in capability or compatibility.

## ActiveX Control Pad

Coding ActiveX controls into a Web page by hand can be a tedious process. Each ActiveX control may have several attributes and a number of parameters that need to be specified. At a minimum, each must have a Class ID, a number with five fields and a total of 32 places; an error in any one of these 32 entries can "break" the control.

To simplify the process of ActiveX coding, Microsoft has developed the *ActiveX Control Pad,* a utility for adding ActiveX controls to your Web page. For a technology still in its infancy, the Control Pad is surprisingly easy to use and full-featured. Figure 2.6 shows a window within the Control Pad listing ActiveX controls and their specifications. Adding a control is simply a matter of pointing and clicking.

The ActiveX Control Pad is a much richer application. It makes a very serviceable HTML editor. Figure 2.7 shows the initial screen when you open the Control Pad, which lets users automatically create the outline of an HTML document with the minimum required tags. The Control Pad's online Help includes a fully hyperlinked reference to HTML, up to the current Version 3.2 draft standard.

HTML will be taken to a new level of sophistication with the incorporation of style sheets. Style sheets, likely to be part of the HTML 3.3 draft standard, provide detailed specifications for how the elements of a page are to be laid out, the fonts and sizes to be used, and so on. With style sheets HTML will finally allow something close to the fine-tuning of page layout that document-processing languages in desktop publishing already allow. Style sheets also signify the point at which hand-coding HTML will simply become too laborious for documents of any sophistication, and Web designers will

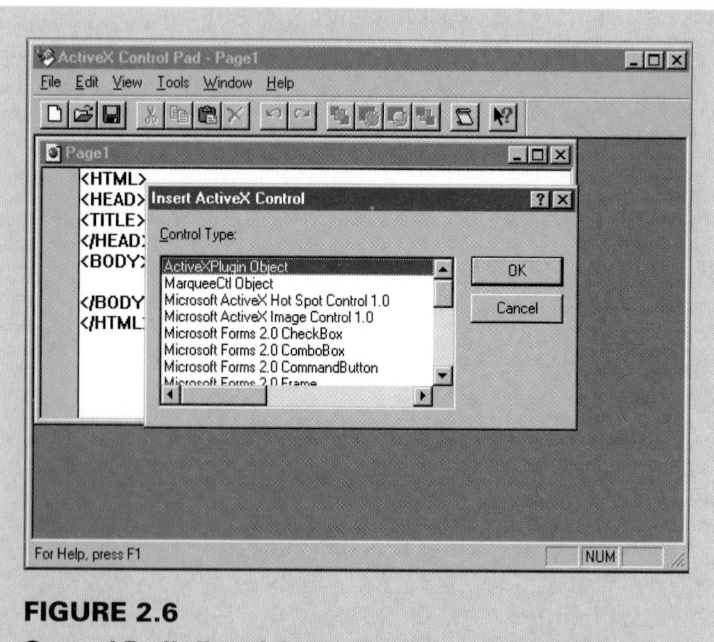


**FIGURE 2.6**
**Control Pad's list of ActiveX controls for insertion.**

require some sort of helper program. Internet Explorer 3.0 includes support for style sheets, and most browsers will in the near future.

The ActiveX Control Pad provides a much simpler way of fine-tuning HTML than the use of style sheets. You can use the Control Pad's HTML layout control. This control lets you drag and drop HTML elements onto a page, and then configure their size and appearance. Figure 2.8 shows the placement and configuration of a text-area window with optional scroll bars. Once the page elements are laid out to your satisfaction, the Control Pad automatically generates the corresponding HTML.

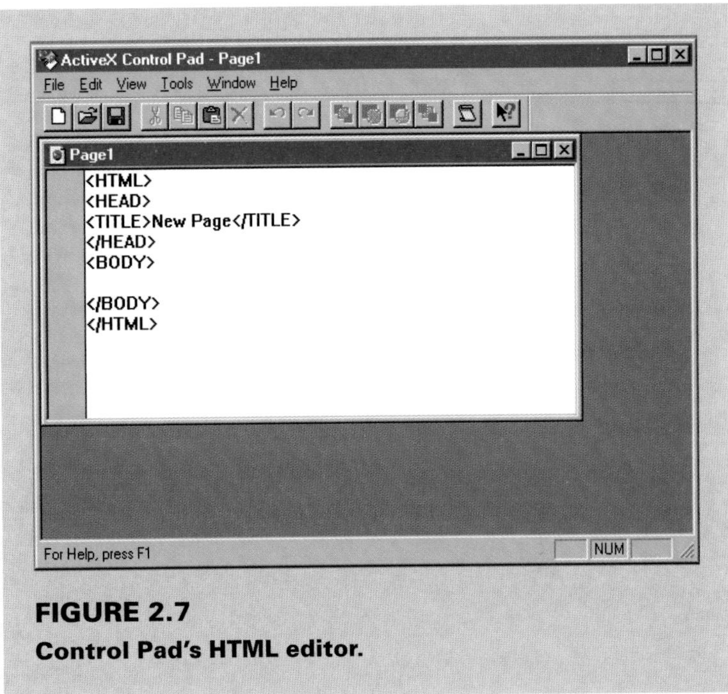


**FIGURE 2.7**
**Control Pad's HTML editor.**

The ActiveX Control Pad also includes a *scripting wizard.* Figure 2.9 shows the HTML for the calculator program we will look at in later chapters, loaded into the Control Pad editor. Notice that when the <SCRIPT> tag appears in the document, the editor places a small scroll icon in the margin next to it. The tool bar also contains the same scroll icon. Clicking on either of these will launch the Control Pad scripting wizard.

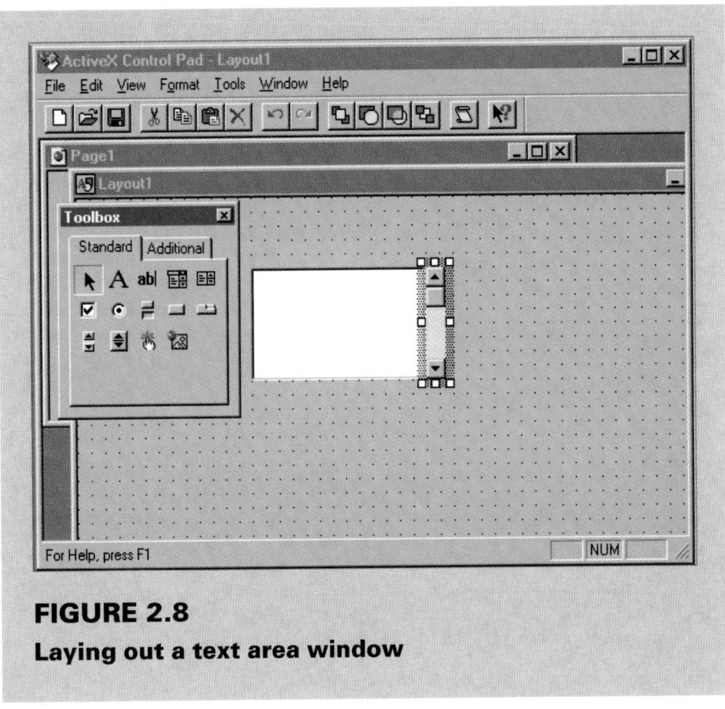


**FIGURE 2.8**
**Laying out a text area window**

The scripting wizard can be set to support either JScript or VBScript: if launched from within a document containing a script, it will set itself to the corresponding language. The wizard opens up three frames, as shown in Figure 2.10. The top two windows show an object hierarchy of the objects in the document being edited. This hierarchy follows a pattern familiar to anyone who

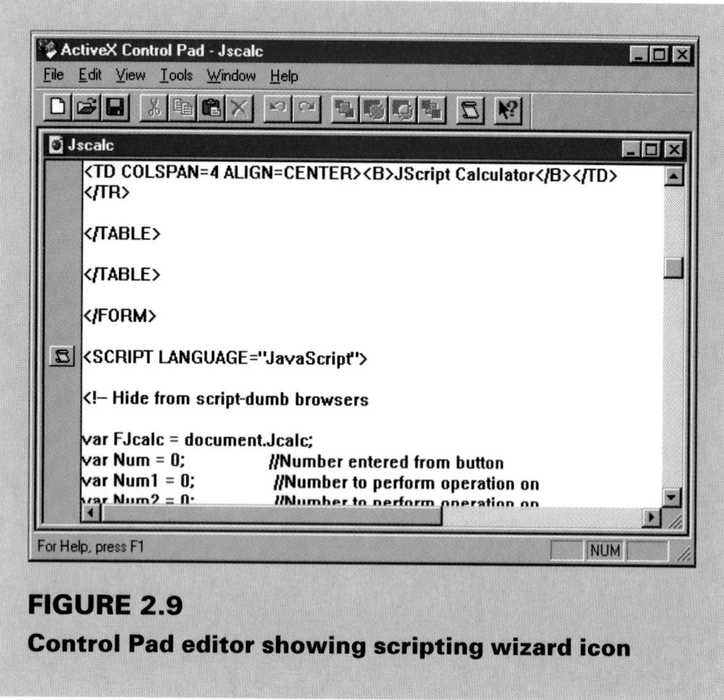


**FIGURE 2.9**
**Control Pad editor showing scripting wizard icon**

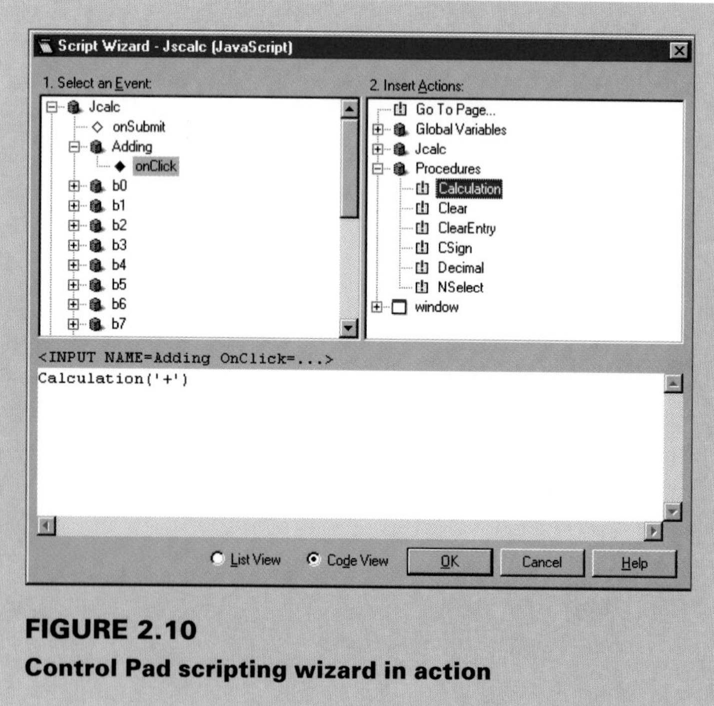


**FIGURE 2.10**
**Control Pad scripting wizard in action**

has used the Windows 3.1 File Manager or the Windows 95 Explorer. The left top frame allows the selection of an event, and the right top frame allows the selection of an action associated with that event. The specific code associated with the action is shown, and can be edited, in the bottom frame.

The scripting wizard does not completely eliminate the need to write JScript code, but it can simplify the task for you and can provide a good visual summary of the elements of your script. A scripting tool is no substitute for learning the language, however. You must know how JScript works before you can return to tools like the ActiveX Control Pad to ease your coding tasks for you. Still, if the Control Pad is any indication of the quality of programming tools that will become available for JScript, then the future of JScript looks bright indeed.

Serving Documents

Counting Hits

Stateless Transactions

Interacting through CGI

Client-Side Scripting

## Chapter 3

# Serving Clients on the Web

We have looked a bit now at the workings of a Web browser, and specifically at some of the key features of Internet Explorer 3.0. Now it's time to step behind the scenes for an overview of how a Web server works, and particularly at how it exchanges information with Web browsers. We will start by looking at how a simple page of HTML is served to a Web browser. Then we'll examine the traditional method for providing interactive elements on the Web, the Common Gateway Interface. Finally, we'll consider the limitations of this approach, and we'll consider how to address those limitations with an exciting new alternative: client-side scripting languages like JScript.

## Serving Documents

Suppose that you have several interlinked HTML files in the same directory of your hard drive rather than on the Web. In other words, you may have a file called foo.html which contains the lines <A HREF = "bar.html"> and <IMG SRC = "foo.gif">, which is in the same directory as the files bar.html and foo.gif. You can open one of these files using the Open File option in your Web browser, and the file will load just fine. You will see a page of fully formatted HTML, with inline images in place and functioning links to documents in the same directory. Most of us are familiar with this basic browser capability. We use it to check our HTML work before putting it online. But ask yourself this: "What exactly do I need a Web server for?" After all, if the browser can open files, follow links, format text, and load images all on its own, what work does the server do? The tasks just described cover the sum total of features on many Web sites.

When you select the Open File option, you are telling your browser to ask the operating system where to find the file in question. This works fine on your hard drive, but not so well over the Internet when the file in question is on another computer, one that may well be running an entirely different operating system. Nor does your operating system know how listen at a communications port, accept a request, and transfer a file via that port.

At its heart, that's what a Web server is: a network-enabled document server that can accomplish these tasks. Figures 3.1 through 3.3 illustrate a brief Web session. Let's look at the corresponding entries in the server access log file; you'll see that a Web server does little more than transfer files:

```
[11/Aug/1996:22:45:55] "GET /~markst/jscript/index.htm HTTP/1.0"
[11/Aug/1996:22:45:56] "GET /~markst/jscript/images/button1.gif HTTP/1.0"
[11/Aug/1996:22:45:56] "GET /~markst/jscript/images/button2.gif HTTP/1.0"
[11/Aug/1996:22:46:19] "GET /~markst/jscript/pcalc.htm HTTP/1.0"
[11/Aug/1996:22:46:49] "GET /cgi-
bin/pcalc.cgi?number1=2&operation=Multiply&number2=2 HTTP/1.0"
[11/Aug/1996:22:46:59] "POST /cgi-bin/pc_comment.cgi HTTP/1.0"
```

The first line can be read as: On August 11, 1996, at 10:45:55 P.M., the server processed a request to get the file index.html from the directory jscript in the Web document directory of user markst.

This series of exchanges has several interesting features. First, almost all the requests are GET requests; in other words, the server's main job is simply transferring files in response to GET requests from Web browsers. Note, however, that a single page can require multiple requests. It takes three requests to load the page index.html, for example, because in addition to the page itself there are two inline graphics (button1.gif and button2.gif) present on the page. Realize also how anonymous these requests are: when a Web browser asks for the file pcalc.htm at 10:46:19, the server neither knows nor cares that this is the same browser that requested index.htm at 10:45:56. The browser can also pass some information to the server, either using a POST request, or appended to the URL of a GET request. Information can also be exchanged between browser and server by a request method not logged here: *HEAD*. The HEAD request

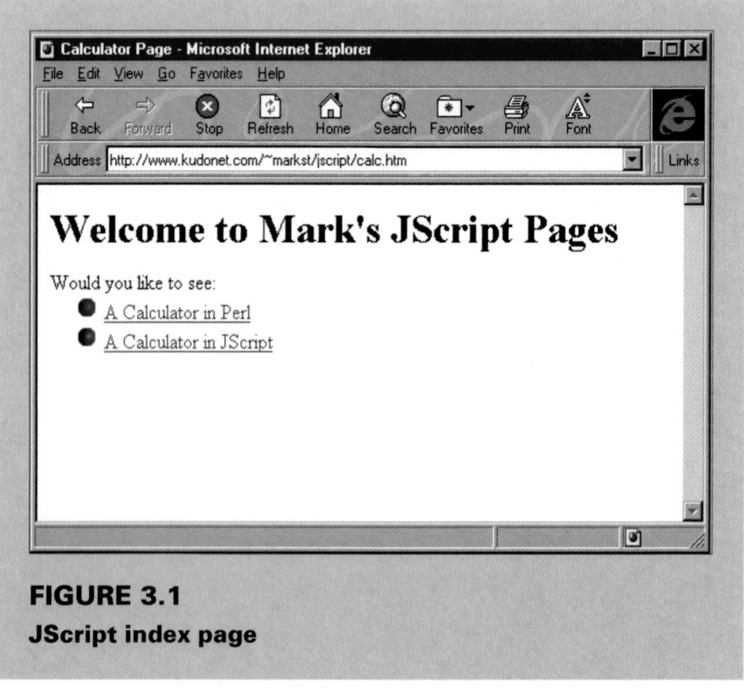


**FIGURE 3.1**
**JScript index page**

asks the server for header information preceding each new file request and, in fact, the browser sends header information of its own each time it makes a request. Let's look at each of these features in more detail.

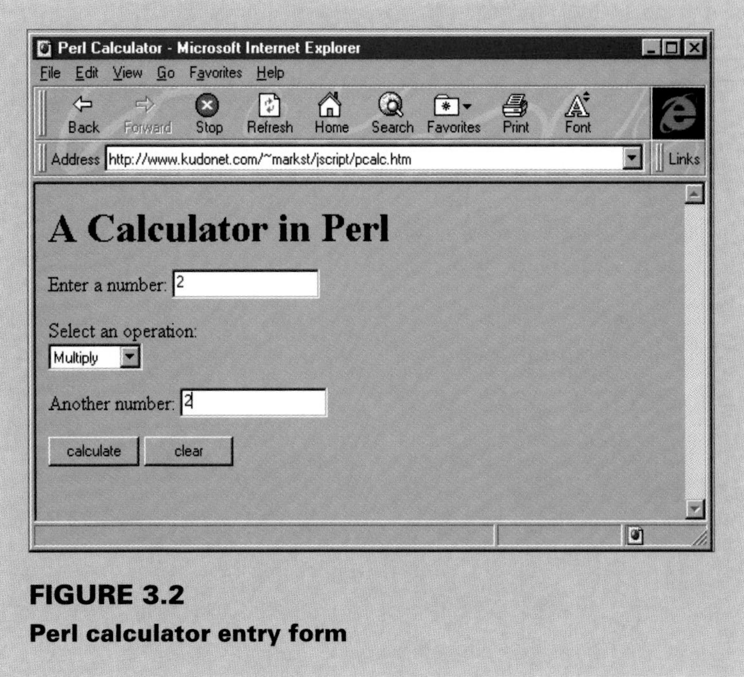


**FIGURE 3.2**
**Perl calculator entry form**

## Counting Hits

In the early hype about the Web, comments were often heard about how a certain site received "10,000 hits a day" or "1,000,000 hits a week," as if this were some objective measure of its popularity. These days people view the Web with a bit more skepticism, and you are likely to hear a response like "Are those raw hits or real hits?" when such wild numbers are thrown around. What's that about?

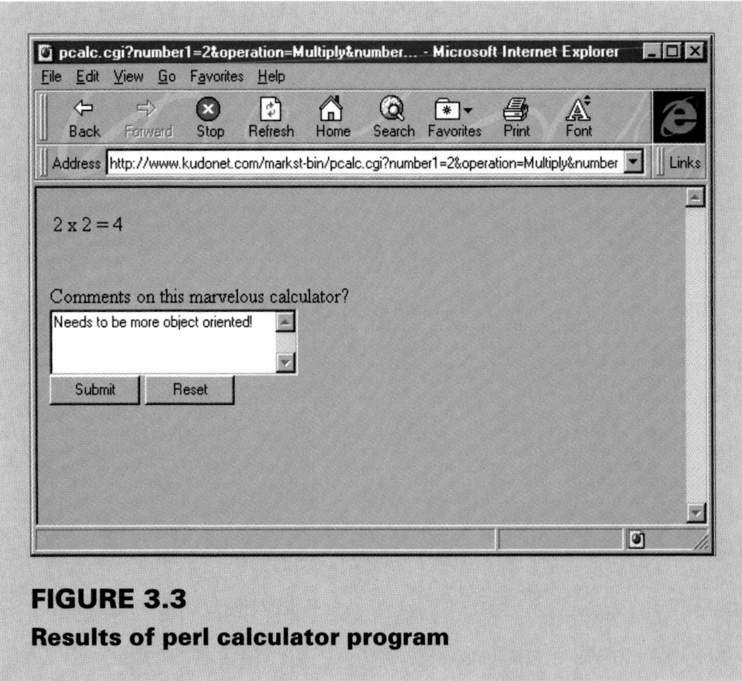


**FIGURE 3.3**
**Results of perl calculator program**

Our log file sample has six requests in it. This represents six *raw* hits. In other words, each request is a hit. When people talk about hits they most often mean raw hits, because the number of raw hits is easiest to count. This number corresponds directly to the number of lines in the access log file. Indeed, you can get the number of raw hits without even opening this file, simply by querying the operating system for the number of lines in the file. Yet even though raw hits is the easiest number to use, it is misleading.

We know, for example, that even though our log file sample shows six raw hits, this represents only four actual pages loaded, since two of the hits correspond to images on a page. If we take the image file requests out of the access log, then we are left with four hits. These are the *real* hits. This is a vital difference, because raw hits can be manipulated. Suppose, for example, I added to index.htm several hundred one pixel by one pixel transparent images. The page would load a little slower, and its appearance would be the same. However, my raw hit count would now go up dramatically every time the page was accessed.

So are real hits the real story? Unfortunately, life on the Web is not so simple. Browsers may cache files. Another server may cache files for browsers behind a company firewall, or for browsers from a commercial online service. These factors can cause the count of real hits to underestimate the number of times a page is viewed. Web pages can also be "hit" by Web bots, automated programs that roam the Web tabulating and indexing Web sites. These hits are not of interest to advertisers, since they do not represent hits in which a potential customer is viewing the page. These are not trivial issues. Advertisers want an accurate and objective measure of Web site activity to assess the merit of advertising on a given site. New tools are being studied to deal with this problem. For now, though, real hits are about as real as it gets.

For our purposes, another feature of the hit count needs to be considered. The two GIF images do nothing more for the page index.html than provide bullets for a listing—pretty, colored bullets, yes, but still mere bullets. We could save server time and server processing resources by eliminating the <IMG> tags in index.htm that refer to these images, and instead using a bulleted list. While the savings here would be rather small, the principle is an important one: since the browser already knows how to draw a bullet—that's part of the basic HTML syntax—it requires less effort for the server to transfer a "draw bullet" instruction than to transfer an image of a bullet from elsewhere.

JScript amplifies this principle tremendously, enabling a wide range of features for which the server can simply send instructions, rather than having to execute a program itself and then send the results.

## Stateless Transactions

At the end of each access log entry you'll see that it says HTTP/1.0. This indicates that the browser is requesting that the document be transferred by means of HTTP (Hypertext Transfer Protocol) version 1.0. The HTTP serving protocol actually provides much higher performance than some of its Internet predecessors, such as FTP (File Transfer Protocol).

During an FTP session the client computer maintains a sustained connection with the server computer. You log in and remain connected for the duration of the session. This mechanism has built-in inefficiencies: while you stare at the screen, reading information, debating which directory to change to, or trying to decide which file you need to get, your computer and the server computer are both idle. Yet because they are still connected, they may well prevent another computer from making a connection.

HTTP, on the other hand, operates in a *stateless* environment. When the server receives a specific request, it responds by transferring a file. Once that transfer is completed, however, the server does not bother maintaining a connection, but instead frees itself up to listen for the next specific request. Thus while you are reading through a Web page, digesting the information, and deciding which link to follow next, the server can busy itself serving up other documents to other clients. With HTTP, there is no idle time, and therefore less inefficiency.

The contrast here is analogous to the relationship between telephone and radio communications. When you make a telephone call, you tie up the line between two phones, and that line cannot be used for any other communications for the duration of the call, even though there may be many pauses when neither party is speaking on the phone. By contrast, a particular radio frequency range may carry many simultaneous transmissions, each fitting into the gaps between the others, because with radio a signal is generated only when there is something to transmit.

HTTP's high performance comes at a price, however. The statelessness of these connections makes them anonymous as well. The server does log an IP address for each client making a request—this is part of the information exchanged when client and server pass header files to each other—but since connections are not sustained, the server has no way of knowing when your browser is making a new request rather than continuing from a previous request. So the client ID information that the server logs does not help it in processing requests. The server is rather like a busy short-order cook taking orders from three waiters that he never sees directly. If Larry, Moe, and Curly are the waiters, they might hear the conversation like this:

Larry: I need a steak and eggs.
Eggs scrambled.
With catsup.
Oh, and coffee.

Moe: Get me a short stack of pancakes, eggs on the side.
Some syrup with that.
Tabasco for the eggs.
Orange juice.

Curly: An order of waffles.
Orange marmalade.
Glass of milk.

Now, to Larry, Moe, and Curly this all sounds very clear and specific. But to our poor cook, it sounds like:

> Get me a short stack of pancakes, eggs on the side.
> I need a steak and eggs.
> Some syrup with that.
> Eggs scrambled.
> An order of waffles.
> Orange marmalade.
> With catsup.
> Oh, and coffee.
> Tabasco for the eggs.
> Orange juice.
> Glass of milk.

Sounds a little confusing, right? So if we want the server to understand that the browser is making one request in relation to an earlier request, we need to add something to the picture. Simple stateless connections may be fast, but they don't give the server enough information.

## Interacting through CGI

Prior to the advent of client-side scripting languages, the only way to add interactivity to the Web was on the server side, by means of the Common Gateway Interface (CGI). Since the server does little more than transfer documents, if it receives a request for anything more complicated, such as executing a program or processing input, it must pass this request off to another program. The server relies on the browser to provide it with the URL of the needed program, and then the server opens a gateway to that program through which it may pass input and receive output to pass back to the browser.

Let's look again at a couple of lines from our access log:

```
[11/Aug/1996:22:46:49] "GET /cgi-
bin/pcalc.cgi?number1=2&operation=Multiply&number2=2 HTTP/1.Ø"
[11/Aug/1996:22:46:59] "POST /cgi-bin/pc_comment.cgi HTTP/1.Ø"
```

Even though one of these is a GET request and the other a POST request, both represent ways of passing input to a program through CGI.

The GET request is, in fact, one the server assembled itself, based on input received from the form pcalc.html. Since that form specifies the GET method, the server knows to look for the program specified by the form and to GET that program, passing input to it by appending the input to the URL, and waiting for output. Because of either the directory (cgi-bin) or filename extension (.cgi) of the program requested—this depends on server configuration—the server knows that the file pcalc.cgi is an executable program that will receive input, and from which the server should receive output to return to the browser.

In this case the program in question is a small Perl script that performs the calculation. The script reads from the environmental variable QUERY_STRING to get input. This variable contains the section of the URL after the "?". The script parses this input and passes the parsed result to variables for the program to process.

The POST method differs from GET in how it passes input. Rather than appending the input to the URL, the POST method passes input directly to the program as standard input. This method has advantages, because the variable QUERY_STRING may have an upper limit on length. An unexpectedly long line of input from a form could overrun this length, causing errors in the execution of the program. The GET method has advantages because it need not be explicitly called from a form. All GET requests are the same to the server: it doesn't care whether or not they originated from a form. So a plain HTML page with this link in it:

```
<A HREF=/cgi-bin/pcalc.cgi?number1=2&operation=Multiply&number2=2>
```

will produce exactly the same results as the form pcalc.html would as it was filled out in Figure 3.3.

Our GET request in this example was generated by the server, based on input from a form. What about our POST request? What form did this request come from? The short answer is the form in Figure 3.3. But look at the log file: which entry corresponds to this page? The answer, of course, is that none of the entries do, because this form is not an HTML file, but a dynamically generated page of HTML generated as output from the script pcalc.cgi. People often speak of HTML pages, HTML documents, and HTML files interchangeably, as if these were all the same thing. *Page* is used somewhat ambiguously to refer to either a file or a document. An HTML document is a body of text that begins with the tag <HTML> and ends with the tag </HTML>. Every document has a source. The source of an HTML document typically is an HTML file, but need not be. The source could be a CGI program or, as we will see, a client-side script, that generates dynamic HTML.

Dynamic HTML provides one key to maintaining state in a stateless environment. Because the output can be made conditional on the results of the program, the dynamically generated document can contain information based on the previous document that called the program. This document could call another program, and thus information could be sustained from document to document to document.

If you've ever encountered an online store while browsing the Web, its shopping cart program probably used just such a sequence of dynamically generated HTML. You probably began by filling out a form asking for information about yourself, and that form most likely assigned you a unique ID number, usually passed to the form-processing program using the HIDDEN input type. As each dynamic document was generated thereafter, it contained that unique ID in a hidden field, along with IDs for any items you selected, so that at the end of your session the store knew what items were selected, and by whom.

CGI connections can get quite complicated. In a normal, non-CGI exchange, the browser sends a header file with some identifying information about itself, a HEAD request for a similar header file from the server, and a GET request for the file needed (see Figure 3.4). The server then sends back its own header information, along with the requested file. Simple enough. With CGI, on the other hand, the server must not only receive the request from the browser, but then open CGI,

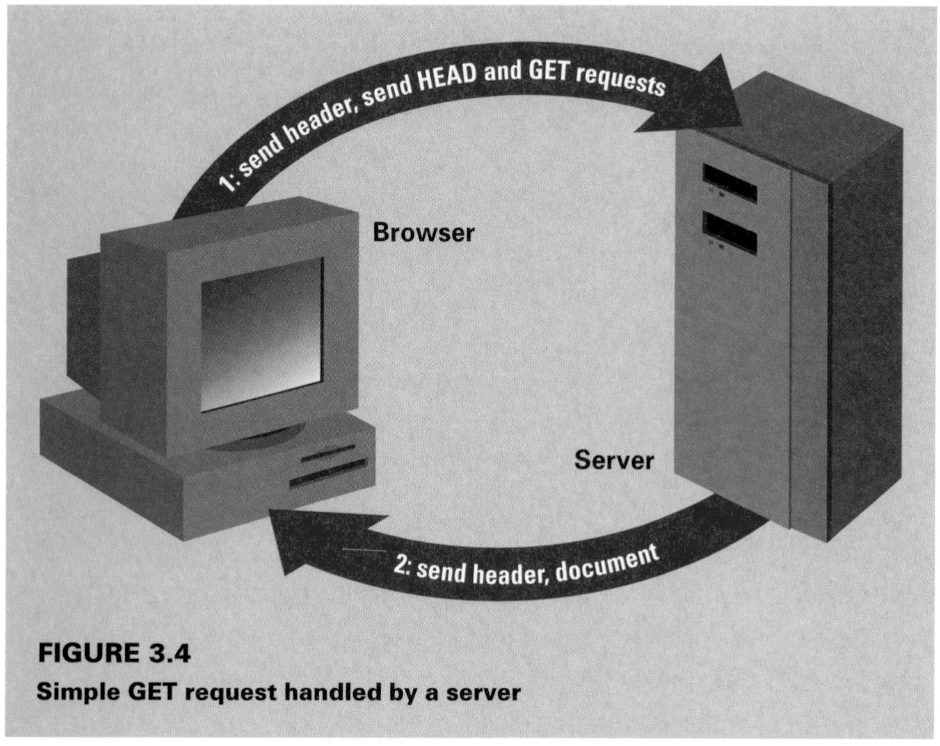


**FIGURE 3.4**
**Simple GET request handled by a server**

request that the system run the requested program and, if the original CGI request came by POST method, pass the forms input to the requested program through CGI as standard input (see Figure 3.5). The server must then wait for the program to execute, receive the results of that program, close CGI, and send the results to the browser as output. Complicated, but powerful.

This mechanism enables the Web to take on an interactive mode. Shopping carts, guest books, Web chat, database queries: all of these are interactive features traditionally enabled by means of CGI. The programs that provide this interactivity may be written in any language that will run on the server's operating system. Perl, C, and Visual Basic are all common language choices for this type of programming.

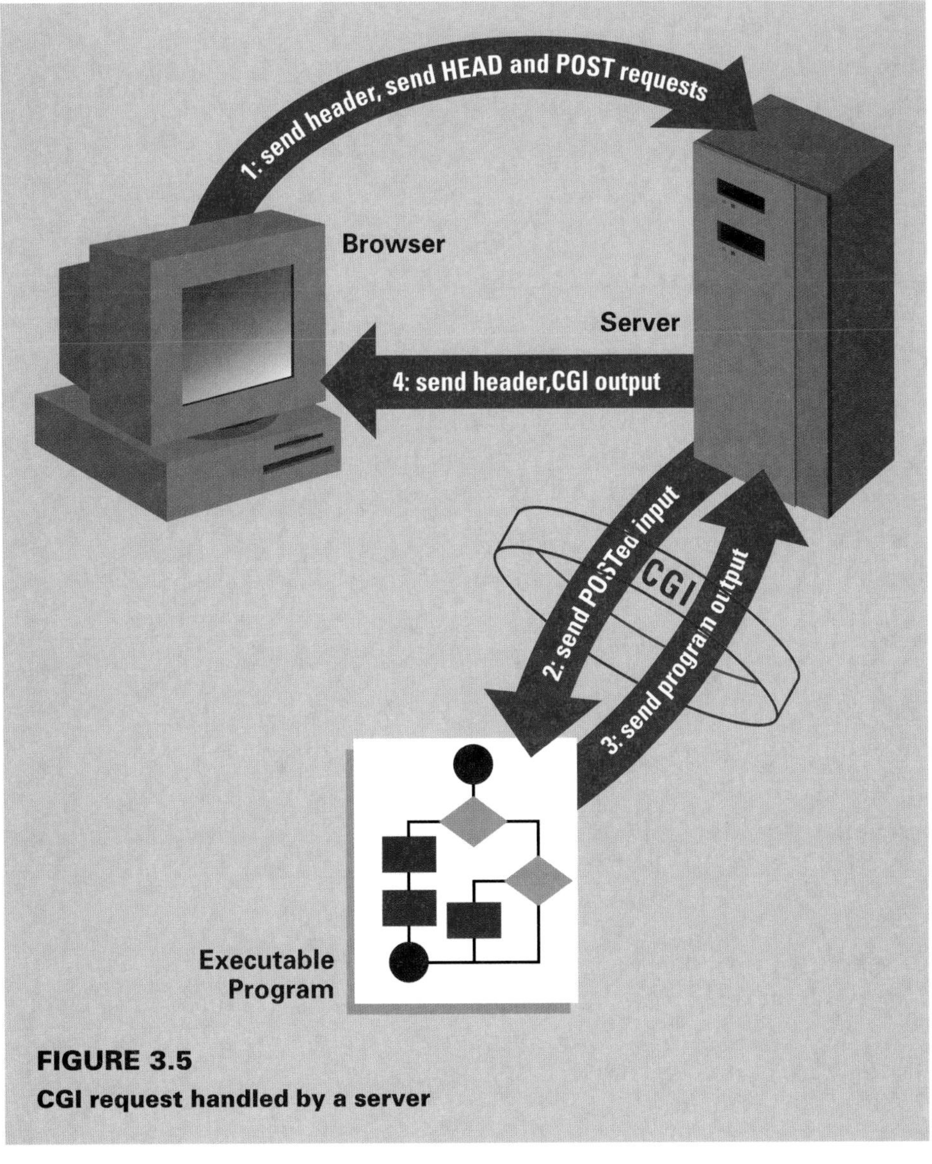


**FIGURE 3.5**
**CGI request handled by a server**

Yet CGI comes with significant drawbacks. These drawbacks are so severe that, although CGI applications will be with us on the Web for a long time, the most rapid developments in adding interactivity to the Web now come from other sources: Java, Java applets, Microsoft's ActiveX, and client-side scripting languages like JScript.

## CGI Limitations: Adding to Server Load

Recall that one of the main advantages of HTTP over older protocols like FTP is supposed to be the speed and efficiency of stateless connections: Figure 3.4 illustrates a relatively simple and efficient model. Yet introducing CGI introduces a lot of complexities, as you can see in Figure 3.5. Specifically, the server must expend time waiting for the program called through CGI to execute and return its results, and the computer on which the server resides must expend processing resources to actually run the program. What had been a clean and efficient protocol can bog down these resources.

In fact, CGI runs counter to the accepted principles of client-server computing. Client-server computing differs from the earlier server-dumb terminal model of computing because it harnesses the processing power of individual machines on a network in order to distribute the overall workload more efficiently.

For example, on your office LAN you don't have single copy of Microsoft Word residing on the server, and then expect every desktop computer that needs to use Word to access that single copy. That would be inefficient. Instead, shared Word documents may reside on the server, but each desktop machine runs its own copy of the Word software. This is how things function in a good client-server model: small applications are distributed to individual machines on the network; only shared files and large applications requiring greater processing power reside on the server.

With CGI the situation is backwards. All browsers wanting to access a Web server are impeded while the server runs the CGI application. This program may run very quickly, and if all goes well any lag in speed will be negligible. But if the site is a busy one that makes extensive use of CGI, the server may become overburdened.

## CGI Limitations: Opening Up Security Risks

Any time another party sends input to your computer there is a security risk. The risk is especially great with CGI, because the input goes automatically to an executable program without any human intervention or oversight.

Security risks will vary depending on the operating system of the server. A Unix server, for example, offers an easy preliminary level of security through the system of Unix file permissions. However, Unix has a very open system architecture, leaving the system extremely vulnerable once that initial level of security has been breached. The Macintosh operating system, by contrast, has nothing corresponding to file permissions. On the other hand, it is much more difficult for a security breach to get at System resources under the Macintosh operating system.

Security risks will also vary depending on the programming language of the CGI application. C, because of its use of pointers, is the riskiest language. Visual Basic, on the other hand, is comparatively secure.

Consequences of a security breach vary as well. A deliberate and malicious attempt to "crack" the system could result in a loss of data on the server. The severity of the loss would depend on where the Web-server document root is installed relative to other system resources, and where any CGI-enabled directories are installed relative to other system resources. Even an unintentional breach could crash the system if unanticipated input to a CGI application behaved in unexpected ways.

Overseeing a server running CGI applications is thus an enormous challenge for a system administrator, particularly if people other than the system administrator develop and install CGI applications on the server. Each application has to be thoroughly tested and debugged, not only for its expected input, but also in ways that anticipate all manner of nonstandard input sequences, whether deliberate or unintentional. This required level of oversight places an enormous burden on administrators.

## CGI Limitations: Who Can Access CGI?

Because of concerns about server load and security, many system administrators respond by denying users access to CGI.

If you administer a server yourself, you need to consider alternatives to CGI. For some applications CGI will remain essential for the foreseeable future, but any opportunity to lighten the load on a server or reduce the security risk to a server deserves serious consideration. If some of the tasks accomplished now by CGI could be accomplished by another means, then your server will perform better.

If your Web pages reside on someone else's server, you may not have unrestricted access to CGI. Many companies providing Web hosting services have a generic library of CGI applications they have already written, which you can make use of, but which you cannot add to or modify. Typically these preset CGI applications offer nothing more than processing the input of an HTML form, allowing you to designate an HTML page to be presented in response to the form submission, and e-mailing you a message containing the results of the form submission. While this information can be useful, it does not allow for real-time interactivity.

Many companies providing Web hosting services do not allow access to CGI at all. If you nevertheless want to add life to your Web pages, if you want them to be more than a passive online catalog, you need an alternative to CGI to bring interactivity to the Web.

## Client-Side Scripting

A fully functional Web server can take up less than one megabyte of disk space. As a mere document server it is a lean, efficient, and powerful program. Today's Web browsers take up three megabytes or more of disk space. These are feature-rich programs capable of handling a variety of tasks, and data types that range from text to images to animation. It makes sense, then, to try to harness browser programs to make use of these features, distributing the processing load to the many browsers rather than centralizing it on a smaller number of servers.

In the next chapter we will begin our look at this alternative: client-side scripting languages. These are program instructions written into HTML pages, much like HTML instructions are written into HTML pages. When downloaded to a scripting-enabled browser like Internet Explorer, they are immediately run by the browser. These scripting languages are limited—neither VBScript nor JScript offers all the features of a full language like Visual Basic. They do, however, offer enough power to create an alternative source of interactivity for your Web pages.

Because a JScript program is executed on the browser rather than the server, JScript programs place much less burden on the server than traditional CGI programs. Processing load is distributed off the server, as it should be in a true client-server computing environment.

Because a JScript program is executed on the browser, any program input from the user remains on the browser and hence poses no security risk to the Web server. While downloading executable content to a browser raises new security concerns for the computer on which the browser runs, these concerns have been addressed by limiting the instruction set of the JScript language, in particular by limiting its file input and output capabilities.

The limitations of JScript can also have another advantage. If your background is primarily as a Web designer rather than programmer, the prospect of learning a full programming language can be daunting. JScript offers a much more manageable slice of the larger programming environment. While somewhat more complicated than HTML, JScript will quickly reveal many familiar HTML elements, and you will find that your background in HTML gives you a head start on the new challenge of designing scripted Web pages.

A Simple
Structured Program

Who's in Control?

A Simple Object-
Oriented Program

Structure-Driven versus
Event-Driven Programs

User-Friendly
But Programmer-Tough

# Chapter 4
# Thinking in Object Terms

Every successful revolution brings about a new status quo. With the PC revolution, this status quo must have been reached some time in the mid 1980s when, for the first time, the number of people using computers who were not programmers exceeded the number of people using computers who were programmers.

This new status quo raised new issues. Suddenly issues of design, layout, and user interface became an important part of applications development. Software companies needed designers and artists, not just programmers. New terminology emerged with the new issues: people began to talk about graphical user interfaces (GUIs) and object-oriented applications.

The revolution we know today as the World Wide Web has reached a similar stage. From the early days of the Web when pages were just passive HTML documents with occasional CGI calls to structured programs, we have moved on to demand greater interactivity and a more object-oriented environment.

Object-oriented scripting with JScript requires a very different frame of mind than traditional structured programming does. For programmers, changing mindsets can be difficult. Fortunately, someone coming from a design background should take more easily to object-oriented scripting. JScript provides a natural extension of the design techniques you use with HTML.

## A Simple Structured Program

To understand what an object-oriented program can do uniquely well, we need to understand what structured programs do not do well. To start with, let's look at a section of a very simple structured program: a Perl calculator similar to the script we used in Chapter 2. This program runs from the command line rather than being called from a Web form through CGI, but otherwise it is essentially the same program. Figure 4.1 shows a simple terminal session that corresponds to the Web session we ran in Chapter 2. If you are unfamiliar with Perl, don't worry. The points to

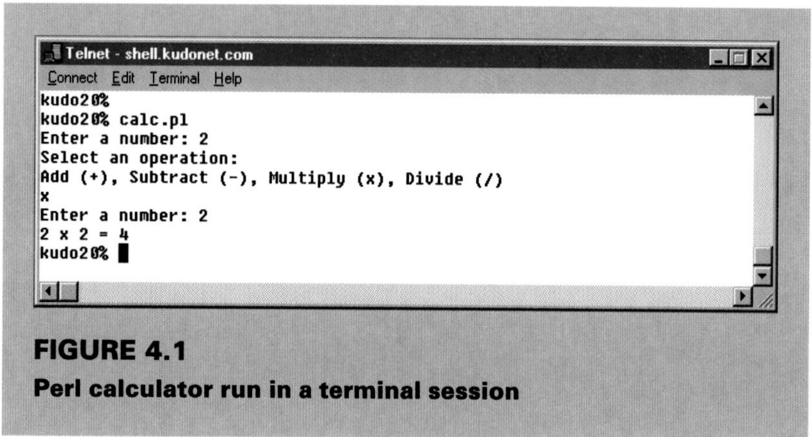


**FIGURE 4.1**
**Perl calculator run in a terminal session**

be made here are basic enough, and the Perl code general enough, to apply to any structured programming language.

Here is our Perl calculator:

```
#!/usr/bin/perl
#This script takes two numbers, $n1 and $n2, as
#input, an operation $op to be performed on them
#as input, and returns the result of $n1 $op $n2.
#
#We'll go through three iterations of a loop to validate
#input, one iteration for each item to be input.
#
for ($i = 1; $i <= 3; $i++) {    $proper_input = "false";
#
#The variable $proper_input acts as a flag; when
#it gets reset to true, we'll know we have proper
#input for that item; until then, we repeat the
#following loop.
#
while ($proper_input eq "false") {
#
#if we are at iteration 1 or 3, we ask for a number;
#otherwise, we ask for an operation.
#
if ($i != 2) {
   print "Enter a number: ";
} else {
```

```
print "Select an operation:\n";
print "Add (+), Subtract (-), Multiply (x), Divide (/)\n";
}
$_ = <STDIN>;
chop($_);
#
#if we are on iteration 1 or 3, we check our input
#string to see that it contains only numbers;
#otherwise, we check for the symbol for a valid
#operation. In the event of an error, we inform
#the user. Otherwise, we change the input flag.
#
if ($i != 2) {
   if (/[^0-9]/) {
      print "That's not a number!\n";
      } else {
      $proper_input = "true";
      }
   } else {
   if (/[^+-x\/]/) {
      print "That's not a valid operation!\n";
      } else {
      $proper_input = "true";
      }
   }
}
#
#Now we pass our validated input to the correct
#variable, depending which iteration we are on.
#
if ($i == 1) {
   $n1 = $_;         }
   elsif ($i == 2) {
      $op = $_;
      } else {
      $n2 = $_;
      }
      #
```

```
        #We reset the flag to validate the next item
        #
        $proper_input = "false"
        }
    #
    #Finally we actually perform the calculation, depending
    #on which operation the user asked for.
    #
    if ($op eq "+") {   $n3 = $n1 + $n2;   }
    elsif ($op eq "-") {   $n3 = $n1 - $n2;   }
    elsif ($op eq "x") {   $n3 = $n1*$n2;   }
    else {   $n3 = $n1/$n2;   }
#
#And last of all, we print out the results.
#
print "$n1 $op $n2 = $n3\n";
```

The logic here is simple (see Figure 4.2). The program uses three input items: two numbers, and the operation to be performed on them. Each input item must be checked to see that it is a valid form of input; the program simply loops until it receives proper input. Once proper input is verified, the program checks to see which condition obtains: add, subtract, multiply, or divide. It then performs the associated operation, and prints the results.

This program is very rigid. Events must happen in a particular sequence, and it is the program, not the user, that determines that sequence. Nor can there be any backtracking; once a valid variable has been input, the program moves relentlessly forward to the next step. Also, only one mode of interaction is permitted: input to the program must be a sequence of numbers or letters, and output comes only in the form of a sequence of numbers or letters. Finally, a structured program must have a definite beginning and a definite end. In this case the program permits only a single calculation to be performed, not an open sequence of calculations, each starting with the results of the previous calculation as input.

Notice, also, that most of the code in this program labors with input validation. The actual calculations are easy to program, as is the output. Even so, the validation is quite primitive. The program does not check against division by zero, for example, nor does it place an upper limit on the length of an input string. Full validation would add substantially to the length of the program. Indeed, the situation would be much worse in a programming language like C or Pascal. Perl is unusually forgiving and will try to do something useful with almost any form of input.

Of course, many of these shortcomings can be corrected. Input could be more fully validated, and additional control loops could be incorporated that would allow users to backtrack, change their minds, and make corrections to input. One could even embed this program in a higher-level loop to permit carrying over the results of one calculation as input to another calculation. All of this cuts against the grain of structured programming. Structured programs can do these things, but they don't do them naturally.

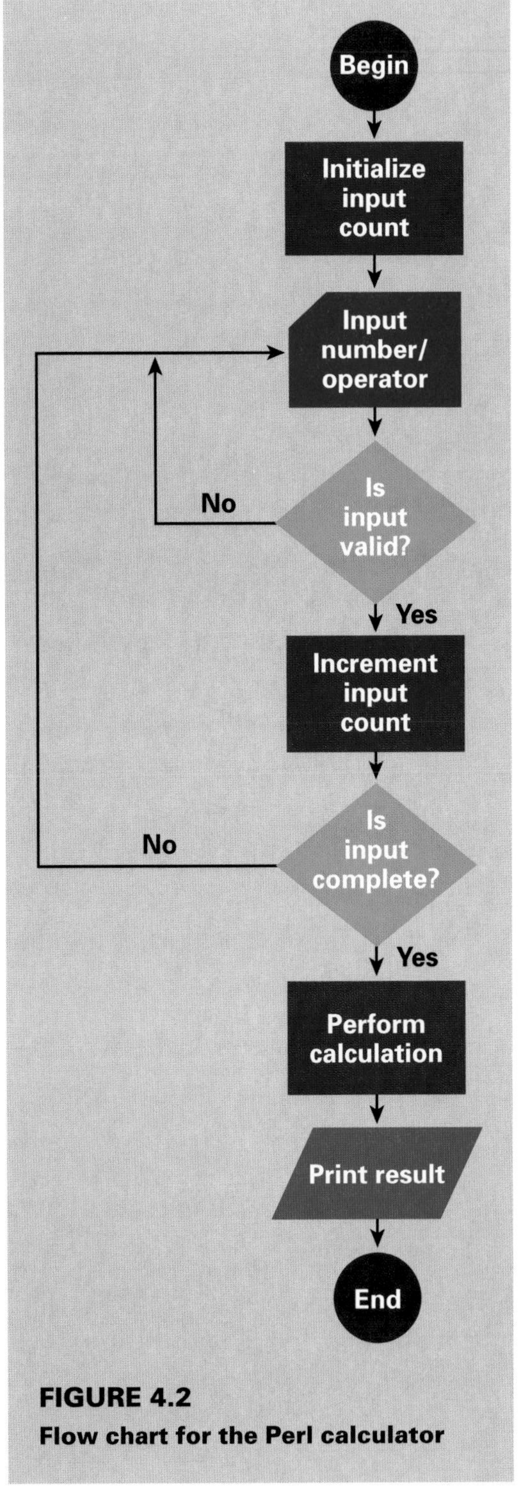


**FIGURE 4.2**
**Flow chart for the Perl calculator**

## Who's in Control?

Who would want to program this way? Structured programming is actually a very powerful programming technique. A more telling question would be: who would want to use this kind of program? To understand the answer, you have to know what makes structured programming powerful, and how it evolved.

When a computer executes a program, it follows a sequence of steps. These steps are followed one at a time, from beginning to end. Each step is an instruction that corresponds to a string (a byte) of 0s and 1s (bits); typical instructions are either 16 or 32 bits in today's computers. Early computers, even early PCs, had only primitive input/output interfaces not much removed from this low level. The Altair, the first PC, had no keyboard and no monitor. Input came from switches set manually to a byte code instruction, and output came from a set of lights that lit up corresponding to an octal number. Even when PCs acquired monitors and keyboards, the windows and icons we take as commonplace remained years away. The I/O (Input/Output) may have come in the form of more familiar numbers and letters, but the mode was still textual rather than graphical, and still fundamentally sequential.

Early programming code was not far removed from the machine code of bytes that computers understand. Assembly language may use words instead of bytes, but its instructions correspond to the lowest level of instructions the computer understands.

Yet this level of programming is very powerful. The more program code resembles machine code, the more efficiently and quickly it will run. Structured program code resembles machine code more than object-oriented program code resembles machine code. Hence the adage:

"The C programming language: combining the power of assembly language with the ease of assembly language."

In other words, what is powerful from the computer's perspective is not necessarily easy from the user's perspective. Ease of use was not an issue in the early days of computing. Computing power was a scarce resource, most users were themselves programmers, and the person most likely to be using a program was the person who wrote it. Programs needed to be fast and efficient much more than they needed to be "user-friendly."

The user interface that stems from this environment is *structure-driven*. In other words, the set of events that constitute the user's interactions with the program is controlled by the program itself, not by the user. Each input/output event originates with a process the program has completed, not with an action the user has taken. In the calculator program, for instance, the program prompts the user for a number or prompts the user for an operation, rather than waiting and expecting user input.

The result is a program that's more efficient than elegant. If one wrote the program, or used it repeatedly, then the clumsiness of the interface would fade with familiarity. Still, it's a user interface that only a programmer could love.

## A Simple Object-Oriented Program

Let's reprogram our calculator, this time using an object-oriented approach. Figure 4.3 shows a calculator created with simple HTML and JScript.

Using this calculator is as simple as using an ordinary pocket calculator. Point the mouse at the numbers to be entered, and click. Corrections can easily be made using the familiar "Clear" and "Clear Entry" buttons. A new calculation can begin immediately with the results of the previous calculation. In other words, none of the shortcomings of the Perl calculator interface are problems here; our JScript calculator operates with a natural, easy user interface.

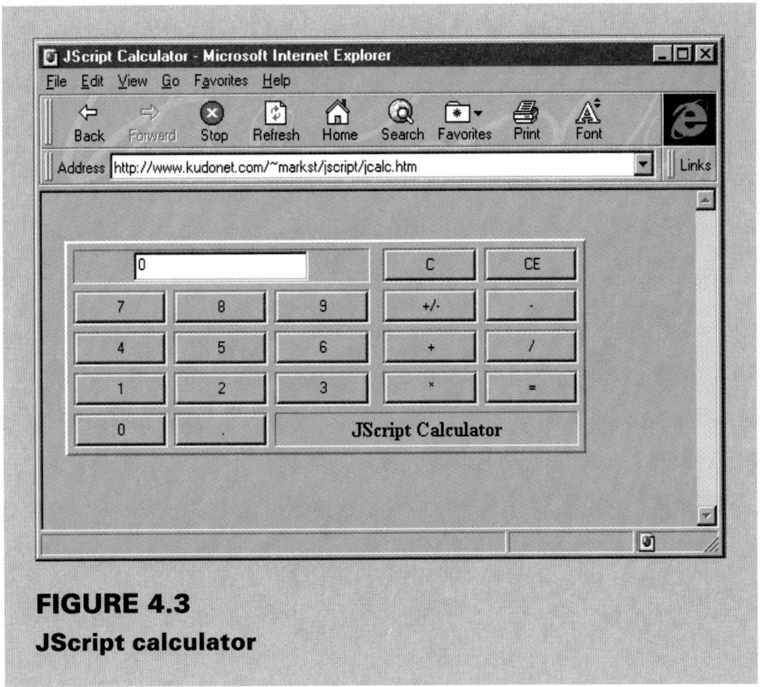


**FIGURE 4.3**
**JScript calculator**

Here is the code that makes this calculator possible. Don't worry if much of it looks unfamiliar. Our goal here is to get a general sense of the object-oriented approach that makes this user interface possible.

```
<HTML>

<HEAD>

<TITLE>JScript Calculator</TITLE>

</HEAD>

<BODY>

<FORM NAME="Jcalc">

<TABLE BORDER=2 WIDTH=50 HEIGHT=60 CELLPADDING=1 CELLSPACING=5>

<TR>
<TD COLSPAN=3 ALIGN=MIDDLE><INPUT NAME="Display" TYPE="Text" SIZE=24
VALUE="0"></TD>
<TD></TD>
```

```
<TD ALIGN=CENTER><INPUT NAME="ClearInput" TYPE="Button" VALUE="  C  "
onClick="Clear()"></TD>
<TD ALIGN=CENTER><INPUT NAME="ClearInputEntry" TYPE="Button" VALUE="  CE "
onClick="ClearEntry()"></TD>
</TR>

<TR>
<TD ALIGN=CENTER><INPUT NAME="b7" TYPE="Button" VALUE="  7  "
onClick="NSelect(7)"></TD>
<TD ALIGN=CENTER><INPUT NAME="b8" TYPE="Button" VALUE="  8  "
onClick="NSelect(8)"></TD>
<TD ALIGN=CENTER><INPUT NAME="b9" TYPE="Button" VALUE="  9  "
onClick="NSelect(9)"></TD>
<TD></TD>
<TD ALIGN=CENTER><INPUT NAME="ChangeSign" TYPE="Button" VALUE=" +/- "
onClick="CSign()"></TD>
<TD ALIGN=MIDDLE><INPUT NAME="Subtracting" TYPE="Button" VALUE="   -   "
onClick="Calculation("-")"></TD>
</TR>

<TR>
<TD ALIGN=CENTER><INPUT NAME="b4" TYPE="Button" VALUE="  4  "
OnClick="NSelect(4)"></TD>
<TD ALIGN=CENTER><INPUT NAME="b5" TYPE="Button" VALUE="  5  "
OnClick="NSelect(5)"></TD>
<TD ALIGN=CENTER><INPUT NAME="b6" TYPE="Button" VALUE="  6  "
OnClick="NSelect(6)"></TD>
<TD></TD>
<TD ALIGN=MIDDLE><INPUT NAME="Adding" TYPE="Button" VALUE="  +  "
onClick="Calculation('+')"></TD>
<TD ALIGN=MIDDLE><INPUT NAME="Dividing" TYPE="Button" VALUE="   /   "
onClick="Calculation('/')"></TD>
</TR>

<TR>
<TD ALIGN=CENTER><INPUT NAME="b1" TYPE="Button" VALUE="  1  "
OnClick="NSelect(1)"></TD>
<TD ALIGN=CENTER><INPUT NAME="b2" TYPE="Button" VALUE="  2  "
```

```
OnClick="NSelect(2)"></TD>
<TD ALIGN=CENTER><INPUT NAME="b3" TYPE="Button" VALUE="  3  "
OnClick="NSelect(3)"></TD>
<TD></TD>
<TD ALIGN=MIDDLE><INPUT NAME="Multiplying" TYPE="Button" VALUE="  *  "
onClick="Calculation('*')"></TD>
<TD ALIGN=CENTER><INPUT NAME="bEq" TYPE="Button" VALUE="  =  "
onClick="Calculation('=')"></TD>
</TR>

<TR>
<TD ALIGN=CENTER><INPUT NAME="b0" TYPE="Button" VALUE="  0  "
onClick="NSelect(0)"></TD>
<TD ALIGN=CENTER><INPUT NAME="DecimalPoint" TYPE="Button" VALUE="   . "
onClick="Decimal()"></TD>
<TD COLSPAN=4 ALIGN=CENTER><B>JScript Calculator</B></TD>
</TR>

</TABLE>

</FORM>

<SCRIPT LANGUAGE="JavaScript">

<!— Hide from script-dumb browsers

var FJcalc = document.Jcalc;
var Num = 0;                //Number entered from button
var Num1 = 0;               //Number to perform operation on
var Num2 = 0;               //Number to perform operation on
var Num3 = 0;               //Results of operating on N1, N2
var NumSet1 = "false";      //Have we finished entering N1?
var NumStart2 = "false";    //Have we started entering N2?
var DecSet = "false";       //Are we using a decimal place?
var Op = '';                //Operation as entered by user
var DoOp = '';              //Operation as accepted by script
```

```
//NSelect is the function which enters numbers from the buttons
//pushed. It has to keep the ever-growing string that is the
//number, and it has to know whether we are entering in the first
//or second number.

function NSelect (Num) {
if (NumSet1 == "false") {
   if ((parseFloat(FJcalc.Display.value) == Ø) && (DecSet == "false")) {
      FJcalc.Display.value = Num;
      } else {
      FJcalc.Display.value += Num;
      }
   Num1 = FJcalc.Display.value;
   } else {
   if (NumStart2 == "false") {
      if (DoOp != '') {
         FJcalc.Display.value = Num;
         NumStart2 = "true";
         } else {
         Clear();
         NSelect(Num);
         }
      } else {
      FJcalc.Display.value += Num;
      }
   Num2 = FJcalc.Display.value;
   }
}

//Calculation is the function that actually performs the
//numerical operations. It has to check to see if the user
//has hit an operation button in a logical place for
//performing an operation, and perform the operation if it
//is valid. This act of accepting a valid operation is also
//how we demarcate taking input for the second number instead
//of the first, so that flag has to be switched here too.

function Calculation (Op) {
```

```
if (NumSet1 == "false") {
   if (Op != '=') {
      NumSet1 = "true";
      DoOp = Op;
      DecSet = "false";
      }
   } else {
   if (NumStart2 == "true") {
      Num1 = parseFloat(Num1);
      Num2 = parseFloat(Num2);
      if (DoOp == '') { DoOp = Op; }
      if (DoOp == '+') { Num3 = Num1+Num2; }
      if (DoOp == '-') { Num3 = Num1-Num2; }
      if (DoOp == '*') { Num3 = Num1*Num2; }
      if (DoOp == '/') { Num3 = Num1/Num2; }
 FJcalc.Display.value = Num3;
      Num1 = Num3;
      Num2 = Ø;
      NumStart2 = "false";
      DecSet = "false";
      DoOp = '';
      if (Op != '=') { DoOp = Op; }
      } else {
      DoOp = Op;
      NumStart2 = "true";
 FJcalc.Display.value = "";
      }
   }
}

//Decimal adds a decimal point to a number string,
//unless one has already been added to that string.

function Decimal () {
if (DecSet == "false") {
   if (NumSet1 == "false") {
 FJcalc.Display.value += ".";
      DecSet = "true";
```

```
        Num1 = FJcalc.Display.value;
        } else {
        if (NumStart2 == "false") {
 FJcalc.Display.value = ".";
           Num2 = FJcalc.Display.value;
           DecSet = "true";
           NumStart2 = "true";
           } else {
 FJcalc.Display.value += ".";
           Num2 = FJcalc.Display.value;
           DecSet = "true";
           }
        }
    }
}

//If we are still working on the first number, then
//this is the same as clear. Otherwise, clear out the
//second number and get ready to start again on it.

function ClearEntry () {
if (NumSet1 == "false") {
   Clear();
   } else {
   Num2 = 0;
   NumStart2 = "false";
   DecSet = "false";
 FJcalc.Display.value = 0;
   }
}

//Clear re-initializes everything.

function Clear () {
Num1 = 0;
Num2 = 0;
Num3 = 0;
NumSet1 = "false";
```

```
NumStart2 = "false";
DecSet = "false";
DoOp = "";
FJcalc.Display.value = 0;
}

//CSign changes the current number from positive to negative, or
//vice versa.

function CSign () {
if (NumSet1 == "false") {
 FJcalc.Display.value = parseFloat(FJcalc.Display.value)*-1;
   Num1 = FJcalc.Display.value;
   } else {
   if (NumStart2 == "true") {
 FJcalc.Display.value = parseFloat(FJcalc.Display.value)*-1;
      Num2 = FJcalc.Display.value;
      }
   }
}

//->

</SCRIPT>

</BODY>

</HTML>
```

The first part of this listing is almost entirely conventional HTML. To create a good layout, you can imagine your design projected against a table grid. Our calculator easily fits this design technique. The buttons and display of the calculator make up the table rows. By making the table grid not only visible, but padded, we achieve a visual effect that looks more like an actual calculator than a table.

Because we want this calculator to be interactive, both receiving and processing input, we embed this table within FORM tags. Each button is specified as an input source, with the values associated with these buttons that we would expect for a calculator.

This form differs subtly from a conventional HTML form, however. The FORM tag lacks a METHOD attribute. Normally this attribute would be required, specifying either POST or GET, as we discussed in Chapter 3, depending on how input is to be passed to an application through CGI. The FORM tag here also lacks an ACTION attribute, which would normally tell the browser the location of the CGI program for processing the form. Since our form will be processed on the client side, neither of these attributes is required. Instead our FORM simply has a NAME attribute, enabling the script to distinguish forms by name later on.

The INPUT tags within this form also differ from the usual tags. TYPE is specified simply as "button," which is not one of the normal options. Also, the INPUT tag contains a new attribute, onClick. This pair, button and onClick, specifies one means of passing input to the script. For the Jcalc script this is the only input source used.

Because browsers ignore HTML tags and attributes they do not understand, these new elements will not cause particular problems with the appearance of the calculator. Figure 4.4 shows how this page appears with an old version of Internet Explorer. The user can see the calculator without any problems in this view, but cannot actually use it unless their Web browser supports client-side scripting with JScript or JavaScript.

What follows the form is the body of the script itself. In this case, it consists of a section of variable declarations and six function definitions. Those familiar with structured programming languages may be puzzled: Okay, we've defined our variables and defined our functions, but where's the program? Welcome to object-oriented programming. The program just *is* those six functions: nothing more, nothing less.

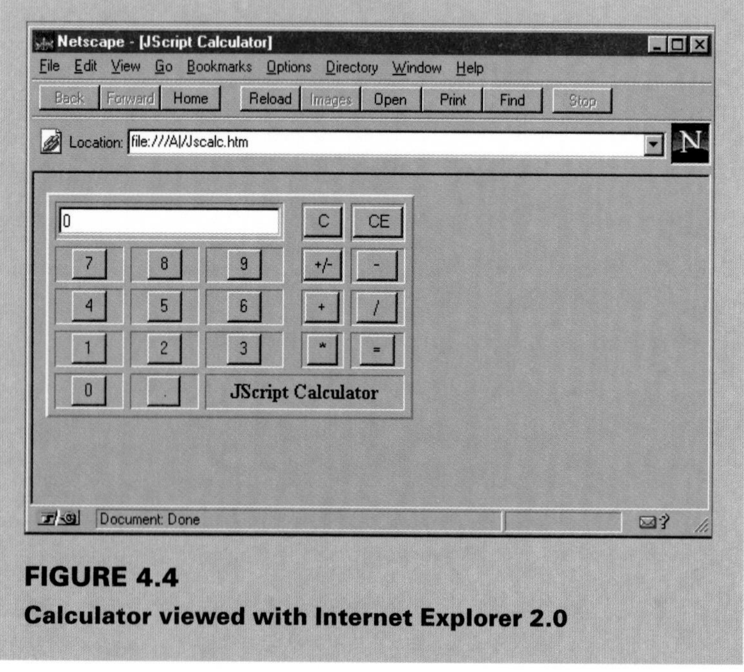


**FIGURE 4.4**
**Calculator viewed with Internet Explorer 2.0**

Each function is the value named by an onClick attribute of some button on our calculator: the numbered buttons call the NSelect function, the arithmetic operator buttons call the Calculation function, the decimal point calls the Decimal function, and the Clear and Clear Entry buttons call the Clear and ClearEntry functions respectively. onClick refers to a click of the mouse while pointing at that button; this is called an *event.* The script must know how to respond to an event, and the value specified by the onClick attribute instructs the script how to respond; this is called an event handler.

In other words, our program consists of a set of possible events—in this case button clicks; and a set of event handlers for those events—in this case six functions for the six types of buttons on our calculator. This sort of program has a decidedly nonlinear aspect. The program has neither a definite beginning nor a definite end, nor must events happen in a unique order. The program could begin with any button click and end with any button click, and the user, not the structure of the program, sets the order in which these events will occur.

## Structure-Driven versus Event-Driven Programs

Object-oriented programs and object-oriented programming are not necessarily the same. Object-oriented programs reflect the emergence of GUIs as the preferred interface between computer and user. The idea is that by having the "objects" on a computer screen resemble familiar, real-world objects, users can depend on their familiarity with these objects to understand how to use programs. The result should be applications with little or no learning curve.

Our calculator illustrates these ideas. Anyone who knows how to use a mouse and who has ever used an actual hand-held calculator will immediately know how to use this program. No explanation or instruction is required.

Of course, this program could have been written using a structured programming approach. JScript has all the familiar elements of a structured programming language, and indeed we see many of these elements at work in the function definitions of this program. In fact, many familiar object-oriented applications are written in large part or even entirely with structured programming code. Frequently, though, structured programming does not fit naturally with object-oriented applications.

Object-oriented programming evolved to meet two needs. In part, it provides a better way of writing reusable or portable code; we will talk more about this feature later. Its other important function is to provide a programming environment whose elements resemble the elements of the applications it is intended to develop.

The Greek philosopher Socrates thought that what was most important about objects was their properties, in particular those properties that were essential. His successor, Aristotle, took a somewhat different view, asserting that what was most important about objects was their purpose, or function. We will incorporate both of these views.

## Properties

A real-world object like a book has a number of properties. A book has a title, an author, and a publisher. These are very essential properties for a book. It also has something called an ISBN number, and a Library of Congress catalog number. Even though all books have these two properties, they seem less essential. Their importance depends on context: in a bookstore, where books are tracked primarily by ISBN number, the ISBN number will be very important, but the Library of Congress catalog number will not be essential at all; in a library, the reverse is likely to be true. In a bookstore price will be an essential property, but in a library it will not. Size and weight hardly seem important, unless you work for a shipping company that must deliver books to a bookstore or library. So what counts as an essential property depends on context.

Think of it another way: objects can also be viewed as containers. What properties are important for an object depend on what that object is contained within. A library is an object, but it is also a container full of books. Indeed, a book is also a container for pages; a page contains words, and so on. Objects have a hierarchy, and their properties depend not only on what the object is, but where it exists within this hierarchy.

A GUI application is not just a collection of objects, but a hierarchy of objects. Figure 4.5 illustrates part of the object hierarchy for the calculator program. For example, the Clear button is contained within a table, which is contained within a form, which is contained within a document, which is contained within a browser window. Each of the containers in this hierarchy has certain properties that are essential to it relative to its place in the hierarchy. The browser window has a location: the current URL. It also has a history: URLs it has recently visited. The document has a type: HTML. This form has a NAME: Jcalc. NAME is an essential property in this context because the form will be handled by a JScript program. In another context—our Perl calculator, for example—the form would be handled by a CGI application. NAME ceases to be an essential property in that context, but instead METHOD and ACTION become essential properties. So it goes all the way down the hierarchy, until we get to the Clear button. This button has the onClick property, which can either be true or false.

## Methods

Objects not only have properties, they have functions: actions which they can perform, or which can be performed with respect to them. We will call these *methods*. Again, what methods are relevant to an object depend on where it is in the hierarchy. A book may be opened or closed; it may also be read. These methods seem to apply generally. A book contained in a bookstore may be purchased, while a book contained in a library may not. Whether purchasing is a relevant method for a book depends on context.

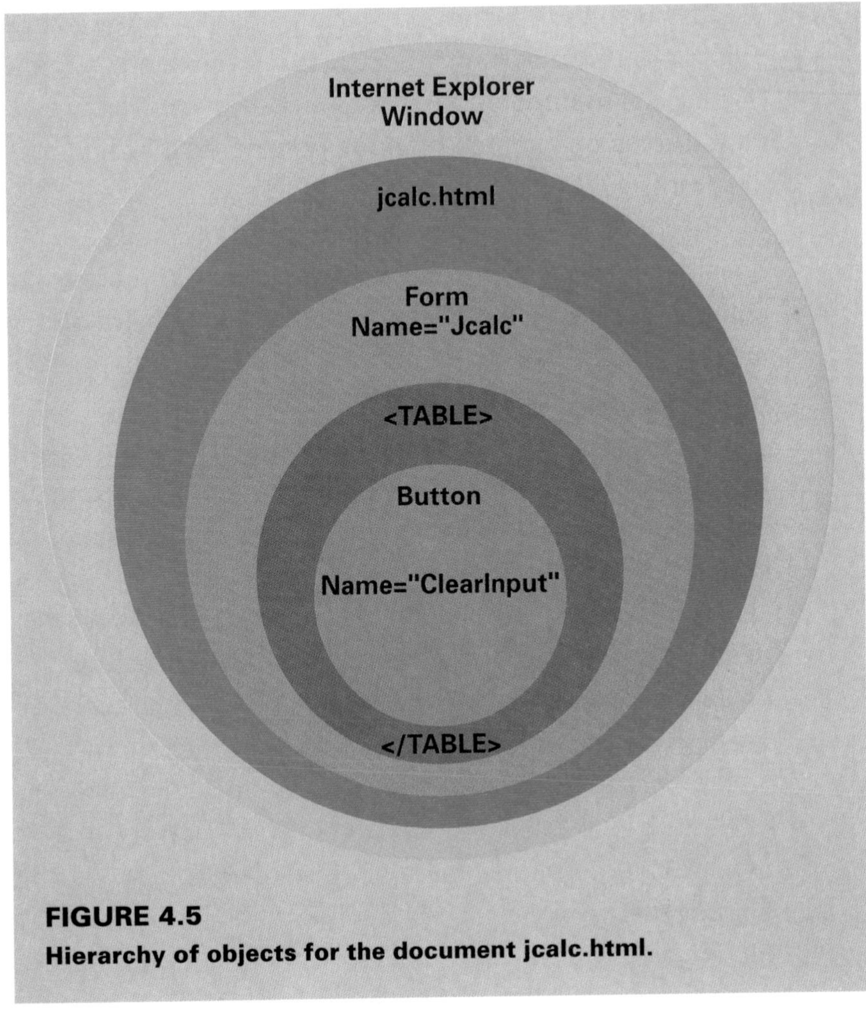


**FIGURE 4.5**
**Hierarchy of objects for the document jcalc.html.**

JScript objects can have methods associated with them as well. Windows may be opened, links may be followed, buttons may be clicked. The results of applying these methods to these objects will depend on context. Some of that context is predefined by the syntax of the JScript language. Each JScript program defines the rest of a particular context.

For the Clear button, the onClick property differs from other properties. In fact, onClick is a method, and thus requires a definition of the outcome of applying that method. In other words, clicking on the button is an event and requires an event handler. Our Clear function is the method that handles this event.

## Events

It was Aristotle who focused on the fact that people are not merely perceivers of the world, but agents in it. We learn the nature of objects not just by focusing our attention on them, but by acting on them to discern their function. These actions are the events that drive an object-oriented program.

A structured program has a definite beginning, and a final state that will signify the end of the program. The structure drives the program toward that final state through its manipulation of data and requests for input. The user enters into this structure as one source of input, but can never really be said to be in control of the program.

By contrast, an object-oriented program really is nothing more than the set of possible events the user can take, and the handlers for those events. With our calculator, we have six types of events: the user can lengthen the number input by another digit or by including a decimal point, change the sign of a number, perform an operation on a pair of numbers, erase the last number entered, or erase all input. No other events are defined, so no other events are recognized. Clicking the mouse outside the calculator or between buttons on the calculator has no effect, for example. Clicking and dragging the mouse has no effect. These are not defined events.

Designing an object-oriented program begins with deciding what types of events you want to occur, and then determining how to handle them. Good design will allow events that feel natural to the user. It would be possible, for example, to program a calculator to input a number any time the mouse passed over a button, with no clicking required. We could do this by making the event onMouseOver an attribute of an object. This would in some sense be "faster" because the extra step of clicking would be eliminated. But it would be a terrible design choice: it goes against the conventions of how users expect buttons to behave, and it would make the interior buttons on a table extremely difficult to use.

If you can design attractive and functional HTML-based Web pages, you can design good JScript events. The design principles are the same: presentation should be clear, the overall look should be attractive, the user's attention should be drawn to key features, and their importance should suggest itself naturally.

## User-Friendly But Programmer-Tough

Structured programming remains popular, even for developing some object-oriented applications, because structured programs are easier to write and debug.

Structured programs are linear. In terms of design, this means the programmer can think one step at a time. In terms of debugging, this means that if a program breaks down it will do so at a particular point. Often determining where a program has failed is the most important step in determining why it failed.

Object-oriented programming is nonlinear. Events do not necessarily happen in a preset order. Event handlers may also need to interact with each other; and the program may need to handle more than one event simultaneously. In terms of design, the programmer needs to think about several events in parallel. In terms of debugging, it will not always be obvious where a program has broken down, nor, given where it broke down, which event caused the problem.

Fortunately we are not learning a full object-oriented language like C++ or Java. Our scripts will be measured in dozens of lines of code, not thousands.

Furthermore, keep in mind that object-oriented programs contain a lot of structured programming under the surface. Each of our functions in the calculator program, for example, is a small structured program.

Finally, object-oriented programs have an important asset that makes programming easier: the objects themselves. Objects are designed to be reusable. While a particular program may be difficult to design and debug, once you have done so you should find that some objects can be ported to other programs. The trio object definition/event specification/event handler can be highly self-contained, and hence easily moved.

This works on many levels. Our calculator has 19 buttons, but requires only six functions because some buttons are similar enough that the functions can be written so generally as to handle more than one button. At a higher level, some of these functions might easily be used with other programs. The Nselect function, for example, could well be reused in other applications. This function builds up a larger numerical string from individual number-button clicks. This is an indispensable function in a calculator, and could be helpful in a variety of other programs that require numerical input.

At an even higher level, full object-oriented programming languages allow objects to be stored in libraries that may be called by any program. The Java language takes this to the extreme, allowing libraries to be distributed across a network. This results in the possibility of programs whose code need not reside on a single computer.

Well-designed JScript should leave the designer with a set of objects and methods that can be reused with little modification. Some aspects of good JScript design depend on following the general principles of good programming; we will discuss these principles in the next chapter. Much of good JScript design, though, depends on planning ahead: portable code results from planning objects that are extensible and reusable. In Chapter 6 we'll put these principles of portability to the test.

Comments on Comments

Flow Control

Modular Design

Debugging

# Chapter 5
# Programming Basics

Society often imposes boundaries on us that are artificial. Programming is a relatively new enterprise. The decades we use to measure its age pale compared to the millennia we need to measure the age of fields such as mathematics or poetry. Consequently, society has had to make some rather hasty decisions about what sort of enterprise programming is, resulting in a classification that may well be inaccurate.

We think that programming is a science, and hence we call the exercise of programming skills "computer science." In the early days this made some sense—the first programmers were often mathematicians, and early programming meant assembly language: thinking in terms of registers and memory addresses, feeling as comfortable with base 16 as base 10 numbers. Yet today's high-level languages like Visual Basic, and scripting languages like VBScript and JScript, have little in common with that first generation of programming languages.

The sad irony is that fine arts students perfectly comfortable with the intricacies of PhotoShop and English majors fluent in HTML nonetheless believe that they cannot program. After all, programming is "scientific" and "mathematical," and society has labeled these as outside the boundary of what a designer or writer can master.

The truth is that someone with the skills to master PhotoShop or HTML is much better prepared to learn JScript than someone with the skills to master assembly language. Programming at this level is not a science—it's an art. Writing programs in JScript is an exercise in composition, and everything your high school English teacher taught you about writing a good essay will apply to writing a good script.

## Comments on Comments

We all remember what a shock it was the first time we had to write a high school research paper. We were not allowed to simply sit down and start writing. We had to have research notes, and they had to be submitted and checked. We had to have an outline, which had to be submitted and checked. We had to submit a rough draft before beginning the final draft. All of this seemed like a lot of unnecessary work. After all, once the final paper was written, the draft, the outline, and the notes could all be thrown away. Yet all this "extra" work did encourage us to organize our thinking, to plan ahead. This process made it easy to move from writing about what we wanted to say to simply saying it.

JScript, like most programming languages, allows programmers to include comment statements in their work. Comment statements are just as extraneous to a program as an outline is to an essay—and just as essential. Two programs that are identical, except that one includes comments and the other does not, will run exactly the same. But comments should be a vital part of how you develop and plan your program.

## Comments for Readability

In writing an essay we are instructed to always think of our words from another person's point of view. While the words you choose may remind you of what you were thinking when you wrote them, another person cannot read your mind; your thoughts must be fully contained in the words themselves.

Programming is no different. Good comments can improve the readability of your script so that someone not privy to your thoughts can read through your code to understand what the program does and how it does it.

Readable, well-commented code can help you as much as it can help others. You may return to a program long after its completion wanting to modify or borrow from it. You may return to a section of a program you have not thought about for some time, suddenly needing to modify it because of changes elsewhere in the program. In these situations you may find it extremely difficult to reconstruct your own thought processes if you have not properly commented within your code.

Look, for example, at the variable declarations in the calculator program:

```
var Num = 0;                 //Number entered from button
var Num1 = 0;                //Number to perform operation on
var Num2 = 0;                //Number to perform operation on
var Num3 = 0;                //Results of operating on N1, N2
var NumSet1 = "false";       //Have we finished entering N1?
var NumStart2 = "false";     //Have we started entering N2?
var DecSet = "false";        //Are we using a decimal place?
var Op = '';                 //Operation as entered by user
var DoOp = '';               //Operation as accepted by script
```

Here a brief comment is included after each variable declaration to explain what the variable is and how it will be used.

These comments make it much easier to decipher what is happening later on in the program. Because variable declaration is done first, these comments are also all grouped together in one place that is easy for someone reading the code to refer back to.

## Self-commenting Code

Most modern programming languages give the programmer great latitude in selecting variable names and function names, and JScript is no exception. These cannot be reserved words (words already used in the syntax of JScript). They cannot contain spaces. These names are case sensitive: foobar names a different variable than FooBar. Keeping these restrictions in mind, you can engage in some very creative naming schemes. Table 5.1 applies some creative naming to the calculator program.

Use this creativity to your advantage. Variable names such as a, b, c, or function names such as f1, f2, f3, will not illuminate the reader as to the purpose of the variable or function.

Take your cue from the JScript event names: onClick, onMouseOver, onSelect, and so on. Anyone familiar with a mouse easily understands what these event names refer to. Let your variable names follow this convention. MyBirthday or My_Birthday is a better variable name than bd; StreetAddress or Street_Address is a better variable name than A1.

To those who object that these naming conventions involve too much typing, remember: you will still spend most of your time while developing a program puzzling over code, not typing.

**TABLE 5.1 THREE CHOICES OF VARIABLE NAMES FOR THE CALCULATOR PROGRAM**

| Poor Variable Names | Better Variable Names | Best Variable Names |
|---|---|---|
| N | Num | NumberEntered |
| N1 | Num1 | FirstOperand |
| N2 | Num2 | SecondOperand |
| N3 | Num3 | NumberCalculated |
| NS1 | NumSet1 | FinishedOperand1 |
| NS2 | NumStart2 | StartedOperand2 |
| D | DecSet | DecimalSet |
| O | Op | OperatorEntered |
| DO | DoOp | OperationToDo |

## Commenting as a Development Process

When writing an essay, an outline provides you with a mechanism for further refining your ideas. You start with a simple outline and revise it to add more detail, until you reach the point when moving from outline to draft should be an easy step.

Programming should follow the same design process. The program should evolve as a series of more-detailed comment statements, without any actual code. When the comments provide a detailed description of the program, writing the actual code should be an easy step. We will look at the development of the calculator program and one of its functions, NSelect, through this kind of process.

## The Calculator Program: Simple Outline

```
//This program presents a visual image resembling
//a pocket calculator, which users can command by clicking on
//buttons to perform simple arithmetic calculations.
```

This is the simplest statement we can make of what the calculator program is, and what it does. It suggests two questions that need to be answered before we can proceed: how are we going to present the calculator image, and how are we going to handle the arithmetic calculations?

The image could be designed in several ways: it could be an image map, a series of inline GIF images, or an HTML table, for example. The calculations could be done through CGI or by client-side scripting, and if client-side scripting is chosen, it could be done using JScript/JavaScript or VBScript. Deciding which options to use does not involve any difficult programming decisions; these are design issues.

Image maps are normally processed through CGI on the server. The current HTML standard makes provisions for client-side processing of image maps, but not all browsers support this standard yet—although Internet Explorer and Netscape Navigator do. Inline GIFs can vary somewhat in appearance and spacing when viewed with different browsers. Tables allow for finer control over the appearance of the page, so we will use a table.

In Chapter 3 we discussed a number of reasons why client-side scripting offers performance advantages over CGI. Currently the only browser that supports VBScript is Internet Explorer. VBScript is a good choice for tasks that it alone can perform, but we will reach a wider audience with our Web page if we use JScript whenever possible.

So now we can expand our outline a bit:

```
//This program presents a representation of a
//pocket calculator rendered as an HTML table.
//
```

```
//Users can perform simple arithmetic calculations
//by clicking on buttons.
//
//These button clicks will be JScript events, and
//the arithmetic calculations will be performed by
//JScript event handlers.
```

## The Calculator Program: Adding Some Detail

These comments are beginning to resemble an outline now. Again, each point in the outline suggests the next level of questions that must be answered before we can proceed. For our table, what will the cells of the table be? For the buttons, which calculations will the calculator allow? For the event handlers, what types of events need to be handled?

We need a display cell on the table that corresponds to a calculator's LED display. We need a clear button and a clear entry button. We need number keys and a decimal point for entering numbers. We'll also need a +/- button for changing the sign of entered numbers. We need an equal sign. We need keys for the operations to perform.

For this calculator, we'll keep the operations simple: no square roots or exponents; no percentages; only addition, subtraction, multiplication, and division.

Given this information, what types of events have we defined? Some of the answers are obvious, but other answers require us to make our first real programming decisions. Each number button clicked is the same type of event. The event will pass a different value to the event handler depending on which number it is, but all number buttons can be handled by the same event handler. Likewise all four arithmetic operations can be handled by the same event handler, passing a different value to the event handler depending on which operation was selected. Clearly a decimal button click is different from any other event and will require its own event handler. Changing the sign of a number is also a unique event and will require its own event handler.

The "clear" and "clear entry" events are very similar. We could use the same event handler for both, and simply have different conditions within the event handler to handle the differences between them. However, all other things being equal, a more modular design is preferable to a less modular design, so we will use a separate event handler for each. This is a programming choice, not a design choice; either approach must yield the same output to the user.

Applying this same logic to the equal sign button, it would appear we should assign it a different event handler. After all, it is quite a different operation from any of the arithmetic operations. This makes sense when we are thinking about a typical sequence of button clicks, like

```
2, +, 3, =
```

The output display that corresponds to these clicks is

```
2, 2, 3, 5
```

Consider a different sequence of button clicks, though:

```
2, +, 3, + 4 =
```

In this case the corresponding output display is

```
2, 2, 3, 5, 4, 9
```

In other words, the calculation and output display triggered by the second + in this case is the same as the calculation and output display triggered by the = in the first case; both events are handled in the same way. Thus the event handler for the arithmetic operations will have to handle the equal sign operation as a special case anyway. There is no reason to make a separate event handler just for the equal sign.

We have identified six event handlers to handle all button click events. Our expanded outline of comments looks like this:

```
//This program presents a representation of a
//pocket calculator rendered as an HTML table.
//The cells of the table will have:
//    a display area,
//    C and CE,
//    the ten digits,
//    a decimal point,
//    +, -, *, /, =
//
//Users can perform simple arithmetic calculations
//by clicking in the appropriate cells. The table is
//a form, and each cell an input area of type Button,
//with the attribute onClick calling an event handler.
//
//These button clicks will be handled by six different
//event handlers; each event handler will be a JScript
//function.
//    Number button clicks will be handled by the
```

```
//    NSelect function,
//    Csign changes the sign of a number entered,
//    C button clicks will be handled by the Clear
//    function,
//    CE button clicks will be handled by the
//    ClearEntry function,
//    Decimal button clicks will be handled by the
//    Decimal function,
//    Clicks on +, -, *, /, or = will be handled by
//    the Calculation function.
```

At this point our outline is almost complete. What remains is outlining each of the six functions. Once they have been outlined, we can move directly to coding the program itself. In the next section we will look at the NSelect function.

## Flow Control

As mentioned in the last chapter, object-oriented programming contains a lot of structured programming beneath the surface. At some level object-oriented programming can be reduced to a series of structured programming tasks. In the calculator program, each function is a small structured program. Part of understanding good programming technique, therefore, requires understanding structured programming.

Structured programs are essentially linear. The challenge is to design a program flow from beginning to end that takes you through the branches needed to handle all the conditions that arise in the program. Programmers have a choice of design approaches here.

Verbal thinkers may prefer to continue the outline technique presented in the previous section. Following this approach, you refine an outline of comments that fully describes the flow control of the program. A full outline yields something called pseudo-code: a body of statements that, though not corresponding exactly to the formal syntax of a programming language, specifies step by step what the program will do. The transition from pseudo-code to program code is straightforward.

Visual thinkers may prefer to use a flow chart design. Following this approach, you diagram the flow control of the program. A full flow chart diagrams each branch and loop that the program goes through; every junction in the diagram corresponds to a specific step in the program.

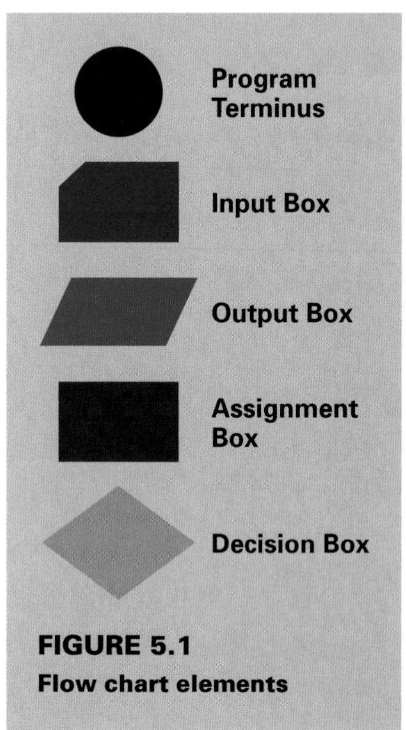


**FIGURE 5.1**
**Flow chart elements**

Flow charts have their own simple syntax (see Figure 5.1). Every element of a flow chart is either a program terminus, an input box, an output box, an assignment box, or a decision box. A program terminus indicates either the beginning or end of the program. An input box indicates a point at which the program receives input from an outside source, either from something the user has entered or from another program. An output box indicates a point at which the program sends output, whether to the screen, to the printer, to a file, or to another program. An assignment box indicates a point at which the program performs an operation and changes the values assigned to variables based on the results of the operation. A decision box indicates a point at which the program will branch to one of several paths, depending on a test condition.

We will look at the development of the NSelect function code using both approaches.

## NSelect: A Simple Outline

```
//NSelect is the function which generates the two
//numbers our calculator will operate on.
//It enters numbers from the buttons pushed,
//it has to keep a growing string that is the number,
//it has to display the number,
//and it has to know whether we are entering in the
//first or second number.
```

Again, each point in this outline and corresponding flow chart (Figure 5.2) suggests a question that must be answered before we can proceed.

How do we know which button has been pushed? This will be a value of the event passed to the event handler. The button for 1 will have the attribute "onClick=NSelect(1)" while the button for 3 will have the attribute "onClick=NSelect(3)" and so on. This says to call the function NSelect and pass to it the value within the parentheses.

How do we add a new digit to our number? Here we have to make a programming choice: do we want to treat our number as a number or as a string of characters at this point? At face value this seems like a silly question—why not treat a number as a number—but in fact at this stage of our program it is easier to manipulate a string of characters than a number. Look at two similar JScript operations for assigning a new value to the variable BuiltString:

```
BuiltString = "a" + "b"
BuiltString = 2 + 3
```

The first operation assigns the value *ab* to BuiltString; it joins the two strings together, or *concatenates* them. The second operation assigns the value *5* to BuiltString; it adds the two numbers together. Now, if our calculator program receives the sequence of button clicks 2, 3, what do we want it to do? We want it to return 23 as a result, not 5. In other words, the function of NSelect is concatenation, not addition. Addition will be handled by a separate function. At this stage, then, we will treat our number as a string of characters to be concatenated with the new input.

How do we display the number? One of our cells in the calculator contains a text entry field called "Display." In HTML a text entry field can start with an initial value; in other words, you can assign some text string to be displayed by default when the text entry window appears. JScript has the corresponding ability to write to a text entry field. Changing the display is as simple as updating the value of the variable assigned to the "Display" object.

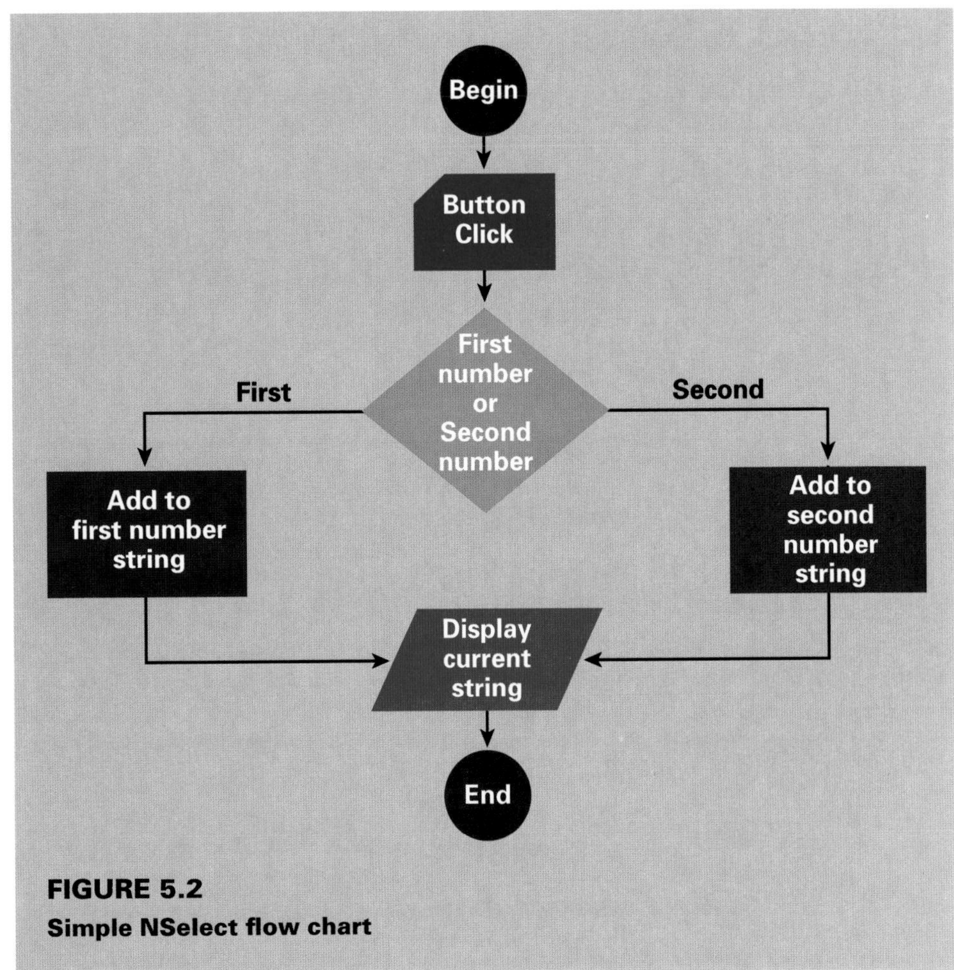


**FIGURE 5.2**
**Simple NSelect flow chart**

When following the outline approach to program development, you can't always see which points of the outline are most important. Flow charts are better at performing this function. Specifically, the biggest programming challenge is almost always filling in the contents of a decision box. We can immediately see from Figure 5-2 that the most important question at this stage is this: How do we know whether we are adding input to the first or second number?

The simple answer would be to have a flag that gets set when the user finishes entering input to the first number, so that we know that further numerical input should be assigned to the second number. We'll call this flag NumSet1. Here the challenges of object-oriented programming loom, however. The real answer is a bit more complicated.

What event signifies the end of input for the first number? Look at these sequences of button clicks:

```
2, +, 3, =
2, 3, -, 1, 7, /, 2, =
4, ., 5, *, 2, =
```

In each case, entering an operation indicates that input to the preceding number has been completed. In other words, a call to the Calculation function signifies that NumSet1 should be set. This illustrates how important it is to keep in mind that object-oriented programming is nonlinear and that events can evolve in parallel. Here a flag for one function (NSelect) will be set from a different function (Calculation). Do other functions place constraints on NSelect? Yes. But let's look first at the state of our outline so far.

## NSelect: A Detailed Outline

```
//NSelect is the function which generates the two
//numbers our calculator will operate on.
//
//The number button clicked on has a value, Num,
//passed to NSelect from onClick.
//
//If the flag NumSet1 has not yet been set, then
//Num is concatenated on the first number string;
//otherwise Num is concatenated on the second
//string.
//
//The value of the text window Display is set to
//the newly concatenated number string.
```

Our flow chart looks more detailed now, but not complete (see Figure 5.3).

Designing for interaction between event handlers is a vital part of object-oriented programming, and an added complication to plotting flow control. We have seen how a flag needed within NSelect must be set from another function. The reverse is also true. Look at these two sequences of button clicks:

```
2, +, +, 2
2, +, 2, +
```

In the first sequence, the second + is erroneous input; it is not a meaningful input entry at this point in the program. Furthermore, such an input sequence could easily happen. Many GUI applications have features that require double-clicking on the mouse to activate, and people often fall into the habit of double-clicking where a single click will suffice. The issue here is not so much a programming puzzle as a question of good interface design. To have a robust interface, our program must know to ignore the second + in the first sequence, but to apply it in the second sequence.

What differentiates these two cases? In both case the second + occurs after the completion of the first number—after the NumSet1 flag has been set. But in the first sequence, the second + occurs prior to the start of input for the second number. We can see, then, that the Calculation function needs to know whether or not input for the second number has commenced, and that this is a flag that will have to be set from within the NSelect function. So we need another flag, which we'll call NumStart2, to be set once we have input at least one number to the second number string.

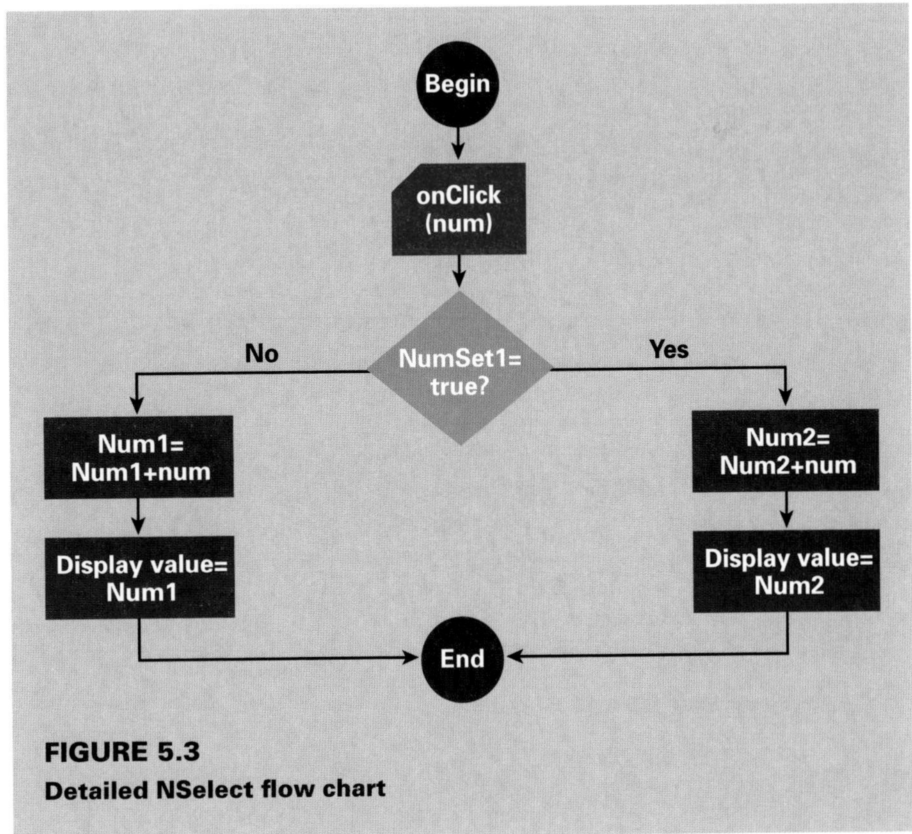


**FIGURE 5.3**
**Detailed NSelect flow chart**

Some other cosmetic details need to be worked

out. Blindly concatenating the new string and displaying the results in the Display window will produce a perfectly functional program, but it will also have some odd display consequences. When we start the calculator, it displays a 0 in this window. As our program stands now, this subsequent button sequence:

```
1, 2, 3
```

would produce this window display:

```
Ø123
```

rather than what we want, which is this display:

```
123
```

Indeed, the only time we want to leave the initial 0 in place is when the next button is the decimal point, so that

```
., 1, 2, 3,
```

will be displayed as

```
Ø.123
```

Here again we find ourselves involved with an interaction between event handlers. Which display method NSelect follows will depend on whether or not a decimal point has been entered, and the DecSet flag will have to be set from within the Decimal function.

Let's look at our completed outline below and the flow chart (Figure 5.4):

```
//
//The number button clicked on has a value, Num,
//passed to NSelect from onClick.
//
//Are we building the first number string, Num1,
//or the second number string, Num2? This
//depends on NumSet1.
//If the NumSet1 = false, build Num1, otherwise
//build Num2.
//
//Building Num1:
//The very first number entered is a special case.
//We'll want to replace the initial Ø in the
//display if this is the first number entered,
```

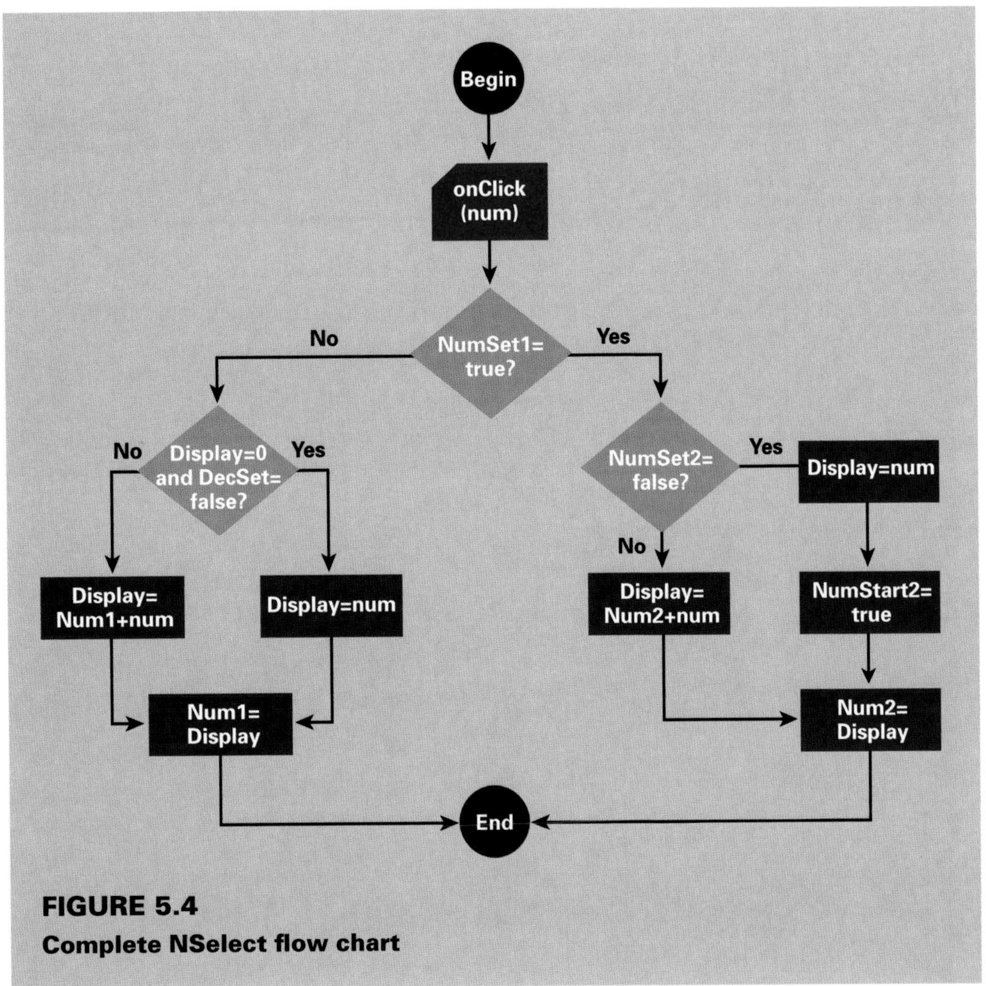


**FIGURE 5.4**
**Complete NSelect flow chart**

```
//unless a decimal point has been entered.
//If Display = 0 and DecSet = false, then
//Display should be set to Num, the number
//just entered. Otherwise, Display = Num1 + Num.
//Now that we've updated the display, update
//Num1:
//Num1 = Display
//
//Building Num2:
//This procedure is parallel to the one above. If
//we are starting Num2, we need to start a fresh
//display; if we are adding more to Num2, we
//concatenate for the new display:
//If NumStart2 = false then Display = Num, and
```

```
//NumStart2 should be set to true, otherwise
//Display = Num2 + Num.
//Num2 = Display.
```

Moving from here to our final program code is straightforward. We can see from our outline which comment statements will remain as comments explaining the function, and which comment statements are pseudo-code that need to be replaced with actual code. A word of caution to those developing code with flow charts: you still need some sort of commentary explaining your final code. Flow charts can, for some, greatly simplify the task of envisioning flow control, but they are not a substitute for the explanatory tips you or another person may need in the future to decipher a piece of old code.

Here is the final code:

```
function NSelect (Num) {
//NSelect is the function which enters numbers from
//the buttons pushed.
//The number button clicked on has a value, Num,
//passed to NSelect from onClick.
//
//Are we building the first number string, Num1,
//or the second number string, Num2? This
//depends on NumSet1.
if (NumSet1 == false) {
//Building Num1:
//The very first number entered is a special case.
//We'll want to replace the initial 0 in the
//display if this is the first number entered,
//unless a decimal point has been entered.
   if ((parseFloat(FJcalc.Display.value) == 0) && (DecSet == false)) {
      FJcalc.Display.value = Num;
   } else {
      FJcalc.Display.value += Num;
   }
   //Now that we've updated the display, update
   //Num1:
   Num1 = FJcalc.Display.value;
   } else {
//Building Num2:
```

```
//This procedure is parallel to the one above. If
//we are starting Num2, we need to start a fresh
//display; if we are adding more to Num2, we
//concatenate for the new display:
   if (NumStart2 == "false") {
 if ((parseFloat(FJcalc.Display.value) == 0) && (DecSet == "false")) {
      FJcalc.Display.value = Num;
      } else {
         FJcalc.Display.value += Num;
   }
   Num1 = FJcalc.Display.value;
   } else {
   if (NumStart2 == "false") {
if (DoOp != '') {
         FJcalc.Display.value = Num;
         NumStart2 = "true";
      } else {
         Clear();
         NSelect(Num);
      }
   } else {
      FJcalc.Display.value += Num;
   }
   Num2 = FJcalc.Display.value;
}
}
```

**NOTE** *You will notice one fork in the flow of this program that is not yet explained: "f (DoOp != '') {". This branch seems puzzling because the function appears to call itself. This is not circular logic; it is an example of a recursive function call. While this is an advanced programming technique that is not often needed, recursive functions can be essential at times. We'll talk more about them later in this chapter.*

## Modular Design

Some programming languages call them subprograms, while others call them subroutines or functions. Some programming languages use more than one of these terms, referring to subtly different operations with each. All of these terms refer to a module of code that may be called from one or more places elsewhere in the program, in which the code module will execute and then return program control to the point in the program from which it was called.

In JScript, the only module type is the function. JScript functions are quite powerful, however, providing all the features you will really need in a module. The calculator program demonstrates the power of modules, since the program consists almost exclusively of function calls. These function calls demonstrate the two key features we need in a module.

First, we can pass values to a function. When either the NSelect function or the Calculation function is called, a value is passed to one of the function variables, Num and Op respectively. In each of these cases only a single value is passed, but nothing prevents us from defining a function that passes more than one value. Thus we can bring input from the program into our function.

Second, we can modify global variables from within the function. In the calculator program *FJcalc.Display* is a global variable whose value gets changed from within the program. Thus any information used in the main program is available to a function, and a function can modify information used in the main program.

You should, then, try to make your programs as modular as possible. Any time that you design two or more sections of a program that will perform identical or similar operations, you should think about defining a function to handle these operations and replacing these sections of code in the main program with a function call.

Modular design can make your programs more readable, more portable, and more efficient. If your comment statements clearly explain what a function does, then it is much easier to read and understand a function call in the midst of a program than it would be to decipher all the statements that make up the function. Well-designed modules, because they are highly self-contained sections of code, will also be reusable with little or no modification in other programs that involve similar operations. And, of course, good modular code helps you write fewer total lines of code to complete a program.

With object-oriented programming, modular design is not an option: it is a necessity. Each event handler must be a program module. Design your event-event handler pairs with care, and you will have an object that can be ported to other programs.

## Recursive Function Calls

You may have noticed a few lines of the NSelect function that were glossed over in the earlier discussion, including a place where the NSelect function calls itself. This sort of self-reference is called *recursion*. It is perfectly permissible syntax in JScript, but you must take care to ensure that these recursive calls actually terminate at some point, or the function will call itself perpetually.

Let's look at a simpler example. Suppose that we want to write a function that will take two numbers, which we'll call *base* and *exponent*, and return as a value base raised to the power exponent. In other words, if base = 2 and exponent = 3, then the result is 2 cubed, or 8. We'll call this function power

```
function power(base, exponent) {
    if (exponent > Ø) {
        return power(base, exponent-1) * base;
        } else {
        return 1;
        }
    }
```

Even though the definition of the power function contains a call to the power function, the definition will still work provided that the nested series of function calls terminates in a defined base case. Our base case here occurs when exponent = 0, in which case the value of the power function is 1.

Working through the case when base = 2 and exponent = 3, we get

```
power(2,3) = power(2,2)*2
```

Since the program does not know the value of power (2,2), it calls the power function again:

```
power(2,2) = power(2,1)*2
```

The program does not know the value of power (2,1), and thus must call the power function again:

```
power(2,1) = power(2,Ø)*2
```

The program still needs a value for power (2,0) and calls the power function again. This time, it gets an answer:

```
power(2,Ø) = 1
```

This gets substituted into the previous unresolved call:

```
power(2,1) = 1*2 = 2
```

This gets substituted back up to the next call:

```
power(2,2) = 2*2 = 4
```

Finally, this gets substituted back to the original function call:

```
power(2,3) = 4*2 = 8
```

The logic behind recursive functions can be difficult to grasp, but they provide a powerful tool that you should be aware of. While an alternative to using recursive functions can usually be devised, they will offer the most direct design solution in many situations.

In the NSelect function, we use a recursive function call to handle the special case when the user follows one calculation immediately with another, rather than terminating the calculation by using the = button. What had been the result of a calculation then occupies the logical place of a user-entered number. Thus we need to shift values accordingly and then call the NSelect function again.

## Debugging

Your English teacher no doubt told you that "writing is rewriting," meaning that most of the time and effort on a writing project goes into rewriting. Likewise with programming, programming is debugging.

Unfortunately, debugging in JScript is a rather primitive task at present. There are no debuggers for you to run your script through, no trace routines you can follow. Even showing the value of a variable on the screen at a given point in the program can be a challenge. Standard output is sent to your browser, and it will display only what it can understand in HTML/JScript terms.

JScript has a few built-in objects that can help with the debugging task. We will look at these when we look at the full JScript syntax in later chapters. One of the advantages, also, of working with a Microsoft language is that if a programming or debugging tool does not exist yet, Microsoft is very likely to write one in the near future. Meanwhile, a few simple guidelines can help simplify the task of debugging.

### Backups

Before making a change in program code, always make a backup copy of the file. The modification you make may not solve the problem. The lines you modified might not even be the source of the problem. Retracing your steps will be easier if you have a backup of the original to which you can return.

### Commenting Out

Rather than simply deleting a line of code and replacing it with an alternative, try "deactivating" the line by inserting a comment marker at the beginning. Then you can insert the new line you want to try below the commented out line. For example, the following lines:

```
//if (Foo = "true") {
if (Bar = "true") {
```

make a good provisional replacement for the line

```
if (Foo = "true") {
```

if you are guessing that this change will solve a problem for you.

## Manual Trace

Proper code will specify a unique course of action under any given circumstance: this is why computers know what to do. You can manually work through this course of action just as a computer would. You'll do it more slowly, and for large programs this approach is impractical, but most JScript programs will be of a length that makes manual tracing manageable.

Write down each variable in your program on a separate line on a piece of scratch paper, and put each display window in your program on a separate line. Next to each variable write its initial value; next to each display window write its initial contents. Then work through your program, step by step. Each time a variable or window display changes, mark the change on your scratch paper. If you are careful, you should be able to maintain a picture of what is going on within your program at each step until you find the problem.

There are some pitfalls to this approach. Authors are notoriously bad at proofreading their own writing. We don't see our own common spelling mistakes, and even more egregious errors often pass us by because we see what we want to see. Debugging is no different. Computers are annoyingly consistent in following instructions; they do only what they are told. People are more liberal in interpreting instructions. Whatever "blind spot" you had in coding the program initially may still blind you when tracing it, so don't be surprised if the laborious process of manual tracing fails to turn up the error.

## Testing Operation Output

Frequently problems arise because an operation does not perform as expected, and hence does not assign to a variable the expected value. Fortunately, there is a resource for testing operation output. This resource is better implemented under Netscape Navigator 3.0 than under Internet Explorer. From Navigator, select Open Location under the File menu option. A dialog box will open, prompting you for a location. Type in **javascript:** and you should see a two-frame window in your browser like the one in Figure 5.5. In the text entry window in the lower frame, where it says *javascript typein*, you may declare variables and perform operations on them. The output from these operations will be displayed in the upper frame. Navigator will keep these operations in memory for the duration of your session, enabling you to see the results of a series of operations.

You can accomplish the same output tests in Internet Explorer by means of Explorer's address entry field on the task bar. Type in **javascript**: followed by the expression you want to evaluate; Explorer should display the results (see Figure 5.6).

For example, Figures 5.7, 5.8, and 5.9 show a sequence of operations that was helpful in developing the calculator program. In this program we need to be able to move smoothly from building a number as a string of characters to handling a number as part of an arithmetic operation. This sequence of operations mimics

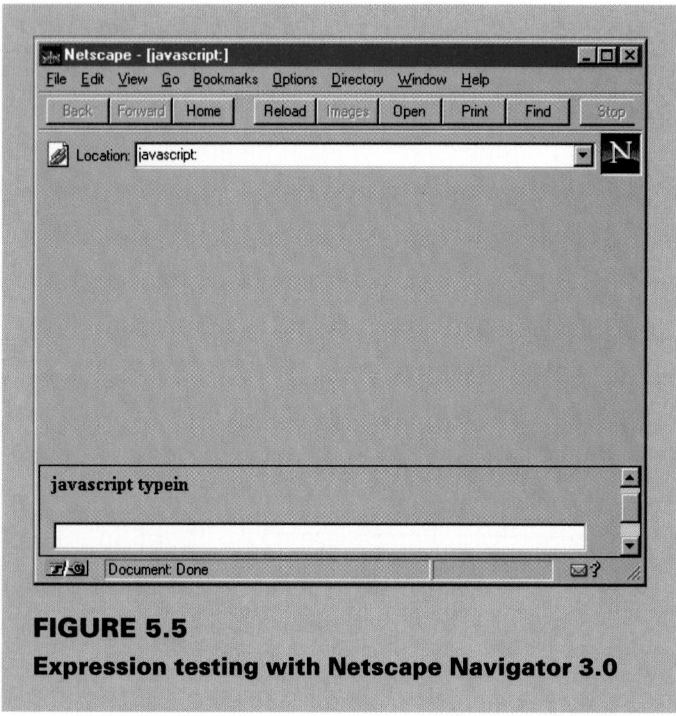


**FIGURE 5.5**
**Expression testing with Netscape Navigator 3.0**

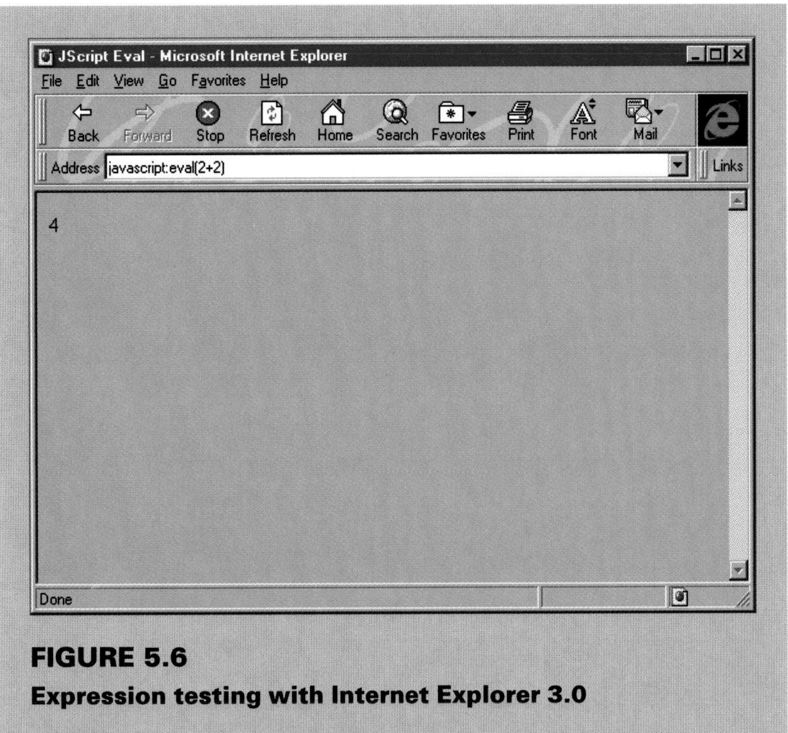


**FIGURE 5.6**
**Expression testing with Internet Explorer 3.0**

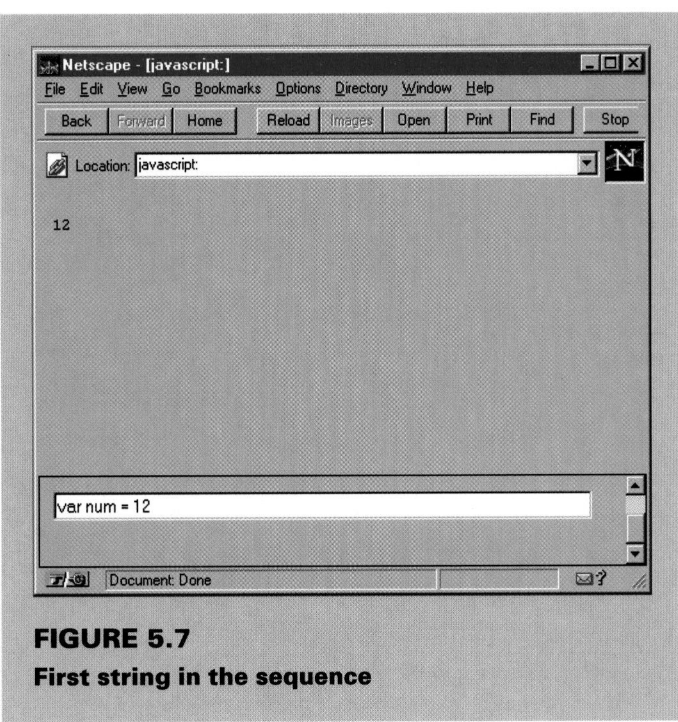


**FIGURE 5.7**
**First string in the sequence**

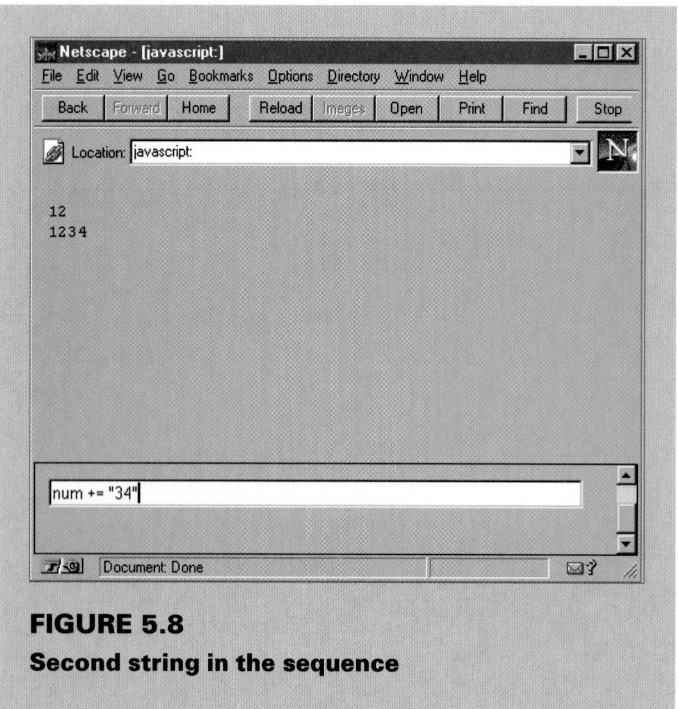


**FIGURE 5.8**

**Second string in the sequence**

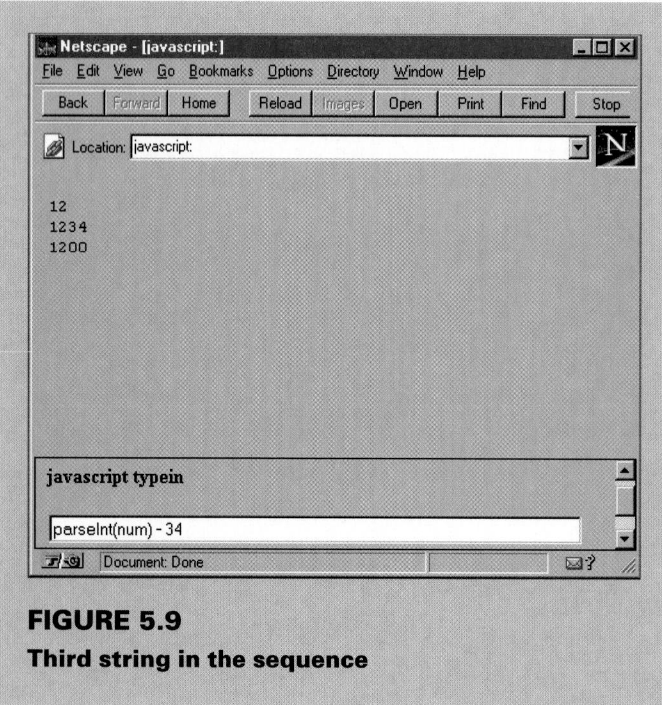


**FIGURE 5.9**

**Third string in the sequence**

what the calculator will be doing, demonstrating that the += operation concatenates a string correctly, and that JScript's predefined parseFloat function properly converts the string to a number.

## Error Messages

Internet Explorer opens an alert dialog box containing an error message when it attempts to execute buggy JScript code (see Figure 5.10). While these error messages won't tell you everything you need to know—you must certainly take the line number references with a grain of salt, for example—they are still helpful in tracking down problems, especially when the problem is a simple syntax error.

### Lack of Closure

Braces {}, single quotes '', and double quotes "" in JScript must all come in pairs. Failure to pair up in any one of these instances will generate an error message. Unclosed quotes will generate something like

```
Unterminated string literal
```

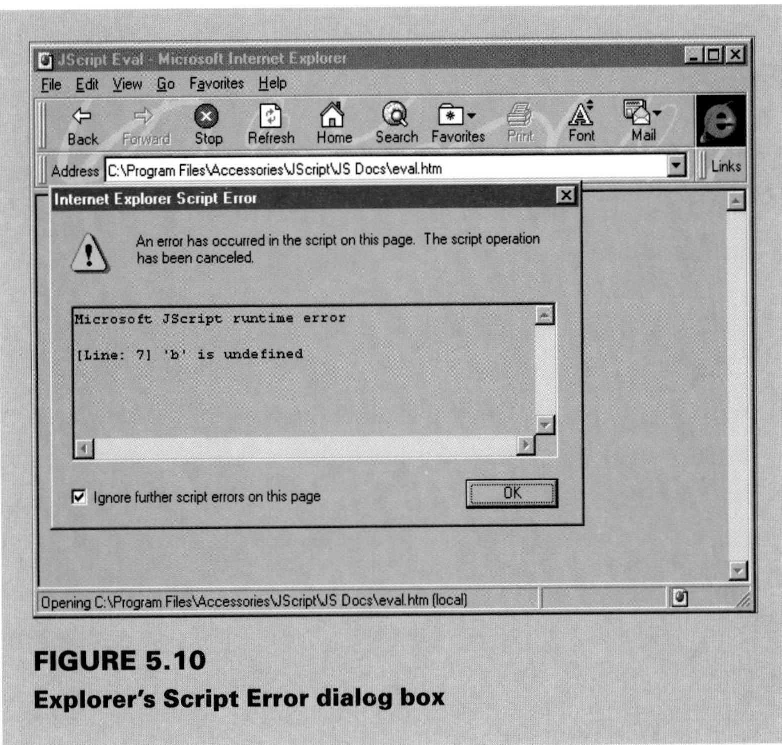


**FIGURE 5.10**
**Explorer's Script Error dialog box**

as an error message. These are usually easy to spot once you know what to look for, as the place where the quotes should begin and end are not widely separated.

An unclosed brace will generate an error message like

```
Missing } after function body
```

Unclosed braces are more challenging to spot because the opening and closing brace may be separated by a number of lines of code, and because brace pairs frequently end up nested within each other.

### Undeclared Terms

Variables and functions must be declared before they can be used in the program. An undeclared variable will generate a message like

```
Var is not defined
```

where Var is the name of the undeclared variable. This problem is easily solved by adding the variable in question to your declarations.

Forgetting to declare a variable can happen easily; but forgetting to declare a function requires a major lapse in concentration. You might think, then, that a message like

```
Fn is not a function
```

would occur rarely. You will, however, also see this message if you mistakenly give a function and a variable the same name. This invalidates the declaration, hence the error message. Speaking from experience, it's not hard to accidentally duplicate function and variable names.

### Mixing Types

As you will see, JScript does not require type definitions. You don't need to worry about declaring a variable as a string variable, an integer variable, a real number variable, or a Boolean variable. JScript will select a type based on the context in which the variable was assigned a value. Should JScript find itself asked to perform a mathematical operation on an item it must treat as a character string, you will get an error message like

```
Var is not a numeric literal
```

This may indicate that the variable the program is trying to operate on is not the one you intended at that point in the program. Alternatively, it may mean that, as in the calculator program, you need to apply the parseInt() or parseFloat() functions.

Static Clock

Visual Clock

Dynamic Clock

The Stopwatch

# Chapter 6
# Introducing JScript: Simple Examples

We have looked at a lot of JScript code at this point, and we have covered a lot of general information about object-oriented programming. However, we have not yet had a formal introduction to the JScript language. In this chapter we will begin that introduction. Hopefully the examples we have looked at so far have prepared you for the more detailed discussion ahead.

We will continue to work from examples, starting with a simple example and enhancing it. This time, however, each example will be accompanied by a detailed look at the JScript code, including specifications for the syntax used, and explanations of the code's function in the example. By introducing a few key elements of JScript in the context of working examples, we will ease into full coverage of the language as presented in the next chapters.

For each example, we will look at three features of the language: objects, data structures, and control structures. Looking at objects, we will consider what elements the program visually presents, and what events the program allows. As regards data structures, we will look at how the program stores and updates information in variables and arrays. And in our examination of control structures, we will look at event handlers and the logic of the program design behind each handler.

## Static Clock

This simple ten-command program displays the current time in the browser window when the document loads. Despite its simplicity, this program has great appeal because it clearly demonstrates what JScript can do that CGI cannot. With CGI, the server can serve a document that displays current time, but only using its own internal clock, and hence only relative to its own time zone. Because of the statelessness of Web transactions, the server would have to explicitly query you about your location to display the time in terms of your own time zone. With JScript, on the other hand, the program automatically displays the time relative to your time zone because JScript runs in the browser rather than the server and uses the client computer's clock (see Figure 6.1).

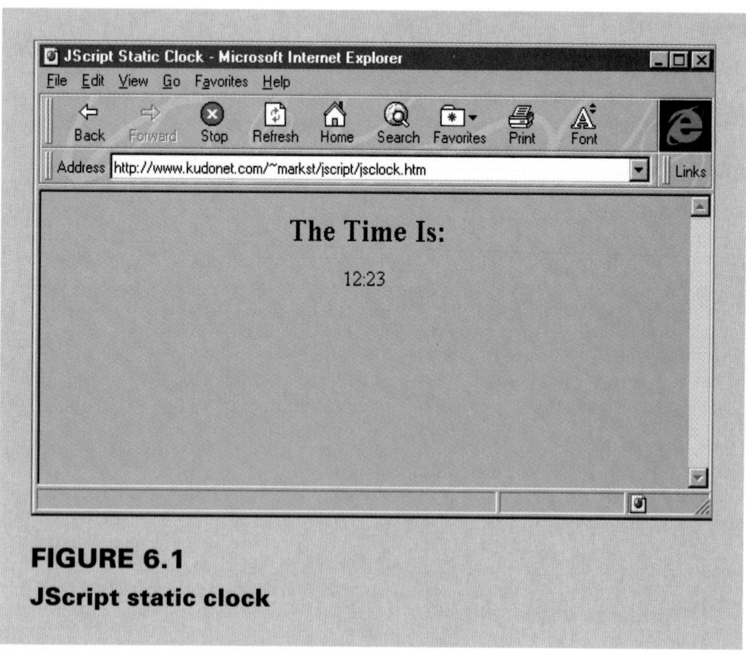


**FIGURE 6.1**
**JScript static clock**

Let's look at the program listing for this Web page.

```
<HTML>
<head>
<title>JScript Static Clock</title>
</head>

<body>
<center>
<h2>The Time Is:</h2>
<p>
<h3>

<script language="JavaScript">
<!-
var hourNow;     //stores the hour
var minNow;      //stores the minute
var timeNow;     //stores the whole result

//This script gets the current time, which
//by default is returned in military 0-24
```

```
//format. If hour is past noon, we'll need
//to subtract 12.
//
//hourNow and minNow must be assigned the
//Date object, so they can use that object's
//methods.

hourNow = new Date();
minNow = new Date();

//Because this is a static clock there are
//no user triggered events. The only event is
//the document loading. The event handler for
//that event will be the Date object's get
//method, by which we'll get the current hour
//and minute.

hourNow = hourNow.getHours();
minNow = minNow.getMinutes();
if (hourNow > 12) {
   hourNow = hourNow - 12;
   }
timeNow = hourNow + ":" + minNow;

//Now we just need to display the results.

document.write(timeNow);

//->
</script>

</h2>
</center>
</body>

</HTML>
```

Your computer stores date and time data in a very complete format, containing more information than we need for our simple clock:

```
Sat Aug 31 12:51:02 PDT 1996
```

This program extracts those elements of the date and time that we need. Then we simply modify them to be displayed in the format we want, and write the result out.

Every JScript program has required features, and these are exhibited in this program as well. The beginning and end of the program code is marked by the <script></script> tags. The <script> tag takes as an attribute the scripting language. While we could have specified the language as JScript, this would confound Netscape Navigator, which only recognizes JavaScript as a scripting language. Since Internet Explorer uses JScript and JavaScript interchangeably, you should always specify the language as JavaScript unless you are using an HTML feature not supported by Navigator.

Browsers that do not support the scripting language will ignore the <script></script> tags, as all browsers do with tags that they do not recognize. This can have the unfortunate consequence that your page will display the program, instead of running the program. To avoid this problem, follow the convention of placing your script within HTML comment tags <!—, —>. Script-aware browsers will assume they are doing script and not HTML at this point, and ignore the comment tags. Script-unaware browsers that have ignored your <script> tag will assume they are still doing HTML, abide by the comment tags, and not display the code of your program.

Every variable and every function that you use in a program must be defined before it is used in the program. Begin each program with a definition section. Variables are defined by a variable declaration statement, which can take either of the following two forms:

```
var varname
var varname = value
```

The first form simply declares the variable as one that can be used in the program. The second form declares the variable and assigns an initial value to it.

Notice that some of the statements in the program end with a semicolon (;). In JScript, the semicolon is used to separate multiple commands on a single line, as in:

```
statement 1; statement 2; statement 3
```

Ending any statement in a semicolon is acceptable, but not required. Because some other programming languages do require a semicolon at the end of every statement, this can be a useful habit even in JScript, but this is a matter of personal style.

## Static Clock Objects

When you see the output of this program, you may not see any objects: we have no buttons, no windows, no input fields. In fact, any Web page containing a JScript program always involves at least two objects: the browser window is an instance of the Window object, and the Web page containing the JScript is an instance of the Document object. Some objects operate "off screen." The History object, for example, retains the URLs your browser has recently visited, but normally operates behind the scenes. The Date object is another object that operates out of view.

This script works explicitly with two objects: the Date object and the Document object. The manipulation of an object is an *event*; the possible event handlers are *methods* of that object.

The Date object supports two general types of methods, *get* and *set*. What can be gotten or set are the various fields of the Date object. Thus, using these methods we can read values from the Date object for year, month, day, hours, minutes, and seconds: this is the get family of methods. Using these methods we can write values for the Date object for year, month, day, hours, minutes, and seconds: this is the set family of methods. Note that setting the date does not change your computer's internal clock; it only changes dates for use within your script.

These methods must be applied to instances of the Date object. The lines

```
hourNow = new Date();
minNow = new Date();
```

create two new instances of the Date object, which we can then manipulate with these methods. Methods must always be specified relative to an object. This is done using the dot syntax hierarchy. You are already familiar with one variation of this syntax from using addresses on the Internet. When you encounter an address like www.foo.bar.com, you understand that this describes a hierarchy: *bar* is in the .com domain, *foo* is one host reachable through *bar*, and *www* is one service supported by *foo*. Similarly, when the clock program uses the following two lines:

```
hourNow = hourNow.getHours();
minNow = minNow.getMinutes();
```

we should read this hierarchically, as getHours applied to the object hourNow, and as getMinutes applied to the object minNow.

Putting all this information together in order to get an exact method specification as we would use it in a program, we need a Date object, we need to know whether we want to get or set, and we need to know which date field we are interested in. Table 6.1 shows how we would fill out the specification for a Date object called thisTime.

Note a couple of things about this table. First, each of the set methods requires a numerical value that the date field will be set to. This is indicated on the table by a variable, *num*. Second, these are not all of the methods supported by the Date objects. There are others, which will be covered in the full syntax specifications in a later chapter. These, however, are the main date methods, and the ones you are most likely to use.

The Document object has its own complexities, and we will see these revealed in later examples. However, the Document object supports relatively few methods: see Table 6.2.

The write and writeln methods both write output to the current document; they require a string or variable containing a string to write. These two methods differ only in that writeln appends a carriage return to the end of its output. This may seem like an irrelevant difference given that HTML ignores carriage returns except after a <pre> tag. However, as a matter of good style you should use writeln just as you put HTML tags on separate lines when composing good HTML.

This method of writing is indelible. Once you have written to a document, you cannot alter or manipulate that output further. From your browser's vantage point,

**TABLE 6.1 BUILDING METHOD SPECIFICATION FOR A DATE OBJECT**

| Date Object | Method Type | Date Field | Specification |
|---|---|---|---|
| thisTime | get | Year | thisTime.getYear() |
| | | Month | thisTime.getMonth() |
| | | Day | thisTime.getDay() |
| | | Hours | thisTime.getHours() |
| | | Minutes | thisTime.getMinutes() |
| | | Seconds | thisTime.getSeconds() |
| | set | Year | thisTime.setYear(num) |
| | | Month | thisTime.setMonth(num) |
| | | Day | thisTime.setDay(num) |
| | | Hours | thisTime.setHours(num) |
| | | Minutes | thisTime.setMinutes(num) |
| | | Seconds | thisTime.setSeconds(num) |

this output is the same as if it had come from an HTML file. Recall the discussion of documents in Chapter 3: a file and a script are two different sources for a document, but in either case a document, once generated, cannot be altered.

The close, clear, and open methods will apply in situations where we are working with frames and trying to handle multiple windows. Note that the open method supports mime types; while it defaults to text/HTML, you can specify others, such as a mime type to load images.

| TABLE 6.2 DOCUMENT METHODS |
|---|
| write(str) |
| writeln(str) |
| close() |
| clear() |
| open(mime) |

## Data Structures and Control Structures

The static clock involves very little in the way of data or control structures. We use only three variables: one for the hour, one for the minute, and one for the overall time. We have only one fork in the program flow: whether or not the hour is in the afternoon.

The use of these variables does illustrate one important feature of JScript. Variables are not declared by type; there is no need within the declaration to specify whether the variable will be a string variable, an integer variable, a real number variable, or a Boolean variable. JScript makes these determinations at runtime based on the context in which the variable is invoked, and indeed one variable can be handled as a different type in different contexts.

The hourNow variable, for example, is treated as both a number and a string. When first assigned a value, that value is a number, and hence we can meaningfully subtract 12 from it if need be. When assigning values to the timeNow variable, however, one of the assigned values, ":", is necessarily a string, and hence all of the values, including the value of hourNow, are treated as strings.

Note that with a potentially ambiguous operation like + JScript must have a default interpretation to resolve ambiguity, and that default interpretation is the numeric operation addition, not the string operation concatenation. Hence, if you have numeric values you wish to concatenate rather than add, you must be sure to force a string context for the operation.

Program flow for the static clock is linear and simple. We read input, assign values, and write out the results: see Figure 6.2. The program makes use of assignment statements, comparison operators, arithmetic operators, and the concatenation operator.

The static clock program does illustrate the syntax for brackets ({}) that JScript programs must follow. Whenever a series of statements must be executed together,

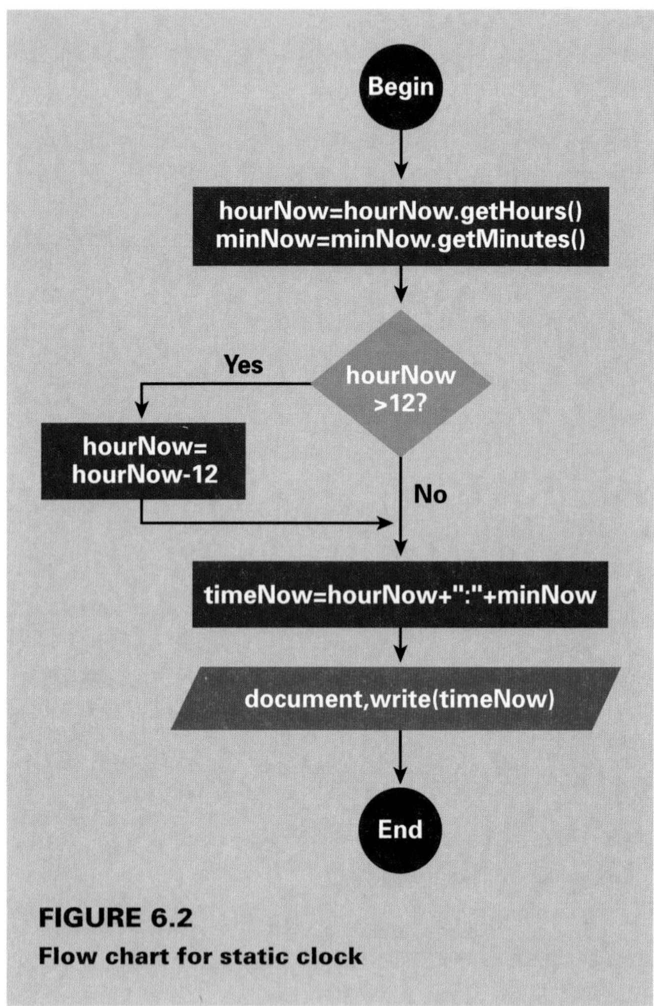


**FIGURE 6.2**
**Flow chart for static clock**

the beginning and end of this statement series must be enclosed within brackets. This occurs when defining a function, and when a program forks as a result of a comparison. Thus in the following program schema:

```
if (test) {
   statement 1;
   statement 2; ...
   statement n;
   }
```

all of the statements *1* through *n* to be executed if test is true must be enclosed in brackets.

### Assignment Statements

Any time that we assign a value to a variable, we do so by means of an assignment statement. The general form of an assignment statement is

```
var = value
```

where var is the name of the variable and value is the value assigned to it. The value may be something we state explicitly, as in

```
var = 10
var = "abc"
```

which will return 10 and abc as values, respectively. Note that if you try the following statement:

```
var = abc
```

then JScript will attempt to find a variable named *abc* and assign its value to var, and will return an "undefined" error if you have no variable named abc.

The value in an assignment statement may also be something that is inferred, either by evaluating a variable or by evaluating an operation. If num is a variable with the value 10, then both of the following would be correct inferred assignment statements:

```
var = num
var = num + 10
```

Several compound assignment statements are permitted as well. The most common are

```
var += value
```

and

```
var -= value
```

which are shorthand for

```
var = var + value
```

and

```
var = var - value
```

If var is "foo" and value is "bar" then the first statement will yield a value of "foobar" for var; the second statement would not be defined in this case. If var is 10 and value is 2, then the first statement will yield a value of 12 for var, and the second statement will yield a value of 8.

## Comparison Operators

"If then" statements and other flow-control statements require some comparison to be made in a test condition to determine what the program should do. JScript defines six comparison operators, shown in Table 6.3: equal, not equal, greater than, less than, greater than or equal to, and less than or equal to.

These comparisons are defined for strings as well as for numbers. String comparisons are case-sensitive, ranking lowercase letters higher than uppercase letters. String comparisons can also

**TABLE 6.3 COMPARISON OPERATORS**

| Operator | Action | Example | Result |
|---|---|---|---|
| == | Equal | 10 == 10 | true |
| != | Not equal | 9 != 10 | true |
| > | Greater than | 9 > 10 | false |
| < | Less than | 9 < 10 | true |
| >= | Greater than or equal to | 10 >= 10 | true |
| <= | Less than or equal to | 10 <= 9 | false |

treat numbers as strings, in which case letters will rank higher than numbers. In other words, "abc" will be greater than "ABC," and "ABC" will be greater than "123".

### Arithmetic Operators

JScript supports the standard arithmetic operations: addition (+), subtraction (-), multiplication (*), and division(/). Two additional operators are supported that may be useful are increment (++) and decrement (−−). These increase and decrease a value by one, respectively. So if num = 1, then these statements

```
var = ++num
var = --num
```

return 2 and 0 for var. The first statement can be read as "increment num and assign the result to var" while the second statement can be read as "decrement num and assign the result to var." Note that this statement produces very different results:

```
var = num++
```

If num = 1 then, after this statement num will be 2, but var will be 1. This result makes sense once you understand that this statement should be read as "assign num to var and increment num."

### Concatenation

The assignment statements

```
var = a + b
```

and

```
var += a
```

can be used with strings as well as with numbers. This is called concatenation, and joins two strings together. If a = "foo" and b = "bar" then in the first statement var will be "foobar". If the second statement is applied to this result, then var will be "foobarfoo".

JScript's default interpretation for + is arithmetic, but if any of the values in the operation is a string value, then all the values will be treated as strings. This is why, in the static clock program,

```
timeNow = 8 + ":" + 30
```

returns a value of "8:30" for timeNow, even though

```
timeNow = 8 + 30
```

would return a value of 38 for timeNow.

## Visual Clock

The static clock does not present an exciting visual display. Our next program will jazz up the output a bit. Rather than displaying a string of numbers, we will display our results graphically, using a round clock face, an hour hand, and a minute hand.

Good programming technique should be subservient to good design. Indeed, once all the design issues are thought through and resolved, what initially may have seemed a significant programming challenge often becomes a matter of simple implementation. In implementing our visual clock, the prospect of graphical programming might seem intimidating. However, let's look at the design issues first.

JScript has no resources for generating graphics dynamically. So however we decide to program our clock, we are restricted to loading one or more static images. Since each hour has 60 minutes, and we have 12 different hours to cover, we could have a library of 720 different images, and have the program select the correct one based on the time. This seems a bit much. Editing 720 different images would be prohibitive, even if each were relatively simple and closely resembled the others.

We can simplify. Rather than displaying all 60 minutes, we could display a new image at five-minute intervals, so that the minute hand, like the hour hand, displays in one of 12 positions. Unfortunately, this still requires 144 images. We need to simplify further.

Ideally we want to be able to use two images, one for the hour hand and one for the minute hand, overlaying one image onto another. Then we would need only 12 + 12, or 24 images, a much more manageable number. The design challenge, then, is to implement an image overlay scheme in HTML.

HTML does make provisions for a background image tiled over a whole page. Inline GIF images placed on the page can have a color specified as transparent, so that the background will show through. But we don't want a tiled image—we want a single background image. This would be difficult to guarantee for a whole page, and would limit what we could do on the page outside the clock. So this approach provides us with a hint, but not yet a solution.

Image overlay provides a powerful design technique, one that can dramatically enhance the Web designer's repertoire. Without a way to control the size and position of both background and foreground images, however, image overlay is a limited tool. Fortunately, Microsoft's Internet Explorer supports an HTML extension that gives us exactly the capability we need. Internet Explorer's implementation of tables not only allows an image to be displayed in a table cell, but also lets a background image be displayed in a table cell, and allows for a different background image to be displayed in each cell of a table. As of this writing only Internet Explorer supports this HTML feature, but it is such an exciting and useful feature that it will likely be adopted in a future draft of the HTML standard.

Our clock can be displayed in this way. We will have a table with only one cell in it, displaying a background image and a transparent foreground image. The background image will be selected from one of 12 possibilities based on the current hour, and the foreground image will be selected from one of 12 possibilities based on the current minute. Here's the program:

```
<HTML>

<head>
<title>JScript Visual Clock</title>
</head>

<body bgcolor=#ffffff>
<center>
<table border=0>
<TR>

<script language="JavaScript">

<!-
//This script displays a visual image
//of a clock on screen, with an hour
//hand and a minute hand indicating the
//current time as of when the clock image
//was generated. The image is displayed in
//a one-cell table.

var i               //iterator for loops
var n               //numeric placeholder for
                    //function calls
var hourNow;        //stores the hour
var minNow;         //stores the minute
```

```
var approxMin;   //stores rounded off minute
var timeNow;     //stores the whole spec
                 //for table cell contents
var hourImage;   //stores hour hand GIF
var minImage;    //stores minute hand GIF

//The hour hand will come from one of 12
//GIF images, as will the minute hand. So
//we'll use two arrays, one for hour and one
//for minute, that will store the URLs to
//the possible GIF images.
//
//We need an array initialization function,
//and then we need to initialize our two arrays.

function MakeArray(n) {
   this.length = n;
   for (i=1; i<=n; i++) {
      this[i] = 0;
      }
   return this;
   }

hourImage = new MakeArray(12);
for (i=1; i<=12; i++) {
   hourImage[i] = i + "hour.gif";
   }
minImage = new MakeArray(12);
for (i=1; i<=12; i++) {
   minImage[i] = i + "min.gif";
   }

//Now we need to get the current time,
//allowing for conversion of hours later
//than noon, and for rounding off minutes
//to the nearest 12th of an hour.

hourNow = new Date();
```

```
minNow = new Date();
hourNow = hourNow.getHours();
minNow = minNow.getMinutes();
if (hourNow > 12) {
   hourNow = hourNow - 12;
   }
minNow = minNow/5;
approxMin = Math.round(minNow);

//Rounding off the minutes can have odd
//results when approxMin has a value of Ø or 12.
//There is no Ø on the clock face to point to;
//this really means point to 12. Likewise,
//12 really means advance to the next hour.

if (approxMin == Ø) {
   approxMin = 12;
   } else {
   if (approxMin == 12) {
      ++hourNow;
      }
   }

//Finally we need to put this together
//into the HTML string that will be the
//cell of our table, and write that
//string out to be displayed.

timeNow = "<td background=\"";
timeNow += minImage[approxMin];
timeNow += "\"><IMG HEIGHT=2ØØ WIDTH=2ØØ SRC=\"";
timeNow += hourImage[hourNow];
timeNow += "\"></td>";
document.write(timeNow);
//->
</script>

</TR>
```

```
</table>
</center>

</body>

</HTML>
```

Figure 6.3 shows the JScript visual clock, the result of running this program.

## Visual Clock Objects

The visual clock employs all the objects that we used in the static clock program. In addition, the visual clock uses Array objects, and uses the Math object. Arrays are a new data structure, and will be discussed in that context. The Math object is referenced in this line, which is used to round off the value of minNow to the nearest integer:

```
approxMin = Math.round(minNow);
```

JavaScript's reasons for invoking object talk at this point are a little obscure, but JScript obligingly follows suit. If we want to have a rounding off function, we can simply use the statement:

```
approxMin = round(minNow);
```

After all, common operations like addition and multiplication do not need to be invoked as methods of an object. JavaScript's syntax conventions make more sense when you realize that the language also has a String object, and that it is quite useful to employ object talk in reference to strings. We naturally think of strings as having properties, such as length, and we naturally think of applying methods to strings, such as lowercase to uppercase conversion. We'll look at the String object in more detail in the next chapter. The point here is that if you are going to have a String object,

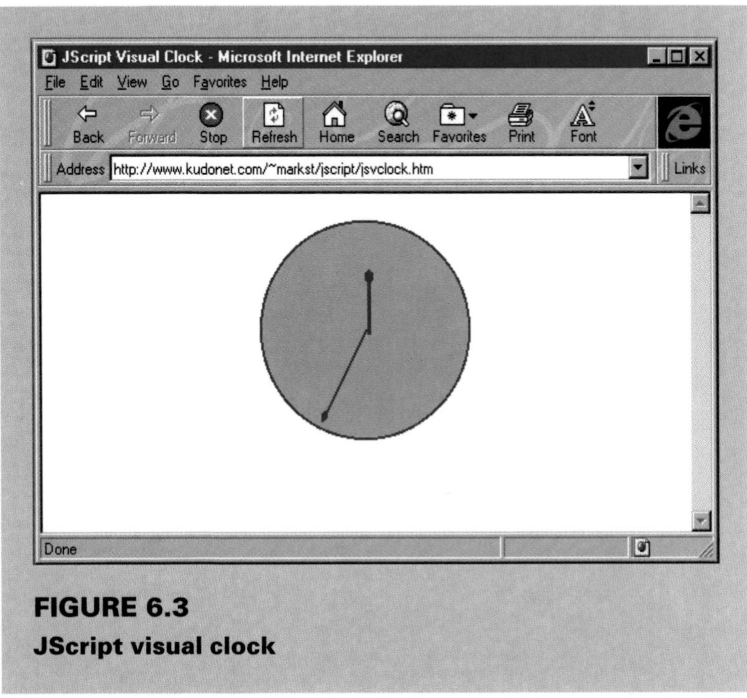


**FIGURE 6.3**
**JScript visual clock**

then for symmetry's sake it makes sense to have a Math object as well. Although the syntax can seem a little strange at first, it does have its own logic once you get used to it.

Objects can have properties and methods. For the Math object, properties are the common mathematical constants. If you want to use pi in a calculation, for example, its approximate value is the value returned by the Math.PI property. The most common Math properties are listed in Table 6.4.

While simple arithmetic operations are basic operators of JScript, more-complex mathematical operations are defined as methods of the Math object. JScript has a full set of mathematical functions, including square root, exponentiation, natural log, trigonometric functions, and hyperbolic functions. If you find yourself using these extensively, then you'll probably be happier programming in a more complex language like Java or C++.

Fortunately the Math object includes a number of useful methods that can enhance anyone's design techniques. Table 6.5 summarizes the most useful of these.

## Visual Clock Data Structures

The visual clock introduces a new data structure, arrays. An *array* is a table of data that can be referenced by an index number that points to a particular data point in

**TABLE 6.4 COMMONLY USED PROPERTIES OF THE MATH OBJECT**

| Property | Constant | Value |
|---|---|---|
| Math.E | e, natural log base | 2.718281828459045 |
| Math.LN10 | natural log of 10 | 2.302585092994046 |
| Math.PI | pi | 3.141592653589793 |
| Math.SQRT2 | square root of 2 | 1.4142135623730951 |

**TABLE 6.5 SOME USEFUL METHODS OF THE MATH OBJECT**

| Method | Function | Example | Value |
|---|---|---|---|
| Math.abs(var) | absolute value of var | Math.abs(-2) | 2 |
| Math.ceil(var) | integer ceiling above var | Math.ceil(1.5) | 2 |
| Math.floor(var) | integer floor below var | Math.floor(1.5) | 1 |
| Math.max(var1, var2) | greater of two values | Math.max(5,10) | 10 |
| Math.min(var1, var2) | lesser of two values | Math.min(5,10) | 5 |
| Math.random() | random number from 0 to 1 | Math.random() | ? |
| Math.round(var) | var rounded off to nearest integer | Math.round(1.8) | 2 |

the table. JScript supports only one-dimensional arrays, tables that can be many rows long but only one column wide. So in JScript an array is like a numbered list, where the index numbers of the array point to the corresponding numbered item on the list.

We use arraylike structures constantly in our day to day lives. Any time you are working with a list of items with an implicit order to the items, you are working with an array. A deck of cards, the TV guide, the days of the week—all of these can be represented as arrays. JScript has some built-in array objects. For example, the Date object is an array, in which each item in the list is a different field of the date, from year down to second. We can also create new arrays, as we do in the visual clock program.

The mechanism for creating arrays is oddly complicated. Just as JScript has a predefined Date object that can be instantiated with the new command to create copies of it, you might expect JScript to have a predefined array object that would enable creation of arrays by simply invoking the new command. Alas, neither JavaScript nor JScript follows this simple solution. Instead, your program must have two parts: an array template function, which creates a generic array object for your program; and an array creation function, which creates a particular array that you want to use in your program.

It's best not to question too deeply why this elaborate process is necessary. The array template function in the visual clock program is called MakeArray, and has been taken verbatim from the developer's guide to JavaScript on the Netscape Web site:

```
function MakeArray(n) {
   this.length = n;
   for (i=1; i<=n; i++) {
      this[i] = Ø;
      }
   return this;
   }
```

This function makes an array object with n elements called MakeArray, initialized with a value of 0 for each element. To create an array from this template, we call this function with the new command, passing to the function a value for the number of elements we want in the array. In the visual clock program, this function is called twice, creating two arrays:

```
hourImage = new MakeArray(12);
minImage = new MakeArray(12);
```

We can then assign values to the elements of these arrays just as we would assign values to any other variable. In this case each element of hourImage will hold a string that is the name of an hour-hand image file, and each element of minImage will hold a string that is the name of a minute-hand image file.

## Visual Clock Control Structures

The visual clock program follows the same general logic as the static clock program with a few variations (see Figure 6.4). We are still reading the current time, setting variables accordingly, and writing out the results. Because we are rounding off the minutes, we need to check for some potential errors that can result from rounding off. Because we are writing out images rather than text, some additional steps are needed. We need a control loop to initialize the arrays that store the image-file data, and we need to build an output statement that will send to the browser the HTML code needed to generate the correct images.

Suppose that we simply divided the minutes of the current time by 12, rounded off the result, and used this as the value for approxMin without further modification. Consider what would happen at 9:01. The value for approxMin would be the result of rounding off 1/5, namely 0. Yet there is no GIF image named 0min.gif to be displayed. In fact, the minute hand on clocks points to 12 when the minute is 0, and so we need to reset the value of approxMin to 12 under these conditions:

```
if (approxMin == 0) {
    approxMin = 12;
    }
```

At the other end of the hour we must also be careful. Consider what happens when the time is 9:59. The value of approxMin would be the result of rounding off 59/5, namely 12. If, however, we simply display the clock based on these values, then the hour hand will point to 9 and the minute hand will point to 12, which will be read as 9:00 when in fact we want a display that will be read as 10:00. So when approxMin rounds off to 12, we need to advance the hour by one:

```
if (approxMin == 12) {
    ++hourNow;
    }
```

We also have to be careful not to run these commands in this order. If we do, then at 9:01 approxMin will be set to 12, and because it is set to 12 hourNow will be incremented to 10. The problem can clearly be seen in the small flow chart in Figure 6.5. We need to return from the assignment box approxMin = 12 after the

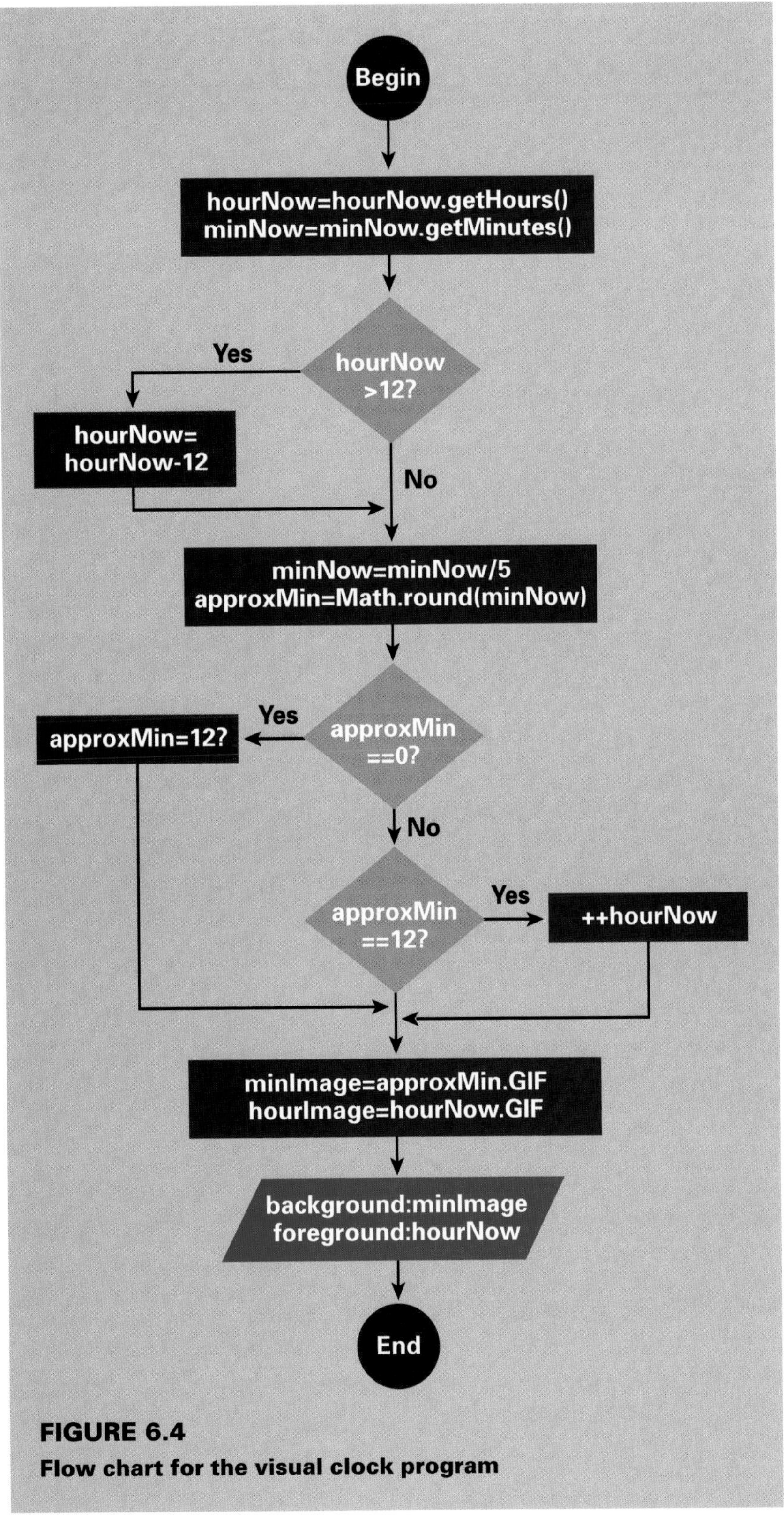


**FIGURE 6.4**

**Flow chart for the visual clock program**

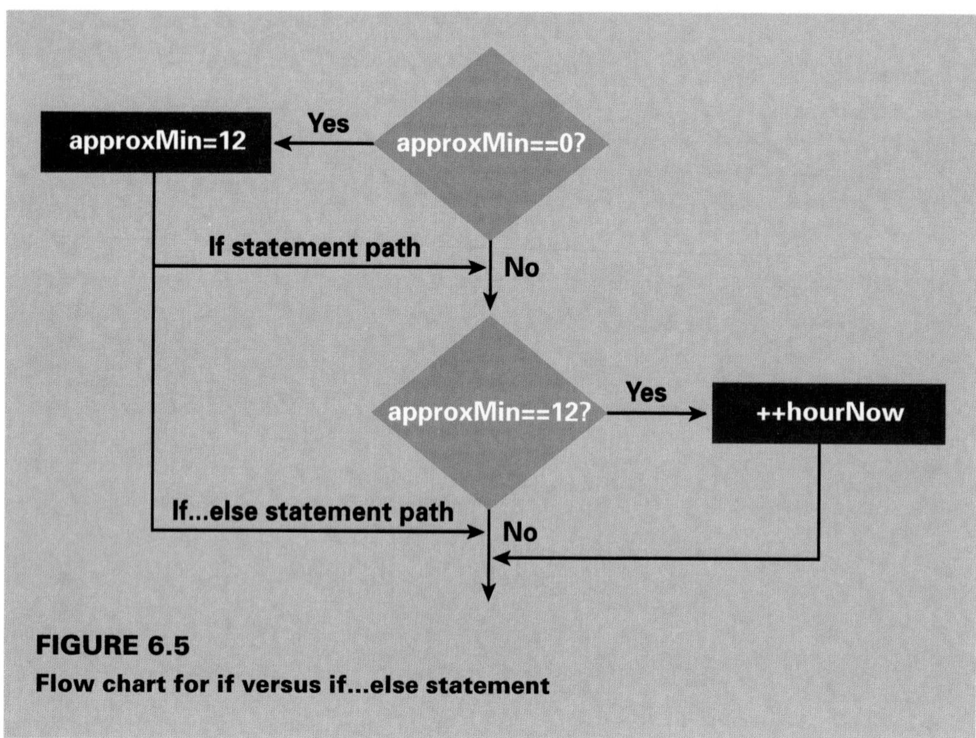


**FIGURE 6.5**
**Flow chart for if versus if...else statement**

decision box appoxMin == 12, not before it. We accomplish this with a variation of the if statement, using the if...else format:

```
if (approxMin == 0) {
   approxMin = 12;
   } else {
   if (approxMin == 12) {
      ++hourNow;
      }
   }
```

The clause following the else statement will only be executed if the original test condition is false. If the time is 9:01, then at the point the program tests that original condition, the condition is true, and hence the else clause is not executed.

The other new control structure introduced by the visual clock is the *for* loop, which we use to initialize the values for the two arrays. An if statement is a simple fork in the program, flowing through the branch one time and then returning to the main program. A for loop repeats the loop a number of times. In flow-chart terms, an if statement returns to the main program downstream, and a for loop returns upstream.

For loop syntax requires three statements in the test condition for the loop: a counter variable set to an initial value, a test condition for when the counter has reached the terminating value for the loop, and an increment or decrement statement that indicates how the counter changes value each time through the loop. In this program, we have a 12 item array to initialize, so we want to step through the loop one item at a time from 1 to 12:

```
for (i=1; i<=12; i++) {
```

## Dynamic Clock

So far we have used the fact that JScript runs client side to display a locally accurate time in the browser, but otherwise we have not displayed anything not available through conventional CGI programs. Let's add a new feature to our static clock program that cannot readily be incorporated using CGI. One of JScript's strengths lies in its capability to add dynamic content to your Web pages. Our new display will be a dynamic display, one that updates the time displayed minute by minute.

Dynamic content is, by definition, event-driven. We will need to make our program more modular by moving the body of the program into a set of functions that will handle events. The initial event occurs when the page loads; we will make this explicit using the onLoad attribute of the <body> tag. The other relevant event will be the lapse of an interval of time. In the context of our clock program, that interval will be one minute. JScript has a built-in function, setTimeout, that can be used for precisely this purpose.

The dynamic clock will also require a new approach to writing output. The write and writeln statements function well when a program's output is static, but because their output cannot subsequently be altered they do not provide a suitable output mechanism for dynamic output. The limitation here stems from HTML, rather than JScript. Think of it this way: what elements of an HTML document can be altered once the document has loaded? Relatively few elements, in fact: buttons such as radio buttons or checkboxes, text entry fields, and textarea entry fields. One other less obvious element that can be modified is the status bar at the bottom of your browser. JScript, then, can only alter the appearance of a document that's already been loaded by altering one of these elements.

The paradoxical result is that we must put an input object on the page if we want to write dynamic output. For the dynamic clock we will display the time in a text input window. This means that we will have to define a form to contain this text window. Because we could potentially have more than one form on a page, we should make use of the name attribute for the <form> tag, and direct our output with reference to that name. This is the same technique we used in the last chapter to display output for the calculator.

Figure 6.6 shows the dynamic clock page; here's the actual code for the program:

```
<HTML>

<head>
<title>JScript Dynamic Clock</title>
</head>

<body onLoad="gettingTime(updateInterval)">
<center>
<h2>The Time Is:</h2>
<form name="clock">
<input TYPE="text" NAME="clockDisplay" VALUE="0:00">
</form>
</center>

<script language="JavaScript">
<!–
var timeID          //what setTimeout returns
```

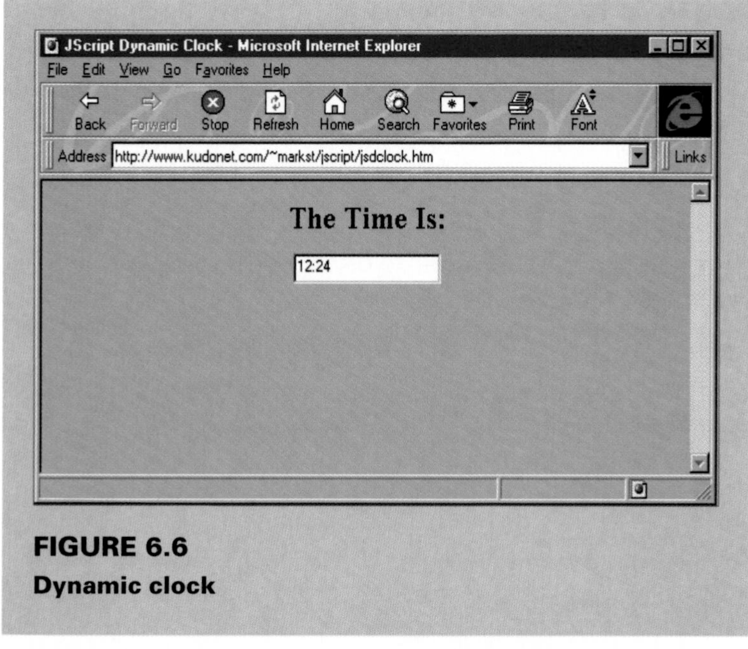


**FIGURE 6.6**
**Dynamic clock**

```
var Fclock          //name of form where output goes
var hourNow;        //stores the hour
var minNow;         //stores the minute
var timeNow;        //stores the whole result
var updateInterval; //milliseconds until next
                    //clock display update.
Fclock = document.clock

//This script gets the current time, and
//updates the time once a minute. The time
//is displayed in a text area window, and
//that display is updated each time the
//current time is updated.
//
//Action is triggered by the onLoad event, an
//attribute of the <body> tag, and this event
//is handled by a pair of functions that
//call each other:

function gettingTime() {
//This function retrieves the current time,
//builds a string to be written showing that
//time, and writes it out to the text window.
//It then calls the checkTime function.

hourNow = new Date();
minNow = new Date();
hourNow = hourNow.getHours();
minNow = minNow.getMinutes();
if (hourNow > 12) {
   hourNow = hourNow - 12;
   }
timeNow = hourNow + ":" + minNow;
Fclock.clockDisplay.value = timeNow;
checkTime(60000);
}

function checkTime(updateInterval) {
```

```
//This function checks the time to
//see when the specified update interval
//has passed, and then calls the
//gettingTime function.

timerID = setTimeout("gettingTime()", updateInterval);
}

//->
</script>

</body>

</HTML>
```

## Dynamic Clock Objects

This program introduces two new objects: the Form object and the Text Input object. We get a clear picture here of the hierarchy of objects in JScript. The Document object has forms as one of its properties. A form is itself an object, and acts as a container for the Text Input object. Finally, the Text Input object has value as one of its properties. Thus, in dot syntax a reference to this value system would look like this:

```
document.form.input.value
```

You have some latitude in referencing forms; the approach you choose depends on what reference mechanism feels most natural to you. Forms can be assigned a name with the name attribute, and this name can be given as a value to a variable. Storing the information in a variable can simplify references you have to make later on in the program, but you should follow a naming convention that makes it clear what the variable is for. Beginning a form name variable with an *f* for *form* might be a useful convention, for example.

The Form object is in fact an Array object. An alternative possibility, then, would be referencing the form by its index number. The first form will have index number 0, the second index number 1, and so on. Thus the first form in a document could be referenced by

```
document.form[0]
```

While this naming scheme offers no mnemonic to help remind you which form this is or what it is for, this naming scheme can have advantages in some programs. For example, if you need a loop to iterate through every one of several forms on your document, then you might prefer referencing forms by array index.

The dynamic clock program has only one form, and its only purpose is to provide a container for the text-input window. Hence, we keep the reference as simple as possible.

The more conventional use for a text-input window would be allowing the user to enter a single line of text, with the event handler for processing this text triggered by an onSubmit event (clicking on a button of type submit). We will see this use of text-input windows in later examples. This object is considerably more versatile, however. The contents of a text-input window are its value, and this value is a property of the object. Thus this value can be accessed at any time, just like the value of any other variable. This value can also be changed at any time by means of an assignment statement, just like any other variable. Thus we can use this object as a means of continually updating information on screen. No explicit write statement is required; the screen updates automatically as soon as we change the value.

We saw a text-input window used this way in the calculator example from the last chapter. We assigned numerical values to variables by reading from the text-input window, and continually updated the numerical string displayed by means of concatenation.

The dynamic clock program is even simpler. Every 60 seconds the value of the input-text window is changed by the statement:

```
Fclock.clockDisplay.value = timeNow;
```

## Dynamic Clock Data Structures

Although this program does not involve any new data structures, it does employ one new technique for handling data. Notice that we have defined a variable called updateInterval, and used it in the definition of the function checkTime. However, when the program runs no value is ever assigned to updateInterval.

This variable functions as a place-holder, enabling us to pass a value to the function checkTime. The actual function call is to checkTime (60000), but the place-holder updateInterval instructs the program how to handle 60000—or whatever other value is passed to checkTime—within the function.

To put it formally, updateInterval is a parameter of checkTime, and 60000 is a value passed to that parameter. Functions can be defined to have no, one, or multiple parameters.

## Dynamic Clock Control Structures

The flow of the dynamic clock program is driven by two events: onLoad and setTimeout. The onLoad event occurs once at the beginning of the program, and setTimeout is a recurring event. The program structure is entirely modular here. Nothing but variable declaration and initialization occurs in the body of the program; the remainder of the program executes within the two functions, gettingTime and checkTime, that are the program's event handlers. While object-oriented programs can be difficult to describe in a flow chart because they can be nonlinear and event driven, the dynamic clock is still a relatively simple program to chart (see Figure 6.7). It still does not allow for user input, and hence the events happen linearly and in a predetermined order.

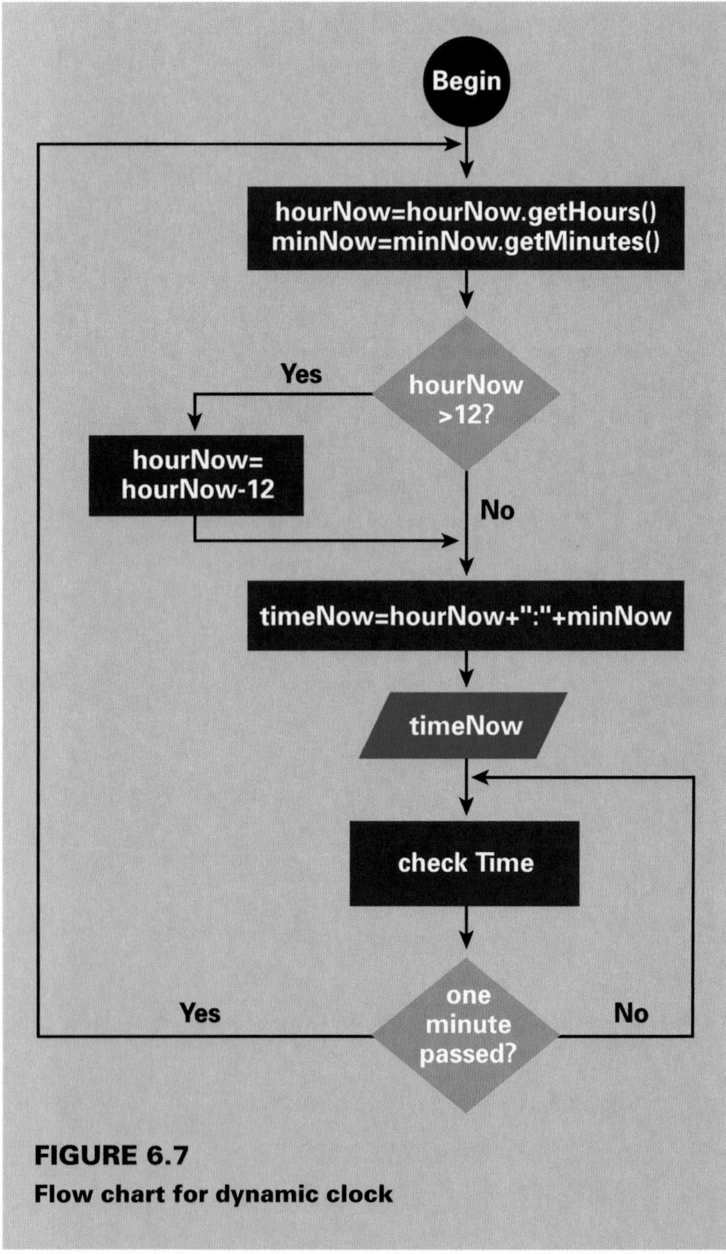


**FIGURE 6.7**
**Flow chart for dynamic clock**

The onLoad event is triggered when the current document has completely loaded into the browser window. It is an attribute of the <body> tag, and specifies an event handler to be run when loading is complete. If you are using a document with frames, you might note that there is no <body> tag. In this case onLoad can be used as an attribute of the <frameset> tag.

The onLoad event has a corollary, which is onUnload. Needless to say, onUnload has limited use in a single-frame window, but proves extremely useful in a window with multiple frames.

The setTimeout function and its companion, the clearTimeout function, provide powerful tools for directing program action when the only event you are waiting for is the passage of a certain interval of time. setTimeout takes two parameters, one the name of an event handler, the other a numerical value specifying the number of milliseconds to wait before calling the event handler.

A document could potentially have several setTimeout functions running simultaneously. Thus the value returned by the setTimeout function would be a numerical value that serves as an ID for that function. The clearTimeout function takes a single parameter, which is the ID of a setTimeout function. When the clearTimeout function executes, that particular setTimeout function's countdown is canceled.

The gettingTime function of the dynamic clock is nothing more than the same JScript code we have used in previous programs in this chapter to get the current time. To this code we have appended a call to the checkTime function, passing a parameter of 60000. The checkTime function is nothing more than an instance of setTimeout. It waits 60 seconds—60000 milliseconds—and then calls back the gettingTime function. These two functions form an infinite loop that bounces back and forth between the two once a minute, and thus updates the clock display once a minute.

This simple program exemplifies a type that can have far more interesting applications, particularly in combination with the clearTimeout function. This logic could be used, for example, to generate a screen-saver program for your computer, with the clearTimeout function providing an interrupt mechanism. The same logic could also be used to present someone browsing your Web site with a virtual slide-show of pages on your site, with the clearTimeout function providing a mechanism for a pause button when they see something they want to view in more detail.

These sorts of applications will require us to program elements that we have not yet incorporated: frames and user input. We'll conclude this chapter by looking at one last clock example that brings both of these elements into play.

## The Stopwatch

Imagine that you have been assigned to replace the high-school track coach for a day. You arrive at the meet just as they are about to start the 1500 meter run, only to discover that you have forgotten your stopwatch. You look dubiously at your watch, which does have a second hand. There are eight runners whose times you must keep track of, however, some of whom may cross the finish line quite close together. Fortunately, though you forgot your stopwatch, you did remember to bring your laptop computer with Windows 95 and Internet Explorer 3.0 installed. With a little help from JScript your problems are solved.

The core of our program is still the Date object, only instead of looking at the time we need to look at time that has elapsed from a starting point. This would be a relatively simple matter if we needed just one time. We could use a display similar to the dynamic clock, adding in a routine to measure elapsed time and adding in a call to the clearTimeout function to stop our timer. However, we need to be able to track multiple elapsed time intervals and still have our stopwatch running.

The best approach will be to use a two-frame window. The upper window will contain the stopwatch, and in the lower window we'll display results. We'll need to be able to start the stopwatch, record an interim result, and stop the stopwatch. In good Windows tradition, we will also allow a help screen to be called up for anyone who doesn't find the operation of the stopwatch self-evident. At the start we have no output, so the lower frame will be blank. The opening stopwatch window is shown in Figure 6.8.

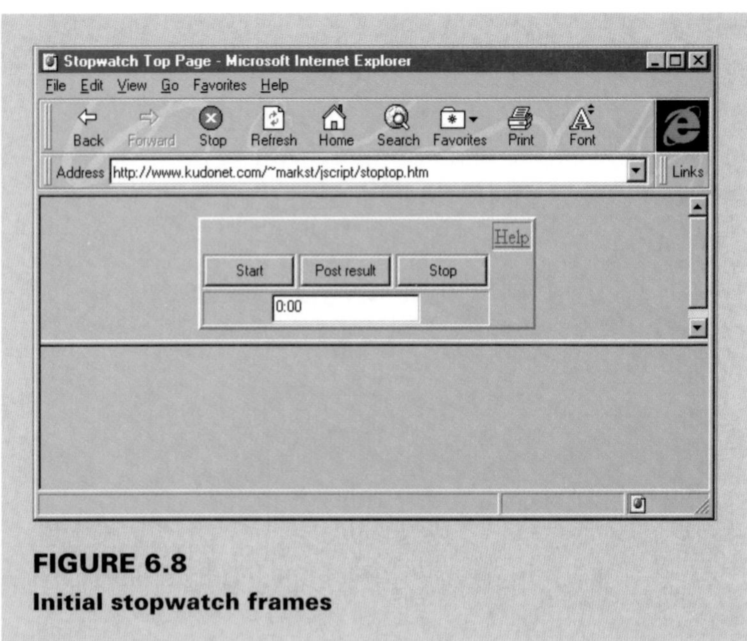


**FIGURE 6.8**
**Initial stopwatch frames**

This program will require a total of four HTML pages: a FRAMESET page, on which the initial frames are specified and URLs given to the pages initially loaded in those frames; the stopwatch page, which contains the actual JScript program; a blank page initially displayed in the lower frame; and a Help page to be displayed in the lower frame if asked for. Figure 6.9 shows the stopwatch with the Help page displayed.

The FRAMESET page is as follows:

```
<HTML>
<HEAD><TITLE>Stopwatch Top Page</TITLE></HEAD>
<FRAMESET ROWS = "50%, 50%">
   <FRAME SRC="stopwach.htm" NAME="topFrame">
   <FRAME SRC="blank.htm" NAME="bottomFrame">
</FRAMESET>
</HTML>
```

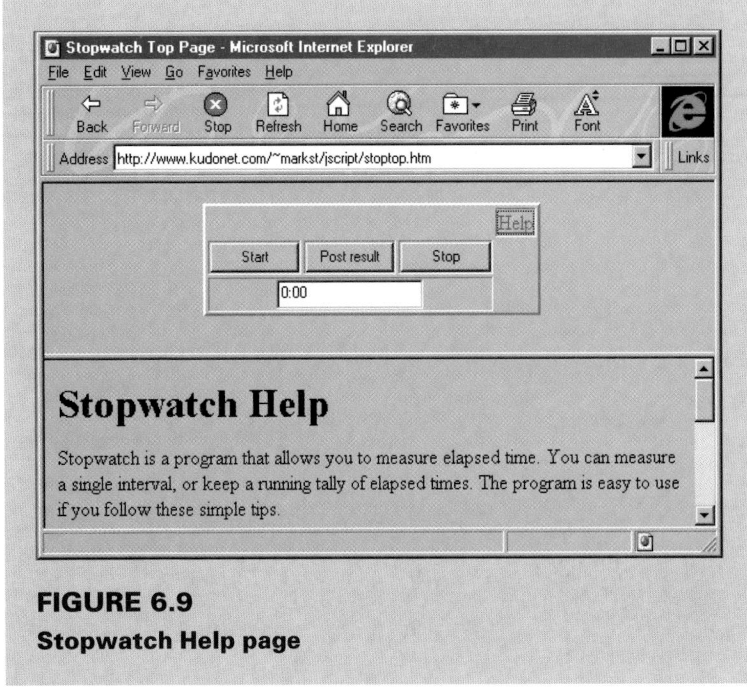


**FIGURE 6.9**
**Stopwatch Help page**

Frames can be assigned a portion of the window in different ways, including assigning each an absolute number of pixels. Because you don't know about the screen sizes of all the browsers that might load your page, the better design choice is using proportional frame assignments whenever possible. If you think your application needs frames specified in pixels, then try to keep the total size within the VGA screen limits, which are 640 by 480 pixels. We've used the optional NAME attribute with the <FRAME> tags. This allows us to refer to frames by name later on. Like the FORM object from the last section, the FRAME object is an array, so you can also refer to a frame by index number.

Realize that the FRAMESET page is present at all times in this program. This is crucial when trying to specify your references in the object hierarchy. This is the top window. In this example, it is also the parent window of the other two frames. Should one of those frames contain another FRAMESET page dividing its frames into further frames, then it would be the parent of those further frames, but still not the top.

The blank page is just a conventional, though sparse, HTML page:

```
<HTML>
<HEAD><TITLE>Blank Page</TITLE></HEAD>
<BODY>
</BODY>
</HTML>
```

Though browsers like Navigator may have internal URLs like about:blank for generating a blank page, this will not work on Internet Explorer. Good crossplatform design should avoid the use of internal URLs.

The help page is also just a conventional page of HTML:

```
<HTML>
<HEAD><TITLE>Stopwatch Help Page</TITLE></HEAD>
<BODY>
```

```
<H1>Stopwatch Help</H1>
Stopwatch is a program that allows you to measure elapsed time. You can mea-
sure a single interval, or keep a running tally of elapsed times. The program
is easy to use if you follow these simple tips.

<P>
<DL>
<DT>Start
<DD>Clicking on the Start button starts the stopwatch running from zero. Any
time you click on the Start button, the stopwatch will start over.

<DT>Post result
<DD>If you want to record an elapsed interval without stopping the clock,
then click on the Post Result button. The current elapsed time will be dis-
played, but the clock will continue to run.

<DT>Stop
<DD>The stop button halts the stopwatch. The final time will register in the
watch display, and will also be posted to the lower frame.
</DL>

</BODY>
</HTML>
```

The stopwatch program is as fully object-oriented as JScript gets. It combines user interaction, simultaneously running events, dynamic content, and dynamic displays. In other words, unless you are careful such a program can be difficult to develop and debug. You should keep several tips in mind.

First, do not use JScript gratuitously. We could, for example, write a JScript function to load the help page, but there is no need to do so. Conventional HTML can perform this function perfectly well, and JScript adds no capability in this situation. You'll see that this is accomplished by using a <BASE> tag in the head of the stopwatch document, since we have only one frame as our output target, and then a simple link tag on the Help cell in the stopwatch table.

Second, take advantage of object portability. Many of the functions used in the stopwatch have been taken with little or no modification from programs earlier in this chapter. We use the same technique for displaying a time in a window, the same technique for polling the clock to get an updated time. The new programming elements are thus kept to a minimum.

Finally, stick to the principles of good modular design. The stopwatch is an entirely modular program, using five functions to handle events. Because it is modular, the program went through several stages of development, bringing one module "on line" at a time.

Start with what you know how to do. From the dynamic clock we know how to display a continually updated time report in a window. This program requires the same feature, with two small differences: the dynamic display is initiated by clicking on the Start button, and the time displayed is an elapsed time, not the current time. Thus we can use the checkTime function from the previous program without change, and the gettingTime function with little change. We add a new function, startTimer, but it only records the current time, which we know how to do from previous programs, and calls the checkTime function. The only additional change required is for the gettingTime function to compare its time to the startTimer time and display the difference.

It is important to realize that this portion of the program can be debugged on its own. Once these functions have been written, you can simply leave the Post Result and Stop buttons inactive while you test out the Start button.

The postTime function involves the most new programming. This function must get a time from a running clock display, and write it out to a different frame window. Even here, however, we are borrowing. Reading a string from a text window into a variable is simple enough; we did this previously with the calculator program. We have also used the write statement before. Our destination is different here, and the hierarchy referenced in the dot syntax must reflect that, but the task is not essentially different.

Again, this function can be tested without yet writing the Stop button event handler. If that Start button works, you can next add and debug this module of code by itself.

Once the other modules work, the Stop button is easy to program. It is really just a special case of the postTime function. Mainly it just needs to halt the stopwatch with the clearTimeout function, and then call the postTime function for the last time. Figure 6.10 shows the results of a complete session of the stopwatch program.

Looking at the code, you should see how much we have built this program out of other parts we had lying around:

```
<HTML>
<HEAD>
<TITLE>Stopwatch</TITLE>
```

```
<BASE TARGET="bottomFrame">
</HEAD>
<BODY>

<FORM NAME="swatch">

<CENTER>
<TABLE BORDER=2>
<TR>
<TD></TD><TD></TD><TD></TD>
<TD><A HREF="help.htm">Help</A></TD>
</TR>

<TR>
<TD><INPUT NAME="start" TYPE="Button" VALUE="Start"
onClick="startTimer()"></TD>
<TD><INPUT NAME="post" TYPE="Button" VALUE="Post result"
onClick="postTime()"></TD>
<TD><INPUT NAME="stop" TYPE="Button" VALUE="Stop" onClick="haltTimer()"></TD>
<TD></TD>
</TR>
```

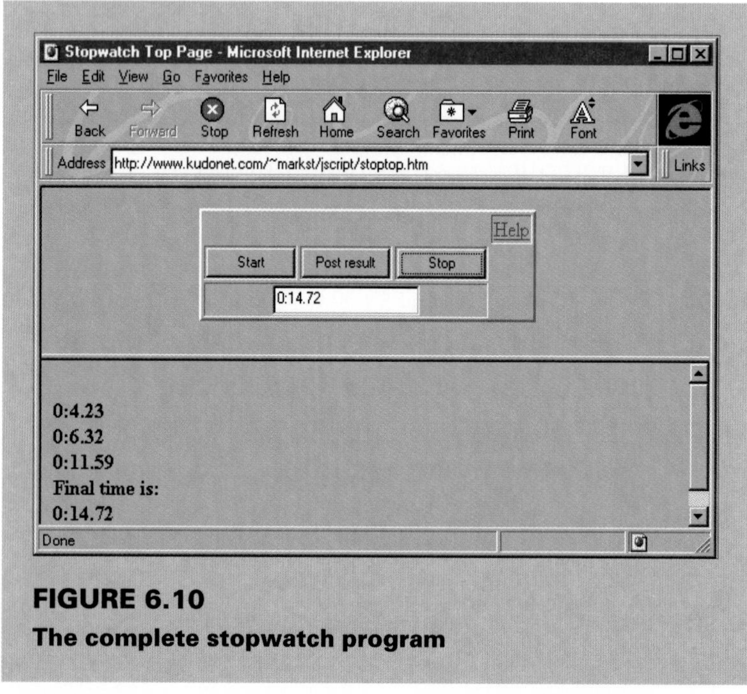


**FIGURE 6.10**

**The complete stopwatch program**

```
<TR>
<TD COLSPAN=3 ALIGN=CENTER><INPUT NAME="Display" TYPE="Text"
VALUE="0:00"></TD>
<TD></TD>
</TR>
</TABLE>
</CENTER>

</FORM>

<SCRIPT LANGUAGE=JavaScript>
<!-

//This script runs a stopwatch in this
//frame (the upper frame) and allows
//times from the stopwatch to be displayed
//in the lower frame. Any number of
//interim times, and a final time, can
//be displayed.

var page;            //string that holds
                     //the HTML page for
                     //the lower frame
var timeList="<B>";  //times to be displayed
var timeBase;        //time when watch starts
var timeNow;         //time now
var secNow;          //seconds of elapsed time
var minNow;          //minutes of elapsted time
var timeDisplay;     //elapsed time
var updateInterval;  //number of milliseconds
                     //until clock is checked again

function postTime() {
//This function takes the time currently displayed
//in the stopwatch window and writes it out to
//the lower frame. It is written as part of an entire
//HTML page, and is appended to the list of previously
```

```
//displayed times, so that the lower window shows all
//the selected times.

timeList = timeList + "<BR>" + document.swatch.Display.value;
page = "<HTML><BODY>" + timeList + "</BODY></HTML>";
top.bottomFrame.document.close();
top.bottomFrame.document.write(page);
top.bottomFrame.document.close();
}

function startTimer() {
//This function gets the initial time and
//then calls the checkTime function to begin
//polling the clock at one second intervals.

timeNow = new Date();
timeBase = timeNow.getTime();
checkTime(1000);
}

function gettingTime() {
//This function gets the elapsed time
//since the base time. Since this number
//is given in milliseconds, some conversion
//needs to be done to express it in the
//form minutes:seconds.
//
//This elapsed time is displayed in the
//the stopwatch window, and then the
//checkTime function is called again.

timeNow = new Date();
timeNow = timeNow.getTime() - timeBase;
minNow = timeNow/60000;
minNow = Math.floor(minNow);
secNow = timeNow % 60000;
secNow = secNow/1000;
timeDisplay = minNow + ":" + secNow;
```

```
Fswatch.Display.value = timeDisplay;
checkTime(1000);
}

function checkTime(updateInterval) {
//This function waits a period of time
//equal to updateInterval, and then calls
//the gettingTime function to get the
//current time.

timerID = setTimeout("gettingTime()", updateInterval);
}

function haltTimer() {
//This function completely stops the stopwatch
//by using the clearTimeout function, and then
//calls the postTime function to display the final
//time in the lower frame.

clearTimeout(timerID);
timeList += "<BR>Final time is:";
postTime();
}

//->
</SCRIPT>

</BODY>
</HTML>
```

## Stopwatch Objects

The stopwatch program really only introduces a few new objects. They are used in these three lines:

```
top.bottomFrame.document.close();
top.bottomFrame.document.write(page);
top.bottomFrame.document.close();
```

One of the objects implicitly referenced here is the window object. Its properties are: status, defaultStatus, self, top, parent, and frames. In these lines we want to send output to the lower frame. We are trying to do this from the upper frame, however; the upper frame doesn't "know" anything about other frames. That information is contained only in a FRAMESET document. We have to trace a path up to the FRAMESET document and then back down to the document in question.

The problem is like accessing subdirectories on your hard drive. If "upper" and "lower" are both subdirectories of "root," then you cannot directly access "lower" from "upper." You must either specify an absolute pathname that reaches "lower," such as "\root\lower," or you must specify a relative pathname, such as "..\lower."

By using the top window property, we are referencing the equivalent of an absolute pathname: from the top, go to the frame of that top document named bottomFrame. If we wanted to use the equivalent of a relative pathname, then we could use a command like this:

```
parent.bottomFrame.document.close();
```

In this case the top window and the parent window—relative to the window in which the stopwatch script resides—are the same.

The other object referenced in these lines is the frames object; frames are both a property of the window object, and objects themselves. Because we used the NAME attribute in the FRAMESET document, we can reference the lower frame by its name. The frames object is also an array object, though, and frames can be referenced by index number as well. In the FRAMESET document, the first frame listed will be assigned frames[0], the next frames[1], and so on. Since bottomFrame is the second frame listed on the FRAMESET document, we could use these lines interchangably with the lines above:

```
top.frames[1].document.close();
top.frames[1].document.write(page);
top.frames[1].document.close();
```

At the beginning of the stopwatch program, the document residing in the lower frame is blank.htm, and before the Start button is clicked the document in that frame may be help.htm. What we want to do is put a new document in that frame that will contain the output from the stopwatch. Thus we need to close whatever document is currently there, write the new document, and close it.

The open and close methods of the document object have no real application to a single-frame window, and indeed can cause some peculiar behavior. In a multiple-frame environment, however, they are vital methods for managing output between windows.

## Data Structures

The getTime method of the Date object returns a value in milliseconds. This is a useful piece of data, but we need to transform it into more readable form. To do this we use some new arithmetic and math methods. Look at these lines of code:

```
timeNow = timeNow.getTime() - timeBase;
minNow = timeNow/60000;
minNow = Math.floor(minNow);
secNow = timeNow % 60000;
secNow = secNow/1000;
```

The method timeNow stores the difference between starting time and current time in milliseconds. We can get the number of minutes from this by dividing by 60000, but this will give us a number in decimal form, such as 3.762. All we really want from this is the 3, the integer portion. The Math.floor method produces the desired result: it returns the closest integer less than or equal to a given number.

All that remains is to calculate the remaining number of seconds after we have divided out the minutes. The modulo (%) operator returns the remainder portion, in integer form, of a division operation. Thus:

```
timeNow % 60000
```

returns the number of milliseconds less than a full minute. Dividing by 1000 yields the number of seconds.

## Control Structures

The stopwatch program illustrates the power of simultaneous events. Even though the gettingTime and checkTime functions are locked in an infinite loop, calling each other back and forth once the user clicks the Start button, this loop does not lock out other program activity or user interaction. The user can still click on other buttons and trigger event handlers, and the program can still carry out other operations.

The stopwatch program brings all the results together that HTML and CGI struggle to achieve alone: user interaction with immediate response through manipulation of on-screen objects like buttons, dynamic display in a continuously updated readout, and dynamic content with an HTML document generated on the fly to be sent to a frame.

The next few chapters provide a comprehensive JScript reference, covering the many elements we have not yet discussed. If the stopwatch example makes sense to you, though, then you have grasped the basics of programming JScript. From here on you are really just refining your tools and skills.

While the fanciful example introduced with the stopwatch program may not have many real-world applications, the stopwatch program can, with small modifications, serve as a genuine Web tool. For example, you could design a script that would have a small frame at the top with the stopwatch running and an input field for entering URLs. The script could then retrieve the specified URL and display the page in a larger lower frame. You would have, in effect, a browser within a browser that keeps track of how much time you spend online. If you are looking for a first programming challenge, you might try to modify the stopwatch into this "browser watch" application. Try it: if you really get stuck, you'll find the answer on the CD-ROM included with this book.

# JScript Object Hierarchy

Window Object

Frame Object

History Object

Navigator Object

Location Object

Document Object

Link Object

Form Object

Element Object

# Chapter 7
# JScript Objects

This chapter and the two that follow provide a complete guide to the objects, data structures, commands, and control structures that make up JScript. While this chapter focuses on the JScript object library, objects that tie in directly to data manipulation, such as the Math and String objects, will be discussed in Chapter 8. JavaScript and JScript are still evolving as scripting languages, so these elements may have changed by the time you read this, and will no doubt continue to change. Current reference information can always be found at the Microsoft Web site, in the developers' pages, and under ActiveX Scripting Interface.

These chapters are intended to be referred to as needed, rather than read through from beginning to end. If you have followed the discussion to this point, you really are ready to begin writing JScript programs on your own. Go ahead—give it a try. If you find yourself unsure of how to do a certain task, or unsure why a particular command or object is not working the way you expect, then you should refer to these chapters. If you are looking for tips on more advanced JScript programs, then look ahead to Chapters 10, 11, and 12.

Many simple questions about JScript objects and commands are answered in Appendix A and Appendix B. Appendix A provides a complete list of all the objects and commands covered in this and the next two chapters, though with no accompanying explanations. Appendix B provides you with a guide to the most frequently used JScript components, together with brief explanations.

## JScript Object Hierarchy

JScript works with ten main HTML objects. Our discussion will be organized around these, presenting other objects as they are contained within these main ten. The top-level object is the Window object. It, in turn, contains the following objects:

- Frame: An array of contained frame windows. Each frame is a window that has its own properties, including a document.

- History: This object is used to access the history list from the browser.
- Navigator: The Navigator object contains information about the browser application.
- Location: Provides information about the location of the window's URL.
- Document: Document in the active window. The Document object contains the following objects:
  - Link: Array of hyperlinks found on the given document.
  - Anchor: Array of anchors found on the given document.
  - Form: Array of forms found on the given document. The Form object contains:
    - Element: Array of objects and intrinsic controls contained in the form.

Each of these objects has properties, and some may have methods as well, including events and event handlers. The properties of some objects may themselves be objects with properties and methods. Each object will be explained following the same format. Each explanation should look like this:

**Name**: name of element

**Description**: brief description of the element and how to use it.

**Usage**: example line of JScript code indicating syntactically correct usage.

**Return Value** (if appropriate): value, if any, returned by invoking this element.

**Applies to**: object to which this element applies.

**Contains**: list of properties, methods, events and event handlers of this element.

Each object will have a section on properties, detailing each property in terms of name, description, usage, and return value. Each object will have a section on methods, detailing each method in terms of name, description, usage, and return value. Each object will have a section on events and event handlers, detailing each in terms of name, description, and usage.

# Window Object

**Name**: Window

**Description**: The top-level object in JScript is a window. The Window object represents the Internet Explorer window, and its methods and properties. Methods and properties of the window object containing a script can be called by that script directly; the two statements listed under "usage" below are thus all equivalent. To access a window by name, the window must be given a name. This can happen in three ways: by using the *window* open method, by creating the window with a name using the <FRAMESET> tag, or by creating the window with a URL using the <TARGET> tag. Once loaded, a window's properties cannot be altered. A new window to be loaded, however, can be customized with options to the *window* open method.

**Usage:**

```
window.document.write("Hello world"); //writes to current document

document.write("Hello world"); //writes to current document
```

**Contains:**

Properties: name, parent, opener, self, top, defaultStatus, status, frames, history, navigator, location, document

Methods: alert, confirm, prompt, open, close, setTimeout, clearTimeout, navigate

Events: onLoad, onUnload

## Properties

**Name**: property

**Description**: Returns the name of the current window. This property is read-only; windows cannot be renamed.

**Usage**:

```
val = name; //assigns name of current window to val
```

**Return Value**: Returns the string containing the current window name, or "null" if none.

**Applies to**: window

**Name**: parent Property

**Description**: Returns the Window object of the window's parent. This property is read-only. The parent of the window is the containing FRAMESET document from which the window was defined. If the current window has no such document, then the parent evaluates to the current window.

**Usage**:

```
parent.frames[2].location = newURL; //changes the third frame defined by the
parent window to newURL
```

**Return Value**: Returns the Window object that evaluates to the parent window.

**Applies To**: Window

**Name**: opener Property

**Description**: Returns the window object of the window that opened the current window.

**Usage**:

```
sourceWin = opener; //assigns opening window to sourceWin
```

**Return Value**: Returns the Window object that evaluates to the opener window.

**Applies To**: Window

**Name**: self Property

**Description**: Returns the Window object of the current window. This property is read-only. This may seem like a superfluous property; the first two lines listed under "Usage" function the same, for example. However, "self" does provide a string that can be the value of a variable. If, in the third line under "Usage," winRef is a variable, then "self" provides one value that variable can take to reference the current window.

**Usage**:

```
document.write("Hello World"); //writes to current window
self.document.write("Hello World"); //writes to current window
winRef.document.write("Hello World"); //writes to window specified by winRef
```

**Return Value**: Returns an object that evaluates to the current window.

**Applies To:** Window

**Name**: top Property

**Description**: Returns the Window object of the top-most window. This property is read-only. The top-most window is the containing window of all frames in the current browser instance.

**Usage**:

```
top.frames[0].location = newURL; //changes the first window defined from the
topmost window to newURL
```

**Return Value**: Returns an object that evaluates to the top-most window. This will return the same value as the parent property if there are no nested frames, and the same value as parent or self if there is only one window. In Figure 7.1, Window 1 is the top of Window 4, but Window 2 is the parent of Window 4.

**Applies To**: Window

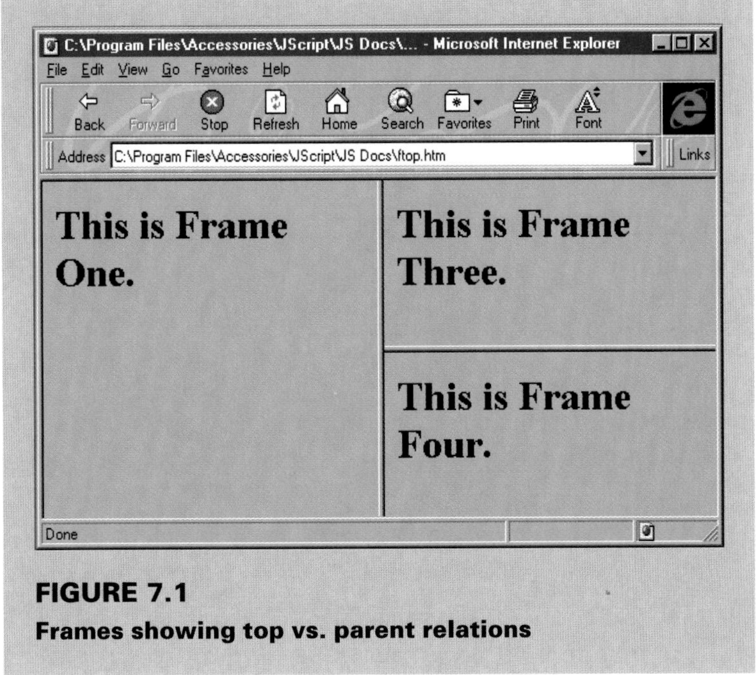


**FIGURE 7.1**
**Frames showing top vs. parent relations**

**Name**: defaultStatus Property

**Description**: Sets the default status text in the lower left portion of the status bar (see Figure 7.2). The status bar is one of the few window elements that can be modified once a document has finished loading.

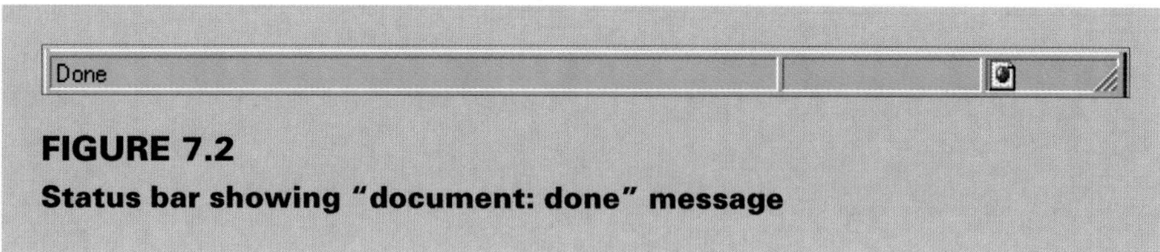


**FIGURE 7.2**
**Status bar showing "document: done" message**

**Usage:**

```
onLoad(defaultStatus="Document done."); //Sets the default message in status
bar to read "Document done" once document has loaded.
```

**Applies To**: Window

**Name**: status Property

**Description**: Sets the status text in the lower left part of the status bar. The status bar is one of the few window elements that can be modified once a document has finished loading. Place messages here with care, however: the browser uses this bar to post status information (surprise!), and will overwrite any text currently in the bar with its message.

**Usage:**

```
onUnload(parent.status = "Bye!"); //Puts the "Bye!" in the status bar of the
parent window when current window is closed.
```

**Applies To**: Window

## Methods

**Name**: alert Method

**Description**: Displays an alert message box. An alert message box contains a message which the user must acknowledge by clicking on the OK button in the box before continuing. The alert Method operates on a string or string variable, and posts this as the message in the alert box. Figure 7.3 shows the output of the command on the following page.

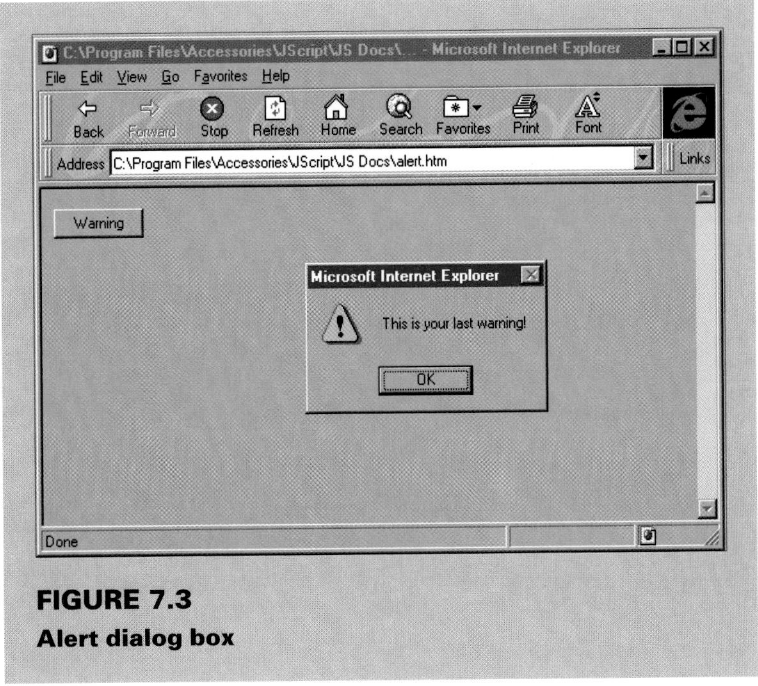


**FIGURE 7.3**
**Alert dialog box**

**Usage**:

```
alert("This is your last warning!"); //opens an alert box and displays this
message, waiting for button to be clicked.
```

**Applies To**: Window

**Name**: confirm Method

**Description**: Displays a message box with an "OK" button and a "Cancel" button. The user must press one or the other to continue. The confirm Method operates on a string or string variable, and posts this as the message in the confirm box. Figure 7.4 shows the output of the command below.

**Usage:**

```
userChoice = confirm("This will end your session.\n" + "Are you sure you want
to continue?"); //Opens a confirm box with this message, and waits for a but-
ton to be clicked.
```

**Return Values**: Returns the user response: TRUE if the user pressed OK; FALSE if not.

**Applies To**: Window

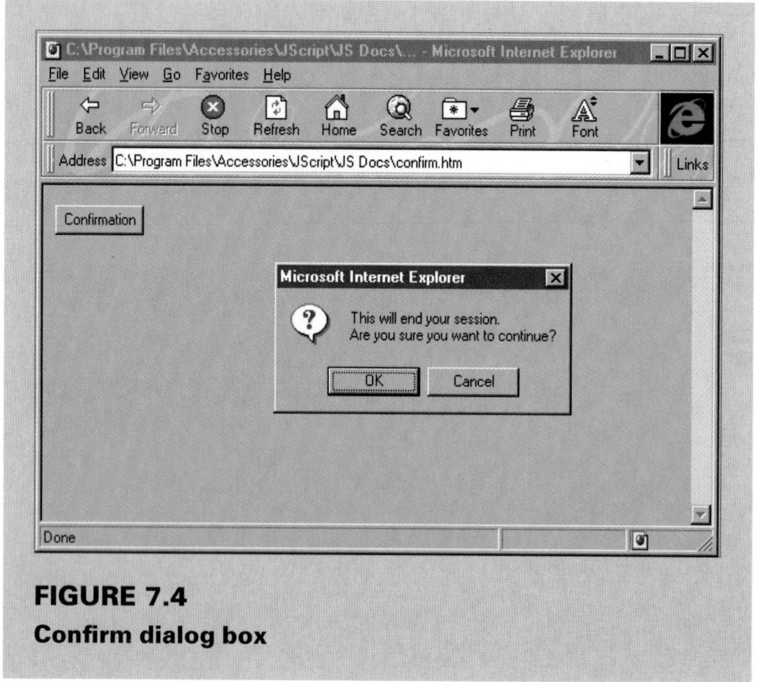


**FIGURE 7.4**
**Confirm dialog box**

**Name**: prompt Method

**Description**: Opens a dialog box with a text-input window, an "OK" button, and a "Cancel" button. The prompt Method operates on two values: the message to be displayed, and the default value to be used as a reply if the user clicks "OK" without typing any input into the text-input window. Figure 7.5 shows the output of the command below.

**Usage:**

```
money = prompt("Please enter your credit card number.", noDice); //Opens
prompt dialog box, displays the message, and waits for a button to be
clicked.
```

**Return Values**: Returns user input if provided and "OK" button clicked, returns default value if no input provided and "OK" button clicked, returns NULL if "Cancel" button clicked.

**Applies To**: Window

**Name**: open Method

**Description**: Creates a new window with a specified URL, name, and optional settings for window features. These three components are each enclosed in

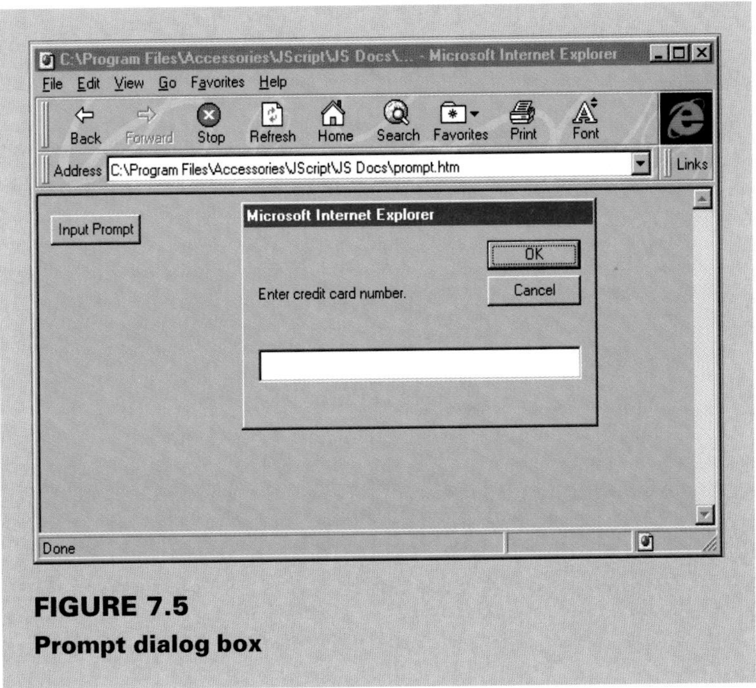


**FIGURE 7.5**
**Prompt dialog box**

quotes, separated by commas, as in: window.open("URL", "name", "option, option, ...").

If no URL is specified, then a blank window is opened. This window can then receive output from a write or writeln statement. Such output should be completed with a document.close() statement.

If no options are specified, then the default window settings for your browser will be used. If any options are specified, then only those options specified will be used. Possible options are: toolbar, location, directories, status, menubar, scrollbars, and resizeable. In other words, if any options are specified, then to have a toolbar on the new window toolbar must be specified, to have a status bar on the new window status bar must be specified, and so on.

On the options list, width and height in pixels may also be specified; if not specified, then your browser's default window size will be used.

**Usage:**

```
window.open("mypage.htm", "window2", "toolbar, location, resizable,
width=300, height=150); //creates a new resizable window, 300x150, loading
"mypage.htm" into that window, with only toolbar and location as features
```

**Applies To**: Window

**Name**: close Method

**Description**: Closes the window. Do not confuse with the document.close() method, which closes output to a document. Applying document.close() to the current window should not cause a problem; applying window.close() to the current window will most likely have undesired consequences.

**Usage**:

```
"window2".close(); //closes the window named "window2"
```

**Applies To**: Window

**Name**: setTimeout Method

**Description**: Sets a timer to execute a statement after a specified number of milliseconds. Typically the statement is a function to be called, but it could be a single expression, or even a list of semicolon-delimited statements.

**Usage**:

```
timerID = setTimeout(liftOff(), 10000); //executes the liftOff function after
10 seconds.
```

**Return Value**: Returns the ID of the timer object. This can be used to cancel the timer using the clearTimeout method.

**Applies To**: Window

**Name**: clearTimeout Method

**Description**: Clears the timer having a particular ID. This action cancels whatever call would have been made when the timer counted down.

**Usage**:

```
clearTimeout(timerID); //clears the timer for the setTimeout method whose ID
value is timerID
```

**Applies To**: Window

**Name**: navigate Method

**Description**: Navigates the window to a new URL. This provides one alternative—there are others—to having the user click on a link to navigate to a new URL. For example, this method can be used in combination with the onLoad event to create a client-side redirect.

**Usage**:

```
<BODY onLoad="redirector()">
//calls redirector function when window finishes loading
function redirector() {
   confMessage = "The document you requested has moved.\n";
   confMessage += "Click on OK to go to its new location."
   goToNewLocation = confirm(confMessage); \\see if OK was clicked
   if (goToNewLocation) {navigate(newURL)); \\if OK, go to newURL
}
```

**Applies To**: Window

## Events

**Name**: onLoad Event Handler

**Description**: Triggered after all HTML has been parsed and processed. Can be used as an attribute of the <BODY> tag, or as an attribute of the <FRAMESET> tag if the document has no <BODY> tag.

**Usage**: see the Navigate method above for a good illustration of onLoad usage.

**Applies To**: Window

**Name**: onUnload Event Handler

**Description**: Triggered when the contents of the window are unloaded. Can be used as an attribute of the <BODY> tag, or as an attribute of the <FRAMESET> tag if the document has no <BODY> tag.

**Usage**:

```
<BODY onUnload="byeBye()"> //calls the byeBye function when the window unloads
```

**Applies To**: Window

# Frame Object

**Name**: Frame

**Description**: The Frame object is very similar to the Window object. The same properties, methods, and events will apply to the Frame object as to the Window object. A Frame object will only be present if frames have been defined within a <FRAMESET> document. Frame is an array object, so frames can be accessed by name or by index number. To access a frame by name, the frame must be given a name as an attribute of the <FRAME> tag that defined it in the <FRAMESET> document. Index numbers are assigned to frames in the order in which they are defined in the <FRAMESET> document: the first frame listed will be frames[0], the next frames[1], and so on.

Frames differ from windows in some ways. A frame will always have a value for the top Property that differs from the value of the self Property, and will always have a value for the parent Property that differs from the self Property. If the frame originates from a nested <FRAMESET> page, then the value of top will also differ from the value of parent.

The frame.open() method also differs from the window.open() method. Frames do not have menus or button bars at the top. Frames also cannot have their size changed; a frame's size is set once and for all by its definition in the <FRAMESET> document. Thus the options list of the window.open() method has no analog in the frame.open() method.

Otherwise frame properties, events, and methods will work like their window counterparts; please refer to the window counterpart for a detailed explanation.

**Usage**:

```
frames[1].document.write("Hello world"); //writes to the second frame
topFrame.document.write("Hello world"); //writes to the frame named topFrame
```

**Contains**:

Properties: name, parent, opener, self, top, defaultStatus, status, frames, history, navigator, location, document

Methods: alert, confirm, prompt, open, close, setTimeout, clearTimeout, navigate

Events: onLoad, onUnload

# History Object

**Name**: History

**Description**: An object that resides below the window in JScript. This object accesses the history list, a list of URLs recently visited by the browser. The History object enables methods for navigating through this list.

From a programming point of view, the logical organization of the History object would be as an array of strings, where each element is a string listing the URL of a site visited. For reasons of privacy, this is not quite the way the History object is implemented. The implementation needs to guard against JScript, in conjunction with a forms submission, passing on information about what sites you have visited without you realizing that this information has been passed on. To avoid this problem, JScript does not permit direct access of URLs on the history list. The only way to reveal a URL from this list would be to load it as the location of a window or frame, in which case the user would be aware of this activity.

**Usage**:

```
reLoad = history.go(n); //navigate to the nth item on the history list.
```

**Contains**:

Properties: length

Methods: back, forward, go

## Properties

**Name**: length Property

**Description**: Returns the number of URLs in the history list.

**Usage**:

```
siteNum = history.length; //assigns the number of URLs to the variable siteNum
```

**Return Value**: Returns the number of entries in the history.

**Applies To**: History

## Methods

**Name**: back Method

**Description**: Jumps back in the history *n* steps. This behaves exactly as if the user has clicked on the back button *n* times. Figure 7.6 shows the output of the commands below.

**Usage**:

```
<INPUT TYPE="button" VALUE="Back 2" onClick="history.back(2)"> //an onscreen
back button; in this case it goes back two items in the history list.
```

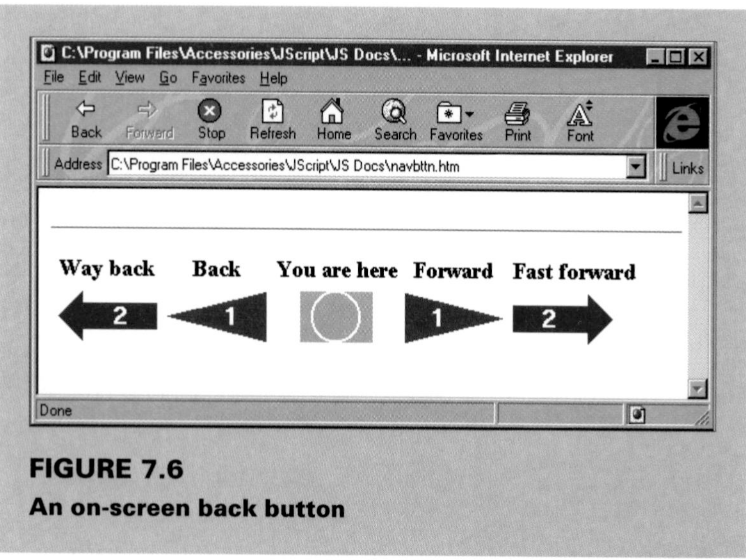


**FIGURE 7.6**
**An on-screen back button**

**Applies To**: History

**Name**: forward Method

**Description**: Jumps forward in the history *n* steps. This behaves exactly as if the user has clicked on the forward button *n* times.

**Usage**:

```
<INPUT TYPE="button" VALUE="Forward" onClick="history.forward(1)"> //an
onscreen forward button
```

**Applies To**: History

**Name**: go Method

**Description**: Navigates to an item on the history list based on one of three ways of specifying that item: by URL, by title, or by number. Fails to execute if no matching item is found on the history list. Title matches the contents of the <TITLE></TITLE> tags from documents, which is what is stored on the history list.

Unfortunately, JScript and JavaScript use different numbering schemes. With Netscape Navigator and JavaScript, numbers are relative to the current document, so go(0) refers to the current document, go(1) is the same as forward(1), and go(-1) is the same as back(1). With Internet Explorer and JScript, numbers are relative to the first document on the history list, so go(0) refers to the first document, go(1) to the second document, and so on.

**Usage**:

```
history.go(1); //navigates to second document on the history list
history.go("mypage.htm"); //navigates to "mypage.htm" if that is on the
history list
history.go("My Home Page"); //navigates to the document titled "My Home Page"
if that is on the history list
```

**Applies To**: History

# Navigator Object

**Name**: navigator

**Description**: An object that resides below the window. The navigator object provides information about the browser in use.

**Usage**:

```
yourBrowserType = navigator.appName; //sets the variable yourBrowserType to
the type of browser you are using
```

**Contains**:

Properties: appCodeName, appName, appVersion, userAgent

## Properties

**Name**: appCodeName Property

**Description:** Returns the code name of the application.

**Usage**:

```
yourBrowser = navigator.appCodeName; //sets the variable yourBrowser to the
application code of the browser you are using.
```

**Return Value:** Returns a string containing the current application code name.

**Applies To**: navigator

**Name**: appName Property

**Description**: Returns the name of the application. Internet Explorer 3.0 currently returns "Microsoft Internet Explorer."

**Usage**:

```
yourBrowserType = navigator.appName; //sets the variable yourBrowserType to
the type of browser you are using
```

**Return Value**: Returns a string containing the current application name.

**Applies To**: navigator

**Name**: appVersion Property

**Description**: Returns the version of the application, including version number and platform.

**Usage**:

```
versionInfo = navigator.appVersion; //assigns version to versionInfo
```

**Return Value**: Returns a string containing the current application version information.

**Applies To**: Navigator

**Name**: userAgent Property

**Description**: Returns the user agent of the application. Internet Explorer 3.0 currently returns "Mozilla/2.0 (compatible; MSIE 3.0A; Windows 95)".

**Usage**:

```
agentInfo = navigator.userAgent; //assigns browser agent to agentInfo
```

**Return Value**: Returns a string containing the current application user agent.

**Applies To**: Navigator

# Location Object

**Name**: location

**Description:** An object that resides below the window. The location object represents the current URL. Properties of the location object can be set as well as read. Consequently, setting any portion of the location object causes the browser to navigate to the newly constructed URL. Given the many properties of the location object, manipulation of this object provides a very powerful programming tool for controlling navigation.

A complete URL consists of a number of elements. The URL begins with a protocol, such as http: or ftp:. This protocol must be directed to search for something, and follows the UNIX convention of delimiting a search with slashes (/), as in "http:/whatToSearchFor/".

In this example "whatToSearchFor" is a host. A host is found by looking for the location of a hostname on the Internet, querying at a particular port, and starting a search from the root of the document tree made available by the host on that port. If our hostname is www.kudonet.com and we are asking for the http protocol, then the default port to query at would be port 80. We want to start our query at the root—in directory parlance / usually indicates the root—of the www document tree. Thus the value we need for "whatToSearchFor" is "/www.kudonet.com:80/".

*These days the "slash slash" of "http://" trips off our tongues so easily we think of it as a single entity. As we see, though, each slash (/) belongs to a different part of the overall URL taxonomy.*

Substituting this in, our whole URL so far looks like "http://www.kudonet.com:80/". We can also follow a pathname within the document tree of that host, as in "http://www.kudonet.com:80/~markst/index.html". Further, we can jump to the middle of that document if it contains an anchor name, as in "http://www.kudonet.com:80/~markst/index.html#js".

Not all of these elements are necessary in a full URL. The default port of 80 is typically assumed, and the server may be configured to use index.html as the default document within a directory. Some browsers will assume the http protocol unless otherwise specified, and most will forgive the omission of trailing slashes. So the following may be a shorter but functionally equivalent version of this URL: "www.kudonet.com/~markst#js".

However, you should be aware of all the elements, even if you do not use them all. The location object has a property for each.

**Usage**:

```
parent.frames[1].location = "http://www.yahoo.com";
//loads the Yahoo home page into the second frame
```

**Contains**:

Properties: href, protocol, host, hostname, port, pathname, search, hash

## Properties

**Name**: href Property

**Description:** href contains the entire URL of protocol, hostname, port (if needed), pathname, and hash (if needed).

**Usage**:

```
if (href != MyHome) { location = MyHome};
//if MyHome contains the URL of my home page, then this command will load my
home page unless it is the current URL.
```

**Return Value:** Returns a string containing the complete URL for the location.

**Applies To**: Location

**Name**: protocol Property

**Description:** Gets or sets the protocol portion of the URL.

**Usage**:

```
if (location.protocol == "http:") {
   location= "ftp://" + location.hostname;
} //If at a web server on a host, attempt to go to the corresponding ftp
server.
```

**Return Value:** Returns a string containing the protocol portion of the URL.

**Applies To**: Location

**Name**: host Property

**Description**: Gets or sets the host and port portions of the URL (hostname:port). The typical port number for http, 80, need not be specified.

**Usage**:

```
location.hostname =  "www.biguniversity.edu"
//navigates to the indicated host
```

**Return Values**: Returns a string containing the host and port portions of the URL.

**Applies To**: Location

**Name**: hostname Property

**Description:** Gets or sets the hostname portion of the URL. Hostname can be specified either by IP number or by name.

**Usage**:

```
hostname = 165.227.52.1
hostname = www.kudonet.com
//These commands navigate to the same host
```

**Return Values:** Returns a string containing the hostname portion of the URL; does not return the IP number.

**Applies To:** Location

**Name**: port Property

**Description**: Gets or sets the port of the URL. While the typical port number for http is 80 and need not be specified, on computers where a Web server is not running as root user, the server will not have permission to listen at any port below 1024. You will occasionally see URLs with higher port numbers, and for these the port number must be treated as an explicit part of the host specification.

**Usage**:

```
location.host = "www.biguniversity.edu";
location.port = "8001";
//these lines navigate to "www.biguniversity.edu:8001"
```

**Return Value**: Returns a string containing the port of the URL. Note that even though it is a number, it returns as a string. Apply parseInteger() to treat it as a number.

**Applies To**: Location

**Name**: pathname Property

**Description**: Gets or sets the pathname in the URL. Navigating by pathname corresponds to what HTML calls a relative URL. This is the location Property most likely to be used, since pathname is all you need to navigate within the same Web site.

**Usage**:

```
if (userChoice == "up") {
   location.pathname = "home.html";
} else {
   location.pathname = "next.html";
} //selects page to navigate to based on value of userChoice
```

**Return Value**: Returns a string containing the pathname portion of the URL.

**Applies To**: Location

**Name**: search Property

**Description**: Gets the search portion of the URL, if specified. Can also be used to set the search portion of the URL. The search portion of a URL is that portion that is sent as input to CGI by the GET method: in other words, appended to the URL after a question mark (?). Setting this portion of the URL can provide a powerful tool for integrating JScript and CGI applications. Recall from Chapter 3 that GET requests do not need to be generated by using an HTML Submit button—they can be generated by navigating directly to the URL of the CGI program. Likewise, in JScript you can send GET requests without use of the onSubmit() event by manipulating the Location object and the search Property.

CGI does not handle characters other than numbers or letters well; other characters may need to be sent as their ASCII code rather than literally. JScript does provide a function, the escape() function, that performs this task, and a function unescape(), that turns ASCII code into literal characters.

**Usage**:

```
location = "big.searchengine.com";
if (userChoice == "author") {
   location .pathname = "cgi-bin/booksearch.pl"
   location .search = "field=author";
} else {
   location .pathname= "cgi-bin/booksearch.pl"
   location .pathname= "title";
} //sends one of these searches:
  //big.searchengine.com/cgi-bin/booksearch.pl?field=author
  // big.searchengine.com/cgi-bin/booksearch.pl?field=title
```

**Return Value**: Returns a string containing the search portion of the URL.

**Applies To**: Location

**Name**: hash Property

**Description**: Gets or sets the hash portion of the URL, if specified. The hash portion follows the hash mark (#), and is used to navigate to a named anchor in the middle of a page.

**Usage**:

```
anchorName = location.hash; //returns the name of the anchor the current
document is loaded to
```

**Return Values**: Returns a string containing the hash portion of the URL.

**Applies To**: Location

# Document Object

**Name**: Document

**Description**: An object that resides below the window. A document begins and ends with <HTML></HTML> tags, and every JScript is contained within a document. Most of the objects visible to the user will be contained within a document, and most of a program's object manipulation will act on objects contained within a document.

The Document object reflects the HTML document currently in the browser and objects on the page: links, forms, buttons, and ActiveX objects. Methods and properties of the Document object must be called in a script by placing *document* first in the statement.

**Usage**:

```
nameOf = document.title; //assigns to nameOf the name of the current document.
```

**Contains**:

Properties: bgColor, fgColor, linkColor, aLinkColor, vLinkColor, location, lastModified, title, referrer, links, anchors, forms

Methods: write, writeLn, open, close, clear

## Properties

**Name**: bgColor Property

**Description**: Gets or sets the current color of the background in a document. The color is expressed in the same hexadecimal notation that HTML uses with the color attributes of the <BODY> tag. This takes the form #rrggbb where rr is a hexadecimal number expressing one of 256 possible red values, gg is a hexadecimal number expressing one of 256 possible green values, and bb is a hexadecimal number expressing one of 256 possible blue values.

Color properties of a document cannot be changed once a document has loaded, nor can they be changed for a pre-existing HTML document. Thus when setting colors, bgColor and the other color properties can only be set for documents that will be generated dynamically with the write() or writeln() functions.

**Usage**:

```
//There's just no telling what color scheme someone
//else has used on their site. But if you show their
//page, and the color scheme conflicts with yours,
//the user could be confused. This code fragment
//illustrates displaying an off-site document in one
//frame, and using its color scheme for dynamically
//generated HTML to a second frame.
frames[0].location = offSiteURL;
frames[1].document.open();
frames[1].document.bgColor = frames[0].document.bgColor;
frames[1].document.fgColor = frames[0].document.fgColor;
frames[1].document.linkColor = frames[0].document.linkColor;
frames[1].document.vlinkColor = frames[0].document.vlinkColor ;
```

**Return Value**: Returns the rgb value of the current background color.

**Applies To**: Document

**Name**: fgColor Property

**Description**: Gets or sets the foreground color in hexadecimal notation: #rrggbb where rr is a hexadecimal number expressing one of 256 possible red values, gg is a hexadecimal number expressing one of 256 possible green values, and bb is a hexadecimal number expressing one of 256 possible blue values.

Color properties of a document cannot be changed once a document has loaded, nor can they be changed for a pre-existing HTML document. Thus when setting colors, fgColor and the other color properties can only be set for documents that will be generated dynamically with the write() or writeln() functions.

**Usage**: see example under bgColor.

**Return Value**: Returns the rgb value of the current foreground color.

**Applies To**: Document

**Name**: linkColor Property

**Description**: Gets or sets the current color of the links in a document in the hexadecimal notation: #rrggbb where rr is a hexadecimal number expressing one of 256 possible red values, gg is a hexadecimal number expressing one of 256 possible green values, and bb is a hexadecimal number expressing one of 256 possible blue values.

Color properties of a document cannot be changed once a document has loaded, nor can they be changed for a pre-existing HTML document. Thus when setting colors, linkColor and the other color properties can only be set for documents that will be generated dynamically with the write() or writeln() functions.

**Usage**: see example under bgColor.

**Return Value**: Returns the rgb value of the current link color.

**Applies To**: Document

**Name**: aLinkColor Property

**Description**: Gets or sets the current color of the *active* links in a document. At present Internet Explorer does not make use of this feature, so aLinkColor has no effect; however, it is supported in Netscape Navigator and so is mentioned here for compatibility reasons.

**Name**: vLinkColor Property

**Description**: Gets or sets the current color of the visited links in a document in the hexadecimal notation: #rrggbb where rr is a hexadecimal number expressing one of 256 possible red values, gg is a hexadecimal number expressing one of 256 possible green values, and bb is a hexadecimal number expressing one of 256 possible blue values.

Color properties of a document cannot be changed once a document has loaded, nor can they be changed for a pre-existing HTML document. Thus when setting colors, linkColor and the other color properties can only be set for documents that will be generated dynamically with the write() or writeln() functions.

**Usage**: see example under bgColor.

**Return Value**: Returns the rgb value of the current visited link color.

**Applies To**: Document

**Name**: location Property

**Description**: Do not confuse the location Property of the Document object with the Location object, which is a window Property. The location Property returns a read-only representation of the location object. In other words, it returns the full URL of the current document.

It makes sense that you cannot set a document location. A document's URL is one of its permanent features; you cannot, with a simple JScript command, move a document around on the Internet.

If you need to read a part of a document's URL, you should be able to do this by manipulating properties of the Location object discussed earlier, rather than the location Property.

**Usage**:

```
whereAmI = document.location; //assigns the URL of the current document to
whereAmI
```

**Return Value**: Returns an object expression that evaluates to the Location object of the document.

**Applies To**: Document

**Name**: lastModified Property

**Description**: Web pages frequently include a line that says something like "Last updated on...." This information can affect how a user evaluates information on a page, but frequent updating by hand places an undue burden on the Web designer, or on the Web server if this information is updated by CGI or its more limited cousin, Server Side Includes.

JScript provides some relief. Ironically, every file carries with it a time stamp for when it was last modified. There's no need for human or server intervention: just let JScript access this time stamp via the lastModified property, which returns the last-modified date of the current page as a string. See Figure 7.7 for an example of a JScript update notice on a page.

Unfortunately, lastModified does not treat this time stamp as the result of a Date object method; if you want to work with part of this string using methods like those available for the Date object, you'll have to do some extra programming.

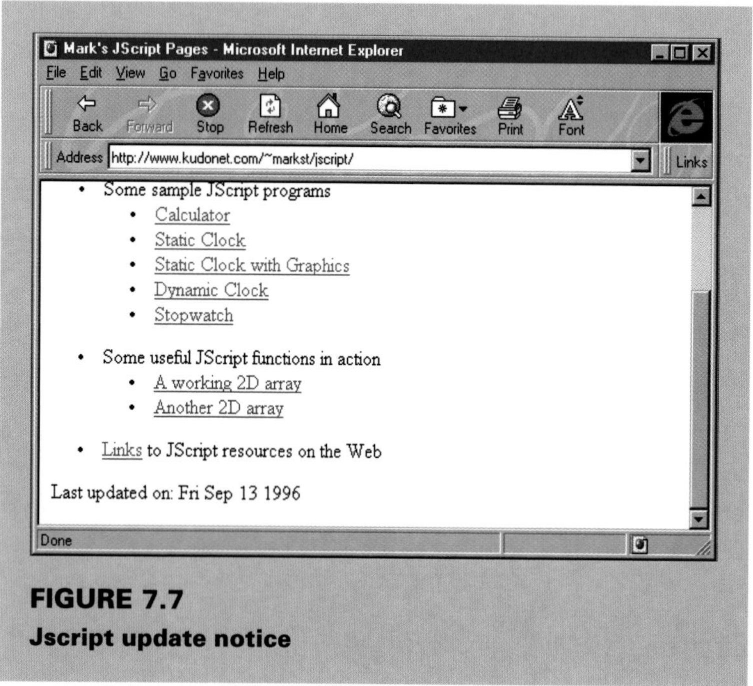


**FIGURE 7.7**
**Jscript update notice**

**Usage**:

```
//This code fragment prints a "Last updated" message
//on the current document.
upDate = document.lastModified;
document.write("<P>Last updated on: " + update);
```

**Return Value**: Returns a string containing the date.

**Applies To**: Document

**Name**: title Property

**Description**: Returns a read-only representation of the document's title, the text between the <TITLE></TITLE> tags.

**Usage**:

```
thisTitle = document.title;
```

**Return Value**: Returns a string expression that evaluates to the title of the document.

**Applies To**: Document

**Name**: cookie Property

**Description**: Gets or sets the cookie for the current document. Under Netsape Navigator, Javascript allows up to 20 cookies per page that can store a string. Under Internet Explorer, JScript only allows one cookie.

**Usage**:

```
myCookie = document.cookie;
```

**Return Value**: Returns a string containing the current cookie.

The cookie is a string expression stored for the current page. Note that setting the cookie overwrites any current cookie information. Also note that you can use string expressions to locate particular information in the cookie string.

**Applies To**: Document

**Name**: referrer Property

**Description**: Similar to the location property, except that it gets the URL of the referring document. The referring document is the one whose link was clicked to reach the current document.

While this property works properly under Netscape Navigator, under Internet Explorer referrer always returns the current URL.

**Usage**:

```
sourcePage = document.referrer;
```

**Return Value**: Returns a string containing the URL of the referring document. Currently returns the URL of the referring document when there is a referrer, and NULL when there is no referrer.

The referrer varies depending on how the user linked to the current document. If a page was reached by explicitly typing in a URL rather than clicking on a link, then referrer should return NULL.

**Applies To**: Document

## Methods

**Name**: write Method

**Description**: Places the given string into the current document. The string is appended to the current document at the current position. The current document must be open; once a document has loaded completely it cannot be written to.

**Usage**:

```
miniDoc = "<HTML><HEAD><TITLE>Mini Document</TITLE></HEAD>";
miniDoc += "<BODY>Hello World!</BODY></HTML>";
document.write(miniDoc);
//writes "Hello World!" to the current document.
```

**Applies To**: Document

**Name**: writeLn Method

**Description**: Similar to write() Method; places the given string into the current document with a new-line character appended to the end.

**Usage**:

```
frameCount = "This is frame " + num;
top.frames[num-1].document.writeln(frameCount);
```

**Applies To**: Document

**Name**: open Method

**Description**: Opens the document stream for output. Cannot be applied to the document containing the script; that document is, by definition, open when it encounters the script. Should be used with frames to open a document in another frame for output.

While the default type of output for open() is "text/html," the open() method can be used to open an output stream for any of the following MIME types: "text/plain," "image/gif," "image/jpeg," "image/xbm," "plugin."

**Usage**:

```
top.frames[1].document.open("image/gif"); //opens second frame for binary
output in gif image format
```

**Applies To**: Document

**Name**: close Method

**Description**: Updates the screen to display all of the strings written after the last open method call. Closes the document to further output. No onLoad event will be executed until the document is closed.

**Usage**:

```
miniDoc = "<HTML><HEAD><TITLE>Mini Document</TITLE></HEAD>";
miniDoc += "<BODY>Hello World!</BODY></HTML>";
frames[1].document.open();
frames[1].document.write(miniDoc);
frames[1].document.close();
```

**Applies To**: Document

**Name**: clear Method

**Description**: The window.close(), document.close(), and document.clear() methods can cause confusion. While the similarity in names might lead one to think that window.close() and document.close() do essentially the same thing, we have seen that this is the wrong conclusion. Window.close() removes the contents of a window from the screen, whereas document.close() simply signals that output to a document has been completed.

The document.clear() Method is, in fact, the method that most resembles the window.close() Method. Document.clear() removes the current document from the window or frame in which it was displayed. To function properly, this method must be applied to a closed document.

**Usage**:

```
frames[2].document.clear(); //blanks out frame three
```

**Applies To**: Document

# Link Object

**Name**: link

**Description**: An object that resides below the Document object. A Link object is constructed for every link that appears in the HTML document. A link is defined in scripting as the anchor tag <A> containing the HREF attribute, as in <A HREF="http://www.microsoft.com">. All properties of the Link object are read-only and are the same as the Location object's properties.

This object specifies all the links for a given document as array elements, in the order in which they occur in the document. In this respect the Link object has a similar structure to the Frame object. The first link in a document can be referenced as document.links[0], the second as document.links[1], and so on. The Link object is referenced as a read-only property array.

**Usage**:

```
top.frames[1].location = top.frames[0].links[3];

//loads the document whose URL is referenced in the
//fourth link of frame one into frame two.
```

**Contains**:

Properties: href, protocol, host, hostname, port, pathname, search, hash

Events: onMouseOver, onClick

## Properties

The properties of the Links object are identical to the properties of the Location object, namely the full URL (href Property) and its constituents (protocol, host, hostname, port, pathname, search, hash). For a detailed description of the behavior of these properties, refer to the Location object.

## Events

**Name**: onMouseOver Event Handler

**Description**: Triggers an event any time the pointer moves over a link. A common use of the onMouseOver event is to display the URL of the link that the pointer is over in the status bar at the bottom of the browser window.

**Usage**:

```
<A HREF="home.html" onMouseOver="window.status=links[0].href">
```

**Applies To**: Link

**Name**: onClick Event Handler

**Description**: Triggers an event any time you click on a link. Keep in mind that clicking on a link triggers an HTML event as well, namely navigating to the linked document. Any script triggered by an onClick event would execute first.

**Usage**:

```
//This code fragment illustrates identifying the
//destination of an offsite jump and displaying a
//"goodbye" message in the status bar.
<A HREF = "www.rivalcompany.com" onClick="lastMessage(linknum)">
function lastMessage(linknum) {
   bye = "Leaving for ";
   bye += links[linknumb].hostname;
   bye += "? Come back soon!";
   window.status = bye;
}
```

**Applies To**: Link

# Anchor Object

**Name**: anchor

**Description**: An object that resides below the document object. An anchor is any occurrence of the <A NAME=> tag, as in <A NAME="Subsection1">. All properties of the Anchor object are read-only. An anchor is that part of a document that can be navigated to by appending the anchor name after the hash (#) in a URL.

This object is similar to the Link object. It specifies all the anchors for a given document as array elements, in the order in which they occur in the document. The first anchor in a document can be referenced as document.anchors[0], the second as document.anchors[1], and so on. The Anchor object is referenced as a read-only property array.

**Usage**:

```
window.location.hash = document.anchors[Ø].name;
//navigates to the first anchor
```

**Contains**:

Properties: name

**Description**: An anchor has only one property, which is its name. This can be read or set.

# Form Object

**Name**: form

**Description**: The Form object represents a form in the HTML document. Forms are kept in the Document object both as an array and by name. The Form object organizes arrays in the same manner as other array objects: the first form in a document is document.forms[0], then document.forms[1], and so on. Forms to be accessed by name must be given one by the NAME attribute of the HTML <FORM> tag.

In HTML forms provide the only means of user input, and hence the only basis for user interaction. JScript piggybacks on this approach. Any elements to be manipulated by the user, or any data to be entered by the user, must be contained within the <FORM></FORM> tags.

In the most typical structure, a JScript program will consist of a number of events specified within a form, and a number of event handlers for resolving those events.

**Usage**:

```
document.forms[Ø].Display.value = "No matching entries found."
//writes a message into a text field named "Display" on the document's first
form.
```

**Contains**:

Properties: action, encoding, method, target, elements

Methods: submit

Events: onSubmit

## Properties

**Name**: action Property

**Description**: Gets or sets the URL to be used to carry out the action of the form, which is the address of the executable program to called through CGI.

**Usage**:

```
cgiAddress = document.forms[1].action;
//assigns the URL for the program called by form two
```

**Return Value**: Returns a string containing the current form action.

**Applies To**: Form

**Name**: encoding Property

**Description**: Forms can be set for a different MIME type output than "text/html." The encoding Property gets or sets the encoding for the form. If no MIME type is specified, "text/html" is used. Note that this is identical to changing the ENCTYPE attribute of the <FORM> tag.

**Usage**:

```
if (document.forms[0].encoding != "text/html") {
  top.frames[1].open(document.forms[0].encoding );
}
//Opens frame two for the MIME type of form one,
//unless form one's encoding is just "text/html"
```

**Return Value**: Returns a string containing the current form encoding.

**Applies To**: Form

**Name**: method Property

**Description**: Indicates how the form data should be sent to the server, as either GET or POST method.

**Usage**:

```
GorP = document.forms[0].method;
```

**Return Value**: Returns a string containing the current form method.

**Applies To**: Form

**Name**: target Property

**Description**: Specifies the name of the target window or frame to display the form results in. This can be especially useful if you do not want a form-results document to overwrite the current window or frame.

**Usage**:

```
resultsFrame = document.forms[1].target;
```

**Return Value**: Returns a string containing the current form target.

**Applies To**: Form

## Methods

**Name**: submit Method

**Description**: Submits the form. Note that this is identical to clicking a form input with TYPE=SUBMIT. This is a powerful JScript method for combining JScript and CGI, because it enables you to customize when form submission occurs, rather than being tied to the click of a SUBMIT button. The code below illustrates one use of this alternative; see Figure 7.8 for the corresponding output.

**Usage**:

```
//This code fragment illustrates turning a clickable
//image into a submit button.
<A HREF = "/cgi-bin/process.pl" onClick="imgSubmit()">
<IMG SRC = "picture.gif"></A>
function imgSubmit() {
```

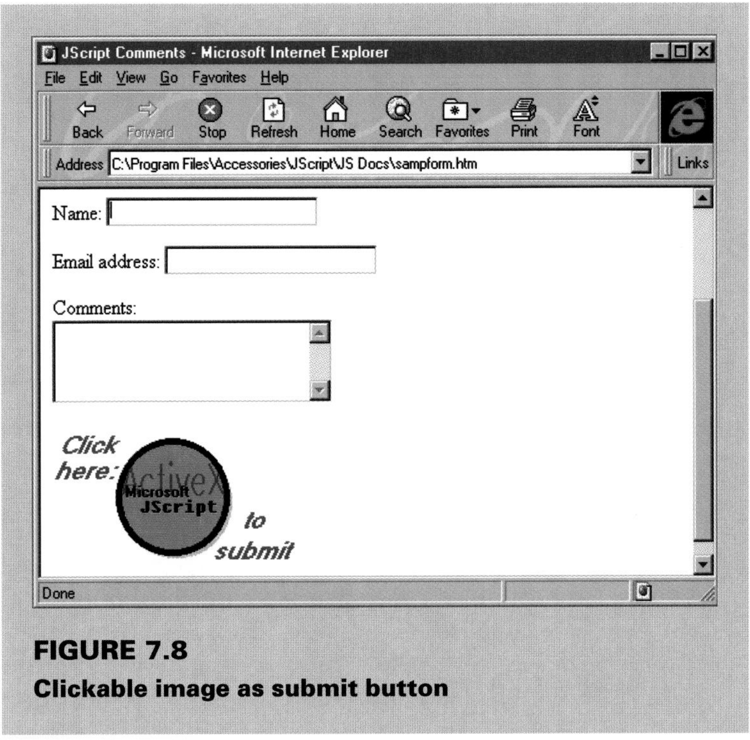


**FIGURE 7.8**
**Clickable image as submit button**

```
    document.forms[0].submit();
}
```

**Applies To**: Form

## Events

**Name**: onSubmit Event

**Description**: Triggered when the form is submitted. This event can be used to prevent the form from being submitted, or it can be used to run additional code before the form is submitted. To prevent the form from being submitted, you must use "return <function>."

**Usage**:

```
form.onSubmit = "return IsValid()";
//Calls IsValid and submits the form if it returns TRUE
//Does not submit the form if it returns FALSE
form.onSubmit = "IsValid()"
//Calls IsValid and submits the form regardless of return value.
```

**Applies To**: Form

# Element Object

**Name**: element

**Description**: An object that resides below the Document object. Elements are intrinsic HTML controls. Controls are placed on a document with the <INPUT> tag. These controls are all of the familiar objects used by HTML for handling user input; see Figure 7.9 for a page illustrating all of these. In JScript the properties of elements can be directly manipulated, and elements can be used to trigger events handled by JScript commands.

Elements are kept in the Form object both as an array and by name. The Form object organizes arrays in the same manner as other array objects: document.forms[0].elements[0] refers to the first element of the first form, document.forms[0].elements[1] refers to the second element of the first form, and so on. Elements to be accessed by name must be given a name by the NAME attribute of the HTML <INPUT> tag.

At present there are some bugs in the implementation of the elements[] array. You may not be able to reference all element types by index number; checkbox options, for example, do not return values if referenced by index number. As a workaround, you can always assign a name to a forms element and reference the element by name.

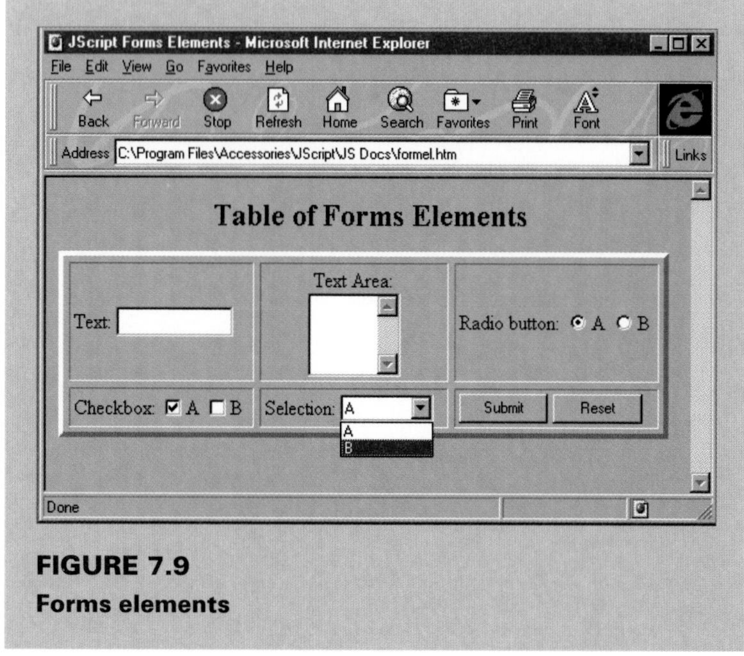


**FIGURE 7.9**
**Forms elements**

**Usage**:

```
//This code fragment illustrates a simple input
//validation step. It checks to see if an element
//has been filled and sends an alert if not.
<INPUT TYPE="submit" onClick="validator()">
function validator () {
   if (document.forms[0].elements[0].value == NULL) {
      warning = "Please complete input before submission.";
      alert(warning);
   }
}
```

**Contains**:

Properties: form, name, value, defaultValue, checked, defaultChecked, length, options, selectedIndex

Events: onClick, onFocus, onBlur, onChange, onSelect

## Properties

**Name**: form Property

**Description**: The form Property is related to, but not to be confused with, the Form object. It gets the Form object containing the element. This can be used to help an event handler keep track of which form a function call came from.

**Usage**:

```
<INPUT TYPE="text" NAME="Display">
<INPUT TYPE="submit" onSumbit="process(document.forms[0].Display.value,
document.forms[0].Display.form)">
//Passes the form ID as well as the display value to
//the process function.
```

**Return Value**: Returns an object expression that evaluates to a Form object.

**Applies To**: All elements except select and hidden.

**Name**: name Property

**Description**: Gets or sets the name of the element.

**Usage**:

```
elementName = document.forms[0].elements[0].name;
```

**Return Value**: Returns a string containing the name of the element.

**Applies To**: All elements

**Name**: value Property

**Description**: Gets or sets the value of the element. This is the most frequently used element property, since this is the property that holds the contents of user input. Also, for text and textarea elements, this field can be written to by JScript simply by updating their value.

**Usage**:

```
userInput = document.forms[0].elements[0].value;
```

**Return Value**: Returns a string containing the value of the element.

**Applies To**: All elements

**Name**: defaultValue Property

**Description**: Gets or sets the default value of the element. This is the value that will be initially displayed, and will be used in the absence of user alterations.

**Usage**:

```
document.forms[0].countryDisplay.defaultValue = "United States";
//In a series of address entry fields, sets the
//default for country to U. S.
```

**Return Value**: Returns a string containing the default value of the element.

**Applies To**: password, text, textarea

**Name**: checked Property

**Description**: Gets or sets the checked state of a checkbox or radio button. This property is somewhat similar to the value Property, which can also be used to get or set these states.

**Usage**:

```
checkState = document.forms[Ø].elements[Ø].value;
```

**Return Values**: Returns 1 if the checkbox or radio button is checked; 0 if not.

**Applies To**: checkbox, radio button

**Name**: defaultChecked Property

**Description**: Similar to the defaultValue Property for text entry, the defaultChecked Property gets or sets a default check for the checkbox.

**Usage**:

```
document.forms[Ø].elements[Ø].defaultChecked = true;
```

**Return Value**: Returns TRUE if the checkbox is checked by default; FALSE if not.

**Applies To**: checkbox

**Name**: length Property

**Description**: Gets the number of options in a select element. This can be useful in setting up an iteration loop to run through each option.

**Usage**:

```
//reads values from select list into the
//optionValue array.
optionCount = document.forms[Ø].elements[Ø].length;
for (i = 1; i <= optionCount; i++) {
   optionValue = document.forms[Ø].elements[Ø].value;
}
```

**Return Value**: Returns an integer specifying the number of options in a select element.

**Applies To**: select

**Name**: options Property

**Description**: An HTML <SELECT> element has the form:

```
<SELECT NAME="someName">
   <OPTION VALUE=val1>text 1
   <OPTION VALUE=val2>text 2
   .
   .
   .
   <OPTION VALUE=valn>text n
</SELECT>
```

where one of the options can also be initialized to be selected, and where its VALUE attribute can be included with the OPTION tag but is not required. Consequently, the options Property is organized as an array, where options[1] corresponds to the first <OPTION>, options[2] corresponds to the second option, and so on.

The options array has its own set of properties: text, value, and selected. Text returns the text string of the option. Value returns the contents of the VALUE attribute, if present. Selected returns "True" if that option has been selected, and otherwise returns "False."

**Usage**:

```
<SELECT NAME="trafficLight">
   <OPTION VALUE="stop">Red
   <OPTION VALUE="slow">Yellow
   <OPTION VALUE="go">Green
</SELECT>
var1 = trafficLight.options[1].text //var1 is now "Red"
var2 = trafficLight.options[2].value //var2 is now "slow"
var3 = trafficLight.options[3].selected //var3 is now false; no option yet se-
lected
```

**Applies To**: select

**Name**: selectedIndex Property

**Description**: Using an iteration loop to check each option for the selected Property would be tedious. Instead, the selectedIndex Property gets the index for the selected option (or the first option selected when there are multiple selected options).

**Usage**:

```
<SELECT NAME="trafficLight">
   <OPTION VALUE="stop" SELECTED>Red
   <OPTION VALUE="slow">Yellow
   <OPTION VALUE="go">Green
</SELECT>
sChoice = trafficLight.selectedIndex; //sChoice = 1
```

**Return Value**: Returns an integer specifying the index for the selected option in a select element.

**Applies To**: select

## Event Handlers

Event handlers script events from objects using the onEvent="event handler" syntax. While an event handler can be any sequence of statements, typically it will be the name of a function. This method can be used for any HTML-intrinsic elements, such as forms, buttons, or links.

**Name**: onClick Event Handler

**Description**: Triggered when the element is clicked. This method works only with button-style elements.

**Usage**:

```
<INPUT TYPE="radio" NAME="resident" VALUE="State resident"
 onClick="checkResidency()">
```

**Applies To**: button, reset, submit, checkbox, radio

**Name**: onFocus Event Handler

**Description**: Using a text-entry area is a two-step process. First, you must bring the cursor into the area by clicking somewhere within the area; then you may begin entering text at the cursor. This act of clicking the cursor into the text area is called focusing. The onFocus event is triggered when the element gets the focus.

**Usage**:

```
<INPUT TYPE="text" NAME="phone" onFocus="AddAreaCode()">
```

**Applies To**: select, text, textarea

**Name**: onBlur Event Handler

**Description**: Once an area has focus, it loses focus when the cursor is moved outside of that area. This loss of focus is called blurring. The onBlur event is triggered when the element loses the focus.

**Usage**:

```
<INPUT TYPE="text" NAME="phone" onBlur="closeFrame()">
```

**Applies To**: select, text, textarea

**Name**: onSelect Event Handler

**Description**: Clicking and dragging over text causes it to become highlighted; this highlighting is called selection. The onSelect event is triggered when the contents of the element are selected.

**Usage**:

```
<INPUT TYPE="text" NAME="name" onSelect="changeCase()">
```

**Applies To**: text, textarea

Representing Data

Data Types

Objects that Are Data-Type Specific

# Chapter 8
# JScript Data Structures

JScript is not a typed language: it does not require that a data type be assigned to a variable or array when it is declared. One perspective on JScript suggests that JScript types on context, looking at the methods to be applied to a data item to determine what type of data it is. Another perspective on JScript suggests that JScript has only one type, the character string.

Both of these perspectives contain an element of truth. JScript does attempt to evaluate data in the context of the methods applied to that data. However, the most important data type in JScript, and the one JScript defaults to in the absence of other information, is the character string.

Initially, we will look at the data structures JScript uses to represent data. The most common data structure is the variable. JScript also has a limited mechanism for defining arrays. JScript's data structures are heavily influenced by the object-oriented aspects of the language. Objects are represented hierarchically; we will examine the dot syntax data structure that JScript uses to represent the object hierarchy.

Once we have introduced data representation, we will look at data types in detail. We will look at the string first, as this is the default data type. As a special case, we will also look at nonalphanumeric ASCII characters. Numbers constitute the other data type most familiar to us. JScript includes facilities to handle several other data types. The most important is Boolean data. We also look at JScript's treatment of MIME types.

Finally, JScript includes three objects not discussed in the last chapter: the String object, the Math object, and the Date object. Because the methods of these objects are important data manipulation methods, they are covered in this chapter.

## Representing Data

The common device for representing data is a variable. Besides single variables, we can also organize variables into indexed lists called arrays. JScript objects also have properties, which function like variables.

## Variables

Data may be presented as either a literal or a variable. To understand the difference, look at these examples:

"abc"

"123"

123

abc

JScript treats the first three as literals: the first two as literal strings and the third as a literal number. When it sees the last example, however, JScript assumes it is a variable. You can test this behavior in your Web browser by typing in the following URL for each expression:

```
javascript:eval(expression)
```

Figure 8.1 shows the results of these evaluations. JScript returns a literal value for the first three, but produces an error message for the last, assuming it be a variable.

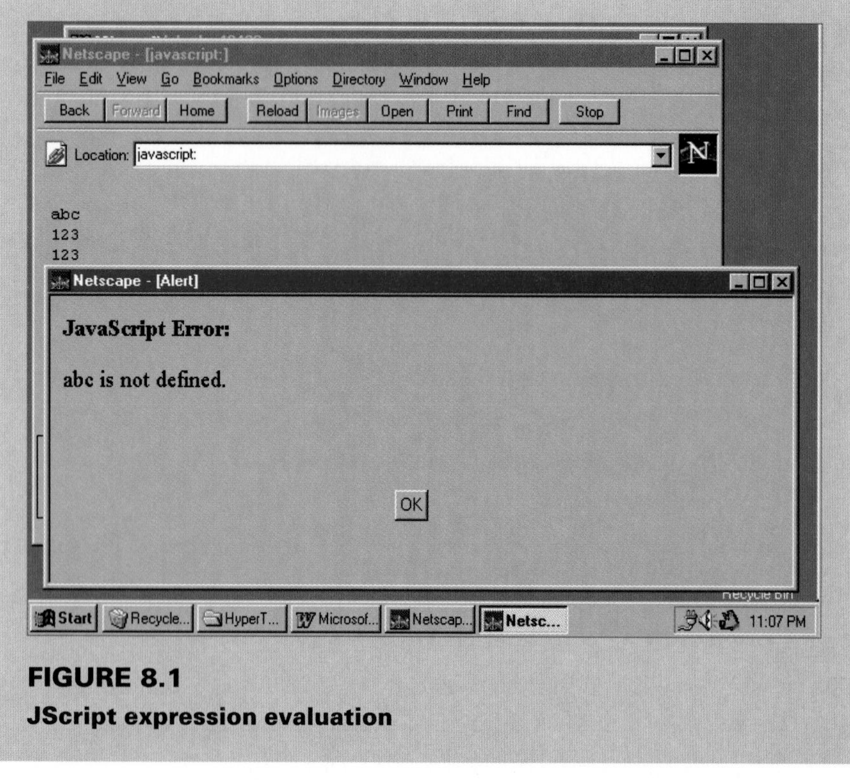


**FIGURE 8.1**
**JScript expression evaluation**

JScript assumes that any expression it encounters that is not part of the JScript command syntax nor the name of a JScript object must either be a literal or a variable. To be a literal, an expression must either be a number or a quoted string of characters; any other string will be treated as a variable.

While a literal, as we've seen in Figure 8.1, evaluates to itself, a variable evaluates to a value. That value can be either a literal or the name of a JScript object. To hold a value, a variable must be declared. In Figure 8.1, the expression abc has not been declared as a variable: hence the error message.

To declare a variable, we use the var command, as in:

```
var abc;
```

A variable may either be simply declared, or declared with an initial value, as in:

```
var abc = "def";
```

A variable declared without an initial value returns the value "undefined" when evaluated.

Initiating a program with variable declaration is a useful convention to follow, but not a requirement. Because JScript is an interpreted language, executing each statement only as the program reaches that statement, a variable's declaration can occur anywhere in the program prior to that variable's use. Take care not to declare a variable twice. Consider the following code fragment:

```
var n = "abc";
var m = "def";
var n;
m = n + m;
```

No error will occur, but JScript will dutifully reinitialize n in this case, returning a final value for m of "undefineddef".

The following code fragment also contains two variable declarations for a variable n, but behaves very differently:

```
function concat(str) {
   var n = "123";
   str = n + str;
}

var n = "abc";
var m = "def";
concat(m);
```

In this case the final value for m is "123def," and the final value for n is "abc." JScript distinguishes between global and local variables. Any variable declared within a function is treated as local to that function. Its value can be assigned and altered within that function, and it can be passed on to other variables, but it has no meaning elsewhere in the program. If, as in this case, a local variable shares a name with a global variable, JScript simply treats these as entirely separate entities. If, on the other hand, the program encounters a local variable outside of the function in which it was defined, the program will terminate with an "undefined" error.

A JScript variable name is legal provided that it is not a literal, and not a reserved word that is part of the JScript syntax. In addition to JScript reserved words, Netscape has reserved some words for future JavaScript development. While these could be used, they are best avoided. Here is the full list of JScript and Netscape reserved words:

abstract
Boolean
break
byte
case
catch
char
class
const
continue
default
do
double
else
extends
false
final
finally
float
for
function
goto
if
implements
import
in
instanceof
int
interface
long
native
new
null
package
private
protected
public
return
short
static
super
switch
synchronized
this
throw
throws
transient
true
try
var
void
while
with

## Arrays

An array is a multidimensional, indexed body of data. While that sounds complicated, the principle is simple and one we use every day. To say the data is indexed just means that each item of data is numbered and has a unique identifier associated with it. To say the data is multidimensional just means that the identifier may be made up of more than one number.

We are most familiar with two types of arrays. A one-dimensional array is a list. It has a first item, second item, and so on. A two-dimensional array is a table. Each item in a table has both a row number and a column number, so specifying a unique identifier requires that we specify both a row number and a column number. Though we rarely think of data presented in anything more complicated than table format, in principle nothing prevents higher-dimensional arrays from being created.

Let's look at an example. We could think of the days of the week as a one-dimensional array, a list. Thus, week[1] refers to Sunday, week[2] refers to Monday, and so on. We could also think of a month as a number of weeks, and thus of a day of the month as a particular day of the week in a particular week of the month. To say that the staff meeting will be held on the third Friday of each month would be like specifying an item in a two-dimensional array of (day, week) as in:

```
meeting = month[6,3]
```

Since the year is a list of months, we could extend this example to a three-dimensional array of [day, week, month]. To say that Election Day is the first Tuesday in November, we could say:

```
Election Day = year[3,1,11]
```

JScript's built-in arrays are only one-dimensional. A forms array, for example, indexes the forms on a document: document.forms[0] refers to the first form of the document. Note that here the first element of the array is forms[0], yet in the example above I used week[1] to refer to the first day of the week. In some contexts, starting an array with 0 will make more sense; in other contexts starting with 1 will make more sense. JScript gives you little choice in the matter, however. Most of JSscript's built-in arrays start with 0, while the easiest way to create user-defined arrays results in arrays that start with 1.

JScript has no built-in array-making function. If you want to include arrays in your script, Netscape's JavaScript documentation recommends including the following as an array-making function in your script:

```
function MakeArray(n) {
//can be used for making arrays of length n,
//starting with 1 as first array element.
this.length = n;
   for (var i = 1; i <= n; i++) {
      this[i] = 0;
   }
   return this
}
```

Any custom array you need in your script can then be created by calling this function. If we want a 10-element array named foo, then we create it with this command:

```
foo = new MakeArray(10);
```

Here are two important questions about JScript arrays: First, why does this MakeArray function work? Second, couldn't a similar function be used to create a higher-dimensional array? After all, JScript's built-in objects seem to contain higher-dimensional arrays of a sort. If, for example, we wanted to reference the third element on the second form of a document, we would use an expression like:

```
document.forms[1].elements[2]
```

which looks very much like a two-dimensional array. To answer these questions, we need to understand the JScript object hierarchy, a worthy data-representation topic in its own right. So let's look at how JScript represents objects, and then return to questions of array creation.

## Object Hierarchy

The philosopher Bertrand Russell noted that we can make a distinction between describing an object in the world and referring to that object. We describe an object in terms of its properties, in the terms that give it meaning to us. We refer to an object by identifying which object in the world it is that we are talking about. One of the enduring puzzles in the philosophy of language is how mere descriptions can ever succeed in referring to objects in the world. Russell felt that in at least some cases the connection between meaning and reference was less puzzling. He called these instances "definite descriptions."

If I say "mountain" you understand the meaning of the word, but may not know what particular mountain, if any, I am referring to. If I say "high mountain" I have made my meaning more specific, but you still may not know what I am referring to. If I say "the highest mountain," however, there can be only one that is that highest: I have given a definite description.

Definite descriptions are not the only unique identifiers in language. Names constitute another linguistic convention that enables us to uniquely refer to objects. For example, because Mount Everest is the highest mountain, when I say "Mount Everest" I refer to the same object as when I say "the highest mountain." In practice we often use a mix of names and definite descriptions to pick out objects in the world, and the definite descriptions we use often reflect a hierarchical scheme. Thus we say things like "the third house on the right on Maple Street" or "the University Avenue exit off of 101." Some of this terminology involves hierarchical descriptors: right vs. left, an ordered sequence of first then second then third, avenues as branches off of highways. Some of this terminology involves names: Maple Street, University Avenue, Highway 101.

JScript's object hierarchy can seem perplexing at first, but it really follows the same linguistic conventions of hierarchical descriptors and names that we use in ordinary discourse. Levels of hierarchy are separated by dots (.), and within a hierarchy objects are picked out either by description — which in JScript means by property, by ordered sequence according to array and index number — or by name. JScript object containment reads from right to left, so this expression:

```
a.b.c[1].d
```

would be read as "d of the second c of b of a".

This notation may start to feel more familiar if you try expressing some ordinary language referents with this syntax. Phone numbers fit naturally into this syntax:

```
areaCode.localPrefix.4DigitNumber
```

Addresses also fit into this syntax:

```
State.zipCode.city.street.number
```

Compared with these examples, the typical JScript object expression may seem more intelligible:

```
document.forms[].elements[].property
```

In ordinary language, we often make relative references without even realizing it. Both the phone number and address schemas above, for example, make no reference to country. In most contexts we can safely assume that our conversation is to be understood relative to the country we are in. Likewise, in JScript object references are normally made relative to the current window, the window in which the script resides. We can refer to other windows by using an absolute reference, in which case our object expression will begin with "top," which refers to the topmost window in the object hierarchy. We can also refer to other windows by using a relative reference, in which case our object expression will begin with "parent," which refers to the window in which the current window was created.

Bertrand Russell identified one other reference mechanism in ordinary discourse. He called this other mechanism "demonstrative reference," and we see it illustrated in the following conversation:

"The phone number is (415) 555-1212."

"Yes, but what country?"

"Why, this country, of course."

In this exchange we have no trouble at all understanding the phrase "this country." We immediately understand the phrase to refer to the current country. If context does not make clear what the current country is, then the demonstrative reference "this" will not work. But Russell understood that in many cases "this" can unambiguously refer to the current object.

JScript includes demonstrative reference as well. You can use the "this" keyword to refer to the current object. You can also use expressions of the form "this.object" to refer to an object contained by the current object. An example will clarify.

Suppose we have a document with two different forms on it, and each form has a text input field on it followed by a button. Our list of objects, then, would be:

```
document.forms[Ø].elements[Ø]
document.forms[Ø].elements[1]
document.forms[1].elements[Ø]
document.forms[1].elements[1]
```

Suppose we want to display the string stored in the variable greeting when the user clicks on the button in the first form. We could handle this with the following HTML and function:

```
<INPUT TYPE="button" onClick="displayGreeting()">
function displayGreeting() {
   document.forms[Ø].elements[Ø].value = greeting;
}
```

This function has two shortcomings. First, writing out an entire object expression is tedious, and a likely place to make a typo that will throw off your program. Second, this function does not adhere to principles of good modular design. We could not use it to display the message in the window on the second form in response to a button click from that form.

Fortunately we can take care of all of this with "this." Since "this" refers to the current object, we can rewrite our buttons and function as follows:

```
<INPUT TYPE="button" onClick="displayGreeting(this.form.element[Ø])">
function displayGreeting(textWindow) {
   textWindow.value = greeting;
}
```

Since "this" always refers to the current object, when "this" is invoked it refers to the button, or element[1] of whichever form the button is on. From that starting point, we can build a reference to other objects. "this.form" refers to the form containing the current object. "this.form.element[0]" refers to the first element on the current form, which is the text field in which we want to display output. We have passed this entire object to the function as a parameter, enabling the function to succinctly perform its task without worrying about object reference.

With all this in mind, we can look again at the MakeArray function, understand its workings, and see if we can extend the function to make multidimensional arrays. Recall that arrays will be created with a statement like:

```
foo = new MakeArray(10);
```

The new command is invoked when we want to make a copy of an object, so this statement makes a new object called "foo". Since "new" is applied to a function, we can conclude that functions are objects. JScript uses the length property to store the length of the array of an array-structured object. "history.length" would return the number of items on the browser's history list, for example. Every function has a length property which, by default, is set to 0, but that can be changed.

Looking at the first two lines of the MakeArray function:

```
function MakeArray(n) {
this.length = n;
```

we can see that the function changes its own length to n. We could say that we have added to the object n properties that can be referenced by index number. These are initialized to 0:

```
    for (var i = 1; i <= n; i++) {
        this[i] = 0;
    }
```

In order to have an object that can be copied with the new statement, the function must return an object as a value. The object to be returned is just the function itself:

```
    return this
}
```

Extending this approach to two-dimensional arrays can be done in a number of ways. We will look at three approaches here. Suppose we wanted to represent the days of the year as a two-dimensional array, with one dimension representing the number of weeks in a year, and the other representing the days of the week. First we need to create an array of weeks. We will make the length of this 53, since a year has either one or two more days than 52 weeks:

```
calendar = new MakeArray(53);
```

Then we need a function for adding days of the week as properties to an object:

```
function weeks(sun, mon, tue, wed, thu, fri, sat) {
    this.sunday = sun;
    this.monday = mon;
    this.tuesday = tue;
    this.wednesday = wed;
    this.thursday = thu;
    this.friday = fri;
    this.saturday = sat;
}
```

Finally, we want to add these properties to the calendar array. We will initialize each value in our array table to 0:

```
for (i = 1; i <= 53; i++) {
    calendar[i] = new weeks(0,0,0,0,0,0,0);
}
```

We have now created a table of data—a two-dimensional array—that we can read values from and write values into simply by referencing the indexes of the table, as in:

```
calendar[24].friday = "staff meeting";
appointment = calendar[15].monday;
```

For many programming purposes, this sort of table will suffice. One of the advantages of arrays, however, is process automation. Rather than using 53 separate steps to initialize the calendar array, a single loop can iterate through the whole array. We cannot, however, iterate through days of the week in this array, because these are named properties, not numbered. To create a two-dimensional array in which each dimension is numbered, we will have to use an entirely different approach.

In some sense, all of this talk of tables and multiple dimensions is just a convenience for the programmer. Your computer will store its information in a linear series of memory addresses no matter what you do. It may transform that data for presentation, but ultimately the data is stored as one long list. We can actually use this kind of transformation technique to reference a one-dimensional array as if it were two-dimensional. To do so, we will create a one-dimensional array, and two functions allowing us to access it as if it were a two-dimensional array.

Our modified array-making function is this one:

```
function MakeTable(rows, cols) {
   this.length = rows*cols;
   this.maxcol = cols;
   for (i = 1; i <= rows*cols; i++) {
      this[i] = Ø;
   }
   return this;
}
```

Any table has a number of cells equal to the number of rows multiplied by the number of columns. We assign a length to our one-dimensional array, then, that's equal to the number of cells the table should have. We also need some information about the number of rows versus the number of columns—otherwise we could not distinguish a 6 x 3 table, for example, from a 9 x 2 table. We've added a property to our array object called maxcol, which stores the maximum value a column number can have.

Since our array only talks in one dimension, but the program will talk in two dimensions, we need a pair of functions to do the translation. One will be called ga, as in get array value, and the other will be called sa, as in set array value:

```
function ga(arr, rows, cols) {
   mc = arr.maxcol;
   val = arr[(rows*mc) - (mc - cols)];
   return val;
}

function sa(arr, rows, cols, val) {
   mc = arr.maxcol;
   arr[(rows*mc) - (mc - cols)] = val;
}
```

To get an array value, we pass the name of the array, the row, and the column to ga as parameters. ga uses the maxcol value of the array to demarcate rows from columns in its list, looks up the corresponding entry on its list, and returns that value. Given a calendar array with rows corresponding to weeks and columns corresponding to days, we could look up a Monday appointment in week fifteen by:

```
appointment = ga(calendar, 15, 2);
```

While somewhat different from the usual array notation, this is still a very readable expression. Unfortunately, we cannot simply apply the reverse to set a value: placing a function on the left side of an assignment statement makes no sense syntactically in JScript. To set a value in the array we must pass the value to be set as a parameter, as in:

```
sa(calendar, 15, 2, appointment);
```

You may want to see all of this assembled into a working program. The following script creates a 3 x 3 array, initializes each element, and writes out the results to the document. The output is shown in Figure 8.2. It should provide an easy basis for writing and implementing tables of other sizes. With some thought, you can also see how to extend these methods to arrays of more than two dimensions.

```
<HTML>
<HEAD><TITLE>2-D Array Tester</TITLE></HEAD>
```

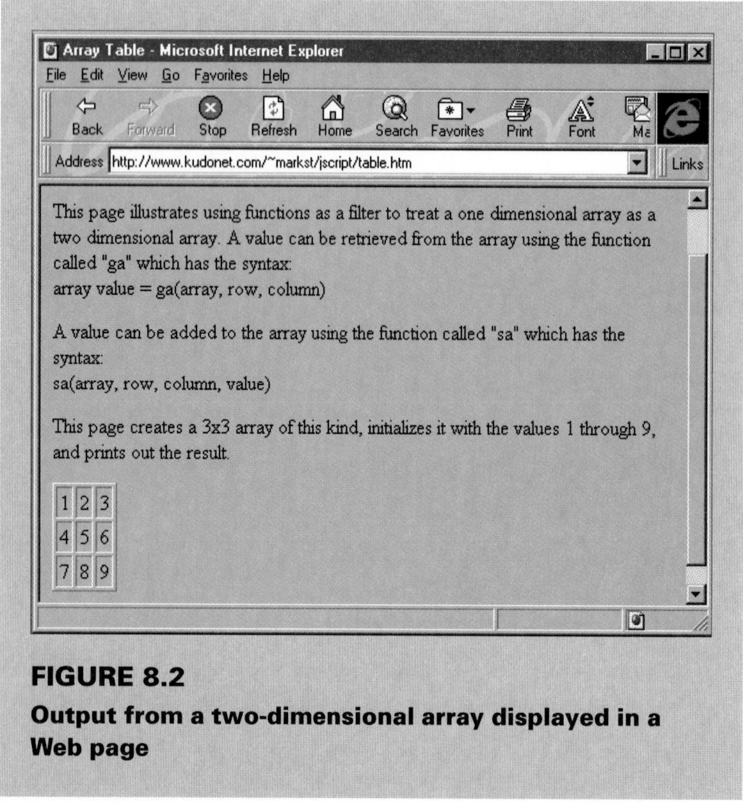


**FIGURE 8.2**

**Output from a two-dimensional array displayed in a Web page**

```
<BODY>
<SCRIPT LANGUAGE="JavaScript">
var rows
var cols
var i
var mc
var val
var msg

function MakeTable(rows, cols) {
   this.length = rows*cols;
   this.maxcol = cols;
   for (i = 1; i <= rows*cols; i++) {
      this[i] = 0;
   }
   return this;
}

function ga(arr, rows, cols) {
   mc = arr.maxcol;
   val = arr[(rows*mc) - (mc - cols)];
   return val;
}

function sa(arr, rows, cols, val) {
   mc = arr.maxcol;
   arr[(rows*mc) - (mc - cols)] = val;
}

table3 = new MakeTable(3,3);
i = 1;
for (n = 1; n <= 3; n++) {
   for (m = 1; m <= 3; m++) {
      sa(table3, n, m, i);
      i++;
      if (m == 1) {msg = "<BR>"} else {msg = "  "};
      msg += ga(table3, n, m);
      document.writeln(msg);
```

```
    }
}

</SCRIPT>
</BODY>
</HTML>
```

One-dimensional arrays can be extended to two dimensions more naturally if we nest one array-creation function call within another., This would create an array of arrays that would be referenced like this: array[row, column]. JScript does permit new properties to be assigned to objects, and the new properties can themselves be objects. Thus the following functions and function calls illustrate the creation of a 3 x 3 table:

```
<HTML>
<HEAD><TITLE>Array Tester</TITLE></HEAD>
<BODY>
<SCRIPT LANGUAGE="JavaScript">
var rows
var cols
var i
var j
var val
var msg

function MakeArray(val) {
   var i;
   this.length = val;
   for (i = 1; i <= val; i++) {
      this[i] = Ø;
   }
   return this;
}

function MakeTable(rows, cols) {
   var i;
   this.length = cols;
   for (i = 1; i <= cols; i++) {
```

```
            this[rows] = new MakeArray(cols);
        }
        return this[rows];
    }

    for (i = 1; i <= 3; i++) {
        table3 = new MakeTable(i,3);
    }

    i = 1;
    for (n = 1; n <= 3; n++) {
        for (m = 1; m <= 3; m++) {
            table3[n,m] = i;
            i++;
            if (m == 1) {msg = "<BR>"} else {msg = "  "};
            msg += table3[n,m];
            document.writeln(msg);
        }
    }
    </SCRIPT>
    </BODY>
    </HTML>
```

JScript really should have built-in array structures so that programmers need not devise each array from scratch. Netscape, in its haste to release JavaScript, has perhaps not had time to fully implement all the features it might want its language to have. Microsoft, in attempting to keep JScript compatible with JavaScript, is constrained by that haste as well. Hopefully future releases of JavaScript and JScript will have a richer array structure. For now, though, mastering the techniques we have described here is essential if you want to bring the power of arrays to your data structures.

## Data Types

JScript's default data type is the string. In the absence of context information to the contrary, JScript will treat a literal as a string. Values can also be treated as numbers, or as Boolean values.

## Strings

Strings are case-sensitive, so that "Hello World" is a different string from "hello world." A string literal consists of any quoted string of characters, as in:

"This is a string"

'another string'

"10"

'3.1415926'

You may use either single quotes or double quotes to enclose your string, provided that the closing quote is of the same type as the opening quote. In assigning a string literal to a variable, JScript strips off the quotes and assigns the contained string as the value of the variable. The variable returns the unquoted value.

Because JScript handles single or double quotes interchangeably, in most cases you need not employ escape characters to signal the inclusion of a quote mark in a string. Suppose, for example, that we want to assign the following Forms element to a variable named val:

```
<INPUT TYPE="submit" VALUE="Submit Now">
```

Because the string we want to assign contains quote marks, we could not use this assignment:

```
val = "<INPUT TYPE="submit" VALUE="Submit Now">";
```

JScript would be unable to correctly parse the quote marks. However, because JScript uses single and double quotes interchangeably, the following assignment will produce the desired results:

```
val = '<INPUT TYPE="submit" VALUE="Submit Now">';
```

## Special ASCII Characters

In some situations you may find that you still cannot easily place quote marks or other special characters in a string variable. Some characters can be forced by means of an escape sequence. An escape sequence is a two-character sequence beginning with a backslash. The backslash notifies JScript that the next character is an escaped character, and should be interpreted according to Table 8.1.

You will have occasion to work with some nonalphanumeric ASCII characters. This need arises most frequently when handling search strings appended to URLs

**TABLE 8.1 ESCAPE SEQUENCE INTERPRETATIONS**

| Escape Sequence | Interpretation |
|---|---|
| \' | indicates a single quote |
| \" | indicates a double quote |
| \b | indicates a backspace |
| \f | indicates a form feed |
| \n | indicates a new line character |
| \r | indicates a carriage return |
| \t | indicates a tab character |
| \\ | indicates a backslash |

that are submitted to CGI by the GET method. Including spaces or other characters can cause problems for the server, and so it is common to represent such characters by ASCII-encoding them.

JScript includes two functions, unescape() and escape(), for handling this type of data. Unescape takes a string which may contain ASCII-encoded characters and returns the string with any such characters replaced by their plain ASCII equivalent. escape() takes a string and replaces any nonalphanumeric characters with their ASCII-encoded equivalents.

Any search strings you intend to submit to CGI should probably be filtered through the escape() function. No harm can be done, and you may avoid causing the server problems on the other end.

## Numbers

Numbers can be either integers or real numbers. Real numbers are usually referred to as floating point numbers in programming parlance; think of it as "numbers with some value floating after the decimal point." A numerical string will be treated as a number; quoting a numerical string causes it to be treated as a string. Thus:

```
val = 2 + 2;
```

returns a value of 4 for val, while

```
val = "2" + "2";
```

returns a value of "22" for val.

A numerical string can include the letter "e" in either in lowercase or uppercase form to indicate powers of ten. Thus

```
val = 2e3;
```

returns a value of 2000 for val, since $10^3 = 1000$, and 1000*2 = 2000.

A sequence of characters returned from a text area or text-input field will automatically be interpreted as a string, even if it contains only numerical characters. In this and some other contexts it may be necessary to force a numerical interpretation on a string. JScript has two built-in functions for this purpose, parseInt() and parseFloat(). parseInt() will return an integer value, if one is available, so that:

```
val = parseInt("12");
```

returns a value of 12 for val. parseFloat() returns a floating point value, if one is available, so that:

```
val = parseFloat("12.3");
```

returns a value of 12.3 for val.

By default JScript represents numbers in base 10, but there may be situations in which you will want to work with either base 8 (octal) or base 16 (hexadecimal). To differentiate, JScript treats numbers with a leading zero as octal, and numbers with the leading sequence "0x" or "0X" as hexadecimal. The first eight octal numbers, then, are

00, 01, 02, 03, 04, 05, 06, 07

The first 16 hexadecimal numbers are

0X0, 0X1, 0X2, 0X3, 0X4, 0X5, 0X6, 0X7, 0X8, 0X9, 0XA, 0XB, 0XC, 0XD, 0XE, 0XF

The A-F values here can also be in lowercase form.

## Boolean Values

As we will see in the next chapter, comparison operations in JScript return a Boolean value: in other words, a value of either true or false. Thus in the following:

```
val = (2 > 3);
```

returns a value of false for val, and

```
val = (1 <= 1);
```

returns a value of true for val.

These values can also be explicitly assigned to variables, as in

```
val = true;
val = false;
```

Boolean literals are case-sensitive, so "TRUE," "FALSE," "True," and "False" will not be recognized as Booleans.

### MIME Types

When sending an output stream to a server, or to another window, it is possible to set the output data type to something other than "text/html". JScript also recognizes "text/plain" as a MIME type, these image type: "image/gif," "image/jpeg," and "image/xbm."

## Objects that Are Data-Type Specific

JScript employs a number of specialized methods for handling string data, numerical data, and data taken from the client computer's internal clock. These methods are part of the String, Math, and Date objects, respectively. These objects are abstract; they have no visible representation on screen. Still, they are structured exactly like other JScript objects, containing properties and methods, and having a domain of objects or data types to which those methods can be applied.

### The String Object

**Name**: string

**Description**: JScript considers each string to be an instance of the String object. Thus whatever properties are defined for it will also be meaningful properties of each string, and whatever methods are defined for it can be applied to each string.

**Usage**:

```
slen = "aeiouy".length;
//assigns slen the length of the indicated string,
//in this case a value of 6.
```

**Contains:**

Properties: length

Methods: toLowerCase(), toUpperCase(), big(), small(), sub(), sup(), blink(), bold(), fixed(), italics(), fontcolor(RGB), fontsize(num), anchor("Name"), link(URL), indexOf(searchString, index), lastIndexOf(searchString, index), CharAt(index), substring(index1, index2)

## Properties

**Name**: length

**Description**: The length property is the number of characters in a string. The string whose length is taken can be either a literal or a variable.

**Usage**:

```
"abc".length;
val = "abc";
val.length;
```

**Return Value**: returns an integer equal to the number of characters in the string.

## Internal Methods

**Names**: toLowerCase(), toUpperCase()

**Description**: These methods change characters in a string from uppercase to lowercase, and from lowercase to uppercase, respectively.

**Usage**:

```
val = "abc".toUpperCase(); //val is now "ABC"
val = val.toLowerCase(); //val is now "abc"
```

**Return Values**: a string whose characters differ only in case from the String object to which the method was applied, returning all lowercase characters for toLowerCase() and all uppercase characters for toUpperCase.

## HTML Methods

**Names**: big(), small(), sub(), sup(), blink(), bold(), fixed(), italics()

**Description**: Each of these methods brackets a string within the HTML tags corresponding to the method, and returns this new, HTML marked-up string.

**Usage**:

```
val = "foo".big() //val is now "<BIG>foo</BIG>"
val = val.italics() //val is now "<I><BIG>foo</BIG></I>"
```

**Return Values**: Returns an opening HTML text format tag, the string, and the corresponding closing HTML tag as a single concatenated string.

**Names**: fontcolor(RGB), fontsize(num), anchor("Name"), link(URL)

**Description**: These methods also mark up the string with the corresponding HTML tags. However, these tags take attributes, and hence the methods take a parameter to set to the attribute. Figure 8.3 shows a document with output from the examples below.

**Usage**:

```
"foo".fontcolor(#FFFFFF)
//returns "<FONT COLOR=#FFFFFF>foo</FONT>"
"bar".fontsize(2)
//returns "<FONT SIZE=2>bar</FONT>"
"foo".anchor("foobar")
//returns "<A NAME = 'foobar'>foo</A>"
"bar".link("bar.htm")
//returns "<A HREF = 'bar.html'>bar</A>"
```

**Return Values**: Returns an opening HTML text format tag with attribute specified, the string, and the corresponding closing HTML tag as a single concatenated string.

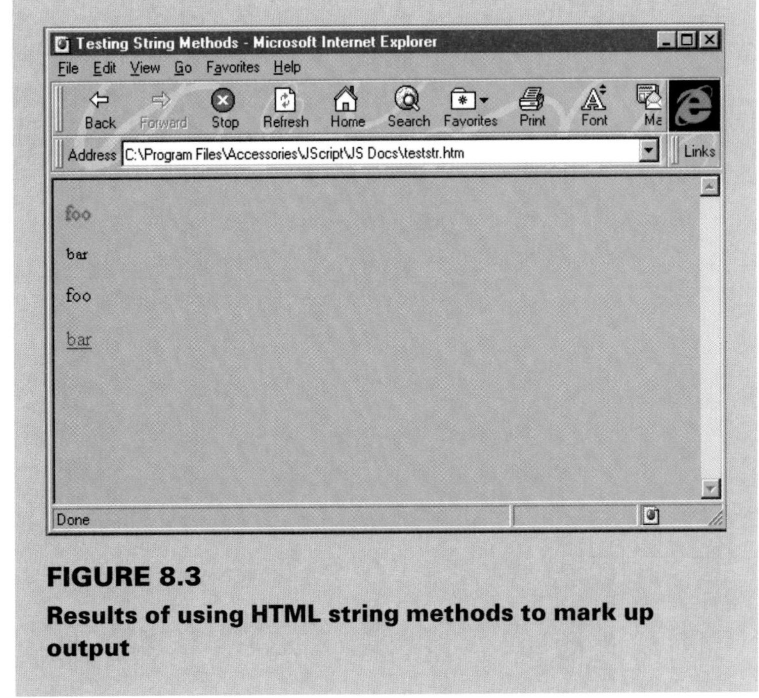


**FIGURE 8.3**
**Results of using HTML string methods to mark up output**

## String Manipulation Methods

**Name**: indexOf(searchString, index)

**Description**: Attempts to match a search string to the target string as a substring of the target string. If a match is found, this method returns the index of the character in the target string that begins the first match. If it is the first character then the index returned is 0, if the second character then the index returned is 1, and so on. If no match is found, then the method returns a value of -1.

Optionally, an index number can be specified as a parameter. In this case, the search for a matching substring will start at the indexed character of the target string.

**Usage**:

```
target = "Peter Piper picked a peck of peppers.";
searchStr = "P";
val = target.indexOfsearchStr); //val = Ø
searchStr = "p";
val = target.indexOfsearchStr); //val = 8
searchStr = "Pi";
val = target.indexOfsearchStr); //val = 6
val = target.indexOfsearchStr, 7); //val = -1
```

**Return Value**: An integer indexing the start of a substring match, or -1 if no match is found.

**Name**: lastIndexOf(searchString, index)

**Description**: This method is identical to the previous method, except that the search scans from the end of the target string to the beginning looking for a match. The index returned is still counted from the beginning of the string.

**Usage**:

```
target = "Peter Piper picked a peck of peppers.";
searchStr = "P";
val = target.LastIndexOf(searchStr); //val = 6
searchStr = "p";
val = target.LastIndexOf(searchStr); //val = 32
searchStr = "Pi";
val = target.LastIndexOf(searchStr); //val = 6
val = target.LastIndexOf(searchStr, 7); //val = 6
```

**Return Value**: An integer indexing the start of a substring match, or -1 if no match is found.

**Name**: charAt(index)

**Description**: Finds the character at the indexed point in the target string, and returns that character. Again, the index of the first character in the target string is 0.

**Usage**:

```
target = "Peter Piper picked a peck of peppers.";
val = target.charAt(4); //val = "r"
val = target.charAt(2); //val = "t"
```

**Return Value**: The character at the indexed point in the target string.

**Name**: substring(index1, index2)

**Description**: Returns a substring of the target string. The substring begins with the character in the target string at index1, and ends with the character in the target string just before index2.

**Usage**:

```
target = "Peter Piper picked a peck of peppers.";
val = target.substring(2,4); //val = "te"
val = target.substring(0,6); //val = "Peter "
```

**Return Value**: The character string from the first indexed character, up to but not including the last indexed character of the target string.

## Supplemental String Manipulation Methods

The string manipulation methods provided by JScript are fairly primitive. This is disappointing, given the pervasiveness of strings in an untyped language. Perl, by contrast, is also an untyped language but meets the challenge by offering an incredibly rich assortment of string-handling features.

Still, JScript does contain all of the raw materials needed to accomplish more-powerful string manipulation tasks. You will have to supplement these basic methods with functions you design yourself.

For example, DOS/Windows users are familiar with certain pattern matching conventions when comparing strings. These operating systems use wild-card characters to match general patterns. Specifically, a question mark (?) is typically used as a wild card to stand for any single character, and an asterisk (*) is typically used as a wild card to stand for any sequence of one or more characters.

Thus "a?c" would be a match for "abc" but not a match for "abbbc." On the other hand, "a*c" would be a match for both "abc" and "abbbc."

This kind of pattern matching can be an invaluable utility for the programmer. Pattern matching becomes especially important when developing Web pages that permit user queries, such as the database application we will look at in a couple of chapters.

In fact, functions to enable pattern matching can readily be constructed from the String object's basic methods. The charAt() method provides an easy way of implementing "?" as a wild card. All we need is a function that checks to see if two strings match, and, where they differ, checks via the charAt() function to see if the character located at the difference is a "?".

The "*" wild card requires a bit more sophistication. We need to take the string containing the "*" and split it into two substrings around the "*". Then the first substring must be matched against an equal length of the beginning of the target string, and the second substring must be matched against an equal length of the end of the target string.

Below is a listing for a program that develops and uses these functions. Figure 8.4 illustrates this program in action.

```
<HTML>
<HEAD>
<SCRIPT LANGUAGE="javascript">
```

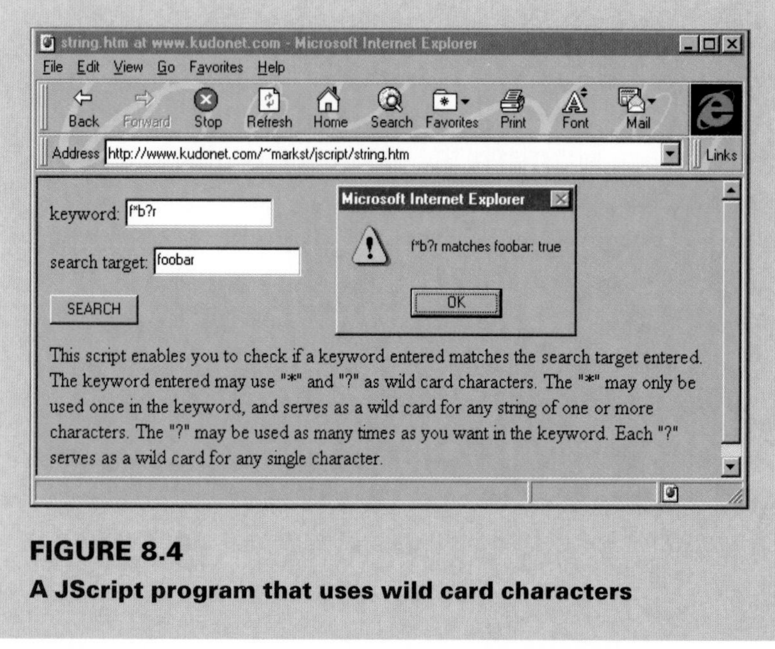


**FIGURE 8.4**

**A JScript program that uses wild card characters**

```
var wildcard; var sTarget; var matching; var msg;
var len; var blen; var elen; var bstr; var estr; var wc;
var startChar; var endChar; var keyword;

function charmatch(startChar, endChar, wc) {
var i; var j=Ø
var wcBuild
var targStartChar = (startChar == Ø) ? Ø : sTarget.length - elen;
for (i = startChar; i <= endChar; i++) {
   if (wc.charAt(i) == "?") {
      wcBuild = wc.substring(Ø, i);
      wcBuild += sTarget.charAt(targStartChar + j);
      wcBuild += wc.substring(i+1, wc.length);
      wc = wcBuild;
   }
   j++;
}
return wc;
}

function SMatch() {
keyword = document.forms[Ø].kywd.value;
wildcard = keyword;
sTarget = document.forms[Ø].targ.value;
matching = false;
len = wildcard.length;
blen = wildcard.indexOf("*", Ø);
elen = len - (blen+1);
if (blen == -1) {
   wildcard = charmatch(Ø, len, wildcard);
   matching = (wildcard == sTarget) ? true : false;
} else {
   wildcard = charmatch(Ø, blen, wildcard);
   wildcard = charmatch(blen+1, len, wildcard);
   bstr = wildcard.substring(Ø, blen);
   estr = wildcard.substring(blen+1, len);
   if (sTarget.substring(Ø,blen) == bstr) {
      if (sTarget.substring(sTarget.length-elen, sTarget.length) == estr) {
```

```
        matching = true;
        }
    }
}

msg = keyword + " matches " + sTarget;
msg += ": " + matching;
alert(msg);
}

</SCRIPT>
</HEAD>

<BODY>
<FORM>
keyword:
<INPUT TYPE="TEXT" NAME="kywd">

<P>
search target:
<INPUT TYPE ="TEXT" NAME="targ">

<P>
<INPUT TYPE="BUTTON" VALUE="SEARCH" onClick="SMatch()">
</FORM>

<P>This script enables you to check if a keyword entered matches
the search target entered. The keyword entered may use "*" and
"?" as wild card characters. The "*" may only be used once in
the keyword, and serves as a wild card for any string of one or
more characters. The "?" may be used as many times as you want
in the keyword. Each "?" serves as a wild card for any single
character.
</BODY>
</HTML>
```

## The Math Object

**Name**: Math

**Description**: JScript mathematical functions not covered by the basic arithmetic operations are handled with the Math object. Properties of the Math object are just mathematical constants. Methods of the Math object are mathematical functions.

**Usage**:

```
Math.round(Math.PI) //returns a value of 3
//The round method rounds off a value to the nearest integer;
//The PI property returns the value of pi,
//hence rounding off pi returns 3.
```

**Contains:**

Properties: E, LN2, LN10, LOG2E, LOG10E, PI, SQRT1_2, SQRT2

Methods: abs(val), ceil(val), floor(val), max(val1, val2), min(val1, val2), random(), round(val), acos(val), asin(val), atan(val), cos(val), sin(val), tan(val), log(val), exp(val), pow(val1, val2), sqrt(val)

### Properties

Table 8.2 provides a complete list of the properties of the Math object, the constant that each property represents, and the value that each property represents that constant with LOG2E, LOG10E, PI, SQRT1_2, SQRT2

**TABLE 8.2 PROPERTIES OF THE MATH OBJECT**

| Property | Constant | Value |
|---|---|---|
| Math.E | e, natural log base | 2.718281828459045 |
| Math.LN2 | natural log of 2 | .6931471805599453 |
| Math.LN10 | natural log of 10 | 2.302585092994046 |
| Math.LOG2E | log base 2 of e | 1.4426950408889634 |
| Math.LOG10E | log base 10 of e | .4342944819032518 |
| Math.PI | pi | 3.141592653589793 |
| Math.SQRT1_2 | 1 over square root of 2 | .7071067811865476 |
| Math.SQRT2 | square root of 2 | 1.4142135623730951 |

### Miscellaneous Math Methods

**Names**: abs(val), ceil(val), floor(val), max(val1, val2), min(val1, val2), random(), round(val)

**Description**: These seven methods perform relatively simple functions, but these are also the functions that are most likely to be useful. Opportunities to use the cosine function or the hyperbolic tangent function are rare, but a good roundoff function or random number generator can prove useful.

**Returned Values**:

abs(val) returns the absolute value of val.

ceil(val) returns the next integer greater than or equal to val.

floor(val) returns the next integer less than or equal to val.

max(val1, val2) returns the greater of val1 and val2.

min(val1, val2) returns the lesser of val1 and val2.

random() returns a random number between 0 and 1.

round(val) returns val rounded off to the nearest integer, rounding up on 1/2.

### Math Methods from Trigonometry

**Names**: acos(val), asin(val), atan(val), cos(val), sin(val), tan(val)

**Description**: These methods perform the basic trigonometric functions, and corresponding hyperbolic functions.

**Returned Values**:

acos(val) returns the hyperbolic cosine of val.

asin(val) returns the hyperbolic sine of val.

atan(val) returns the hyperbolic tangent of val.

cos(val) returns the cosine of val.

sin(val) returns the sine of val.

tan(val) returns the tangent of val.

### Math Methods with Exponentiation

**Names**: log(val), exp(val), pow(val1, val2), sqrt(val)

**Description**: These methods cover the full range of exponential functions. Square roots could also be determined by using a value of 1/2 for the exponent of the power function.

**Returned Values**:

log(val) returns the natural log of val.

exp(val) returns e raised to the power of val.

pow(val1, val2) returns val1 raised to the power of val2.

sqrt(val) returns the square root of val.

## The Date Object

**Name**: Date

**Description**: Lets you work with the date and time stamp from the client computer's internal clock. This provides a string with subfields covering every portion of date and time from year to milliseconds. You can work with the whole string, or subfields of it. Date is stored internally as the number of milliseconds since January 1, 1970 00:00:00. Dates prior to 1970 are not allowed.

A new date object may be created in one of four ways, depending on what format you want the date string returned in:

- dateObjectName = new Date()
- dateObjectName = new Date ("month day, year hours:minutes:seconds")
- dateObjectName = new Date(year, month, day)
- dateObjectName = new Date (year, month, day, hours, minutes, seconds)

Month, day, year, hours, minutes, and seconds are string values for (2). For (3) and (4), they are integer values. (1) creates today's date and time.

**Usage**:

```
today = new Date();
//Returns "Mon Sep 09 10:19:50 PDT 1996"
today = new Date("Aug 1, 1996 6:0:0");
//Returns Thu Aug 01 06:00:00 PDT 1996
today = new Date(1977, 4, 26);
//Returns Thu May 26 00:00:00 PDT 1977;
//note that Jan = 0, Feb = 1, etc.
today = new Date(1984, 8, 30, 14, 30, 0);
//Returns Sun Sep 30 14:30:00 PDT 1984
```

**Contains:**

Methods: getDate(), getDay(), getHours(), getMinutes(), getMonth(), getSeconds(), getTime(), getTimezoneOffset(), getYear(), setDate(val), setHours(val), setMinutes(val), setMonth(val), setSeconds(val), setTime(val), setYear(val), parse(), toGMTString(), toLocaleString(), UTC()

## Getting Date Fields

**Names:** getDate(), getDay(), getHours(), getMinutes(), getMonth(), getSeconds(), getTime(), getTimezoneOffset(), getYear()

**Description**: These methods retrieve particular fields from the Date object. getDate refers to the day of the month; getDay refers to the day of the week. getHours returns a 24 hour value, not a 12 hour value. getTimezoneOffset returns a value in minutes that the client computer's clock is offset from Greenwich Mean Time (GMT), also referred to as the Universal Time Code (UTC).

**Usage**:

```
today = new Date(); //Returns Mon Sep 09 10:58:42 PDT 1996
today.getDate(); //Returns 9
today.getDay(); //Returns 1; note that Sun=0
today.getHours(); //Returns 10
today.getMinutes(); //Returns 58
today.getMonth(); //Returns 8; note that Jan=0
today.getSeconds(); //Returns 42
today.getTime(); //Returns 842291922130; milliseconds since 1/1/70
```

```
today.getTimezoneOffset(); //Returns 420
today.getYear(); //Returns 96; note returns only two digits
```

**Return Values**: Returns an integer value corresponding to the value of the date field in question.

## Setting Date Fields

**Name**: setDate(val), setHours(val), setMinutes(val), setMonth(val), setSeconds(val), setTime(val), setYear(val)

**Description**: These methods are just the reverse of the get methods. They take an integer as a value, and set the corresponding field of the specified Date object according to that value. Note that setting one field can cause other fields to change. If I change the year from 96 to 97, for example, then the match between days of the week and days of the month will change to reflect 1997.

**Usage**:

```
today = new Date(); //Returns Mon Sep 09 10:58:42 PDT 1996
today.getDate(); //Returns 9
today.getDay(); //Returns 1; note that Sun=0
today.setYear(97); //Sets year to 1997
today.getDate(); //Returns 9; still returns the ninth as today
today.getDay(); //Returns 2; weekday has been changed to Tue to reflect 1997
```

## Conversion Methods

**Names**: parse(), toGMTString(), toLocaleString(), UTC()

**Description**: These methods each convert dates from one format to another. parse() converts a string date into a number of milliseconds. toGMTString() does the time zone conversion to convert your local date into GMT. toLocaleString() does the time zone conversion to your local time zone. UTC() converts a comma-delimited set of integers that follow the date format into a number of milliseconds since 1/1/70. parse() and UTC() apply to the Date object. toGMTString() and toLocaleString() apply to an instance of the Date object.

**Usage**:

```
today = new Date(); //returns Mon Sep 09 11:22:06 PDT 1996
today.toGMTString(); //returns Mon, 09 Sep 1996 18:22:06 GMT
today.toLocaleString(); //returns 09/09/96 11:22:06
Date.parse(today); //returns 842293326000
Date.UTC(95,1,1); // returns 791596800000
```

The Main Event

Conditionals

Loops

Operations

# Chapter 9
# JScript Control Structures

Designing and mastering the flow of a JScript program is really an extension of managing the flow of an HTML document. Questions of program design should always be answered in the context of good Web design. One of the first questions you need to answer is how and when to initiate a JScript program at all.

Not every browser supports client-side scripting languages. The release of Internet Explorer 3.0 dramatically increases the number of browsers on the Web with support for scripting. Still, anyone using an older version of Internet Explorer (which currently includes everyone using Explorer on Windows 3.1) or an older version of Netscape Navigator, or Mosaic, or the text-based Lynx browser, cannot take advantage of JScript.

One design decision you face, then, is whether to create two sets of pages for your Web site, one with JScript and one without. This kind of replication occurred frequently in the early days on the Web. At that point the HTML standard still lagged behind Netscape's innovations, and choice of browser by Web users varied more than it does now. At present, HTML standards and browser technology are in much closer alignment. The <SCRIPT> tag should soon be part of that standard. Given that Internet Explorer is and will remain freely available, there really is no excuse for Web users not to run a script-capable browser.

Further, JScript features cannot easily be duplicated in static Web pages. JScript so dramatically extends Web design capabilities that sites without scripting will simply be left behind. On a more practical note, the <SCRIPT> tag lacks a companion tag like the <NOFRAME> tag for browsers that do not support frames.

We are fast reaching the point at which the most dazzling sites on the Web will use scripting as routinely as sites now use graphics. You need not feel guilty about pushing your own Web design in this direction. All the effort needed to maintain a separate set of static pages on your site could be better applied to adding more to the scripts you develop.

One easy courtesy to extend to Web browsers that cannot run JScript is to comment out your scripts. These browsers will ignore the <SCRIPT> tag and attempt to interpret the lines that follow as HTML. Unless you take preventive measures, the result will be a screen full of unformatted text dumped onto the hapless browser. To prevent this you should follow each <SCRIPT> tag with an HTML comment tag(<!—). You should also precede each </SCRIPT> tag with a closing HTML comment tag that is also JScript commented (//—>). Scriptless browsers will then ignore your script text because it falls within comment tags, but script-capable browsers will still execute the script.

**A note about the <NOFRAME> trick:** *While JScript lacks a <NOSCRIPT> tag allowing you to bracket off a section of HTML to be displayed specifically by browsers that do not support scripts, you can still get a reasonable approximation of this using the <NOFRAMES> tag in a particular way.*

*Suppose you have two versions of a page, one called "scriptpg.htm" that uses JScript, and another called "noscript.htm" that offers a static version of the same page. You will need an empty HTML document called something suitable like "blank.htm". Point people to "noscript.htm", but make some changes to it. Remove the <BODY></BODY> tags, and instead include the following:*

```
<FRAMESET ROWS = "0, *">
  <FRAME SRC = "blank.htm">
  <FRAME SRC = "scriptpg.htm">
</FRAMESET>
<NOFRAME>
  [insert HTML for noscript.htm here]
</NOFRAME>
```

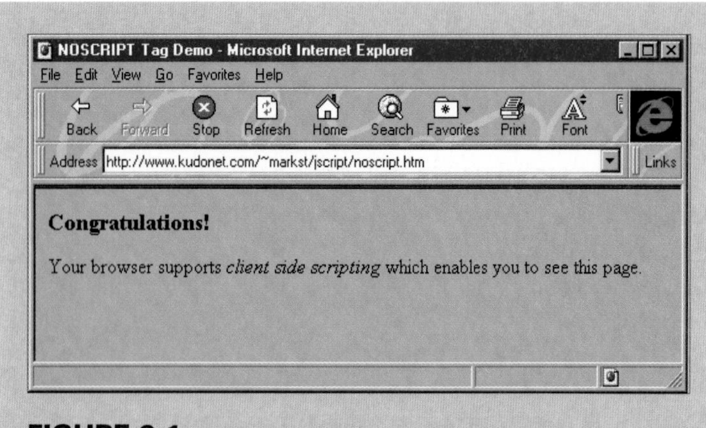


**FIGURE 9.1**
**The "NOSCRIPT" page in Internet Explorer 3.0.**

*Because browsers that can interpret frames are for all intents and purposes the same as browsers that can interpret scripts, those browsers that can support scripts will see a window with an empty 0-pixel-sized frame at the top—in other words, nothing—and the page "Scriptpg.htm". Browsers that cannot support scripts* *will see the contents of the <NOFRAME></NOFRAME> tags. Figure 9.1 shows a rendering of these pages viewed with Internet Explorer 3.0. Figure 9.2 shows a rendering of these pages viewed with Internet Explorer 2.0.*

## The Main Event

How you initiate scripts depends on how you integrate events into your Web pages. Most of the scripts we've looked at so far operate in a single-window frame, and most are embedded within a document with <SCRIPT> </SCRIPT> tags. In fact, JScript commands can be launched in several ways, and JScript execution can take a very distributed form.

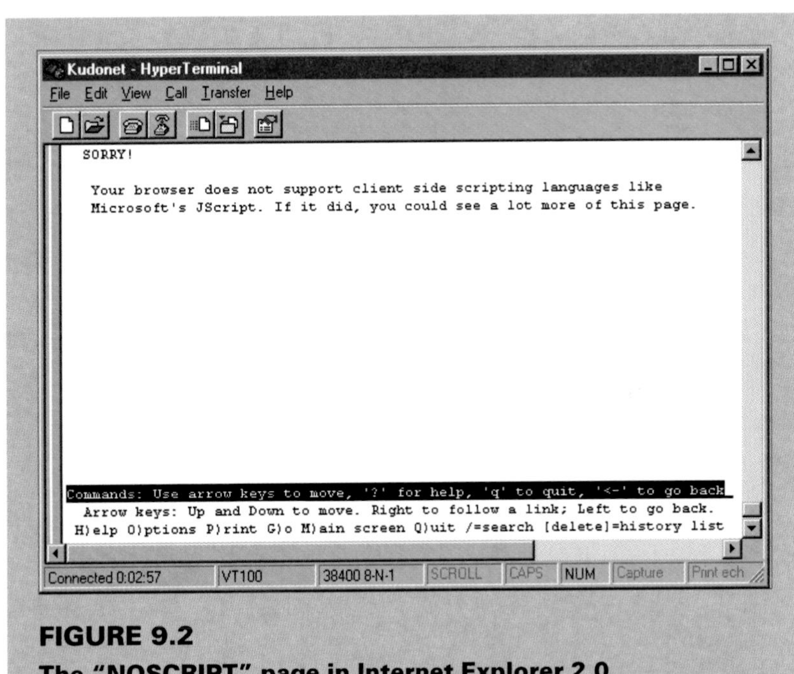


**FIGURE 9.2**

**The "NOSCRIPT" page in Internet Explorer 2.0.**

### Command Line JScript

JavaScript commands can be run directly within Netscape Navigator by entering a URL beginning with "javascript:" into the browser. For example, enter the following URL into the browser:

```
javascript:alert("Welcome to
JScript")
```

You should see the alert box illustrated in Figure 9.3 open up.

This way of launching JScript can be very useful as a debugging tool during program development. It enables you to evaluate expressions and see the results, and to enter some simple display commands to get a preview of how objects will look onscreen. You can enter multiple

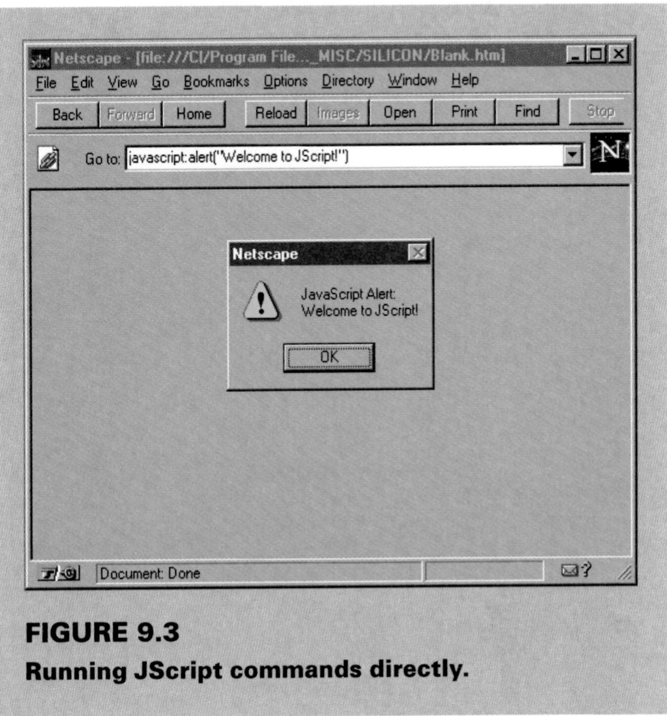


**FIGURE 9.3**

**Running JScript commands directly.**

commands by separating commands with a semicolon (;). This tool is limited by the number of commands you can fit on one entry line.

While this feature may aid development, it is Netscape-specific, and it does not have immediate applications. With one modification, however, we can enhance pages with direct JScript commands that act like small but useful applications, and work with both Internet Explorer and Netscape Navigator. Anything we can type in as a URL can also be used as the address of a link. We can therefore have JScript commands run directly when a link is clicked.

Suppose, for example, that you have linked some pages to your home page, and that you have taken these pages down for further development. You could simply remove the links from your home page, but then users might assume that these pages were permanently gone. Alternatively, you could temporarily replace the links to these pages with the following link:

```
<A HREF="javascript:alert('Temporarily removed for rennovation.\n Please
check back soon.')">
```

Figure 9.4 shows this link in use.

While it is impractical to stuff a large script into a link tag in this manner, we can certainly embed more than one command. A few simple commands can sometimes suffice to solve a problem.

Busy sites sometimes ease the load on the server by load-sharing. Load-sharing mirrors a Web site on more than one server, and then rotates requests among all the mirroring servers to distribute the load evenly between them. Server-side load-sharing routines can be implemented in CGI calls, but the additional processing that CGI requires detracts from the benefits of load-sharing. Load-sharing can be implemented by a system administrator through reconfiguring the server, but this option is neither available nor desirable to all Web designers.

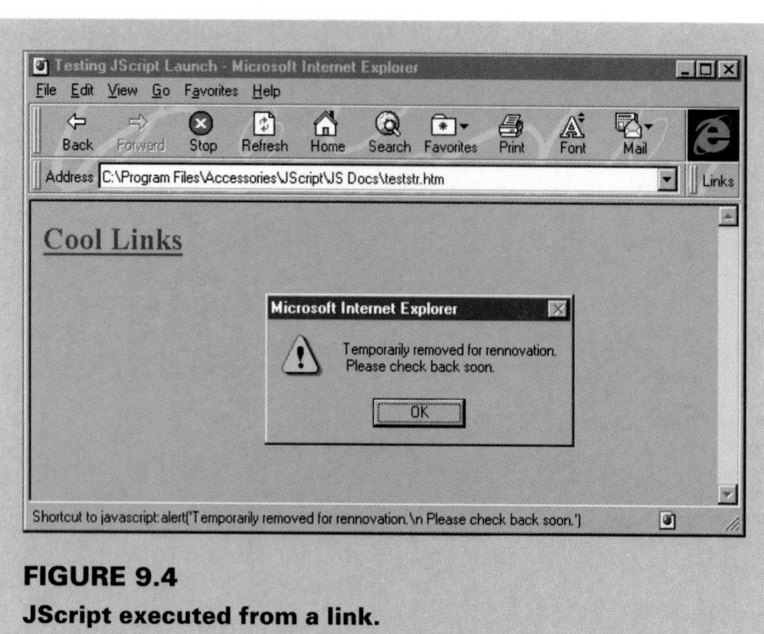


**FIGURE 9.4**
**JScript executed from a link.**

Client-side load-sharing, on the other hand, can be implemented with ease. Suppose we have two mirrors, called "www.mysite.com" and "www.mysite2.com." We will balance the load between them by sending requests occurring on odd-numbered seconds to "www.mysite.com," and requests occurring on even-numbered seconds to "www.mysite2.com." Here is the needed script:

```
t = new Date(); //get the time stamp
t = t.getSeconds() % 2;
//get the seconds, divde by 2, return the remainder
location = (t == 0) ? "www.mysite.com" : "www.mysite2.com";
//shorthand for an if statement. If t is 0, then
//location is set to first value after ? and otherwise
//it is set to the second value.
```

We have only three commands here, which can easily be embedded into a link:

```
<A HREF="javascript:t=new Date(); t=t.getSeconds() % 2; location = (t==0) ?
'www.mysite.com':'www.mysite2.com'">
```

## Embedded JavaScript

More conventionally, JScript commands are contained within <SCRIPT></SCRIPT> tags and embedded in an HTML document. Follow a few simple guidelines when organizing embedded scripts.

Lines in the program will either be part of variable and function definitions, or part of the main program. Your program may not have any lines in the main program if it is completely modular and completely event-driven. Lines in the main program will execute as they are loaded. This can be a source of problems if one line executes before another line it depends on has loaded.

Modular design is preferable. One exception to this is JScript code designed to perform HTML formatting on the fly for the current document as it loads. Once a document has loaded—in other words, once the document is closed—nothing can be altered except forms-input elements. Thus any JScript-generated HTML needs to be created as the page loads.

Otherwise, you should be able to move all of your program code into the module of an event handler, even if it is simply the "onLoad" event to be triggered once the page has completely loaded. If you envision your program as a set of event handlers from the beginning, the design process will proceed more smoothly and it will be easier to produce modular code. You will find it easier to implement your code incrementally, which in turn will make it easier to debug. You will also find it easier to implement portable code, which will aid you in developing other programs.

## Distributed JScript

While we tend to think of a program in terms of a single block of code contained within <SCRIPT></SCRIPT> tags, the JScript you use may be distributed across several documents.

The <SCRIPT> tag allows SRC as an attribute. This means that rather than including the text of your script within the HTML document in which you want it to run, you can store the script in a separate file and reference that file location in the <SCRIPT> tag. Think of it as an inline script being loaded automatically, just as HTML loads inline images automatically from the SRC attribute of the IMG tag:

```
<SCRIPT LANGUAGE="javascript" SRC="myscript.js">
```

Don't use this means of loading scripts gratuitously. Each script loaded this way requires an extra call to the server, and the delivery of an extra file. Your documents will load more slowly, and you'll increase the load on the server. On the other hand, if you find yourself using the same script on several documents, it can make sense to keep the script in a single file that is referenced in each document. This is particularly true if the script is reasonably short.

For example, some pages on your Web site may contain material that is frequently updated, and users may need to know when a page was last changed. If you have a script for generating a "last updated" message on a Web page called "update.js," then this could be included on each Web page simply by including this line:

```
<SCRIPT LANGUAGE="javascript" SRC="update.js">
```

*The SRC attribute for the <SCRIPT> tag suffers from buggy implementation at present. Various reports indicate that it may not work "off-line" on your local hard drive, but only on a Web server; that even on a server, your system administrator may have to configure .js as a recognized file type to serve; that implementation does not work the same under Netscape Navigator as under Internet Explorer. Your experience may vary, and certainly with new versions of Navigator and Explorer coming in the next few months the implementation should improve, but use this feature with care.*

Just as one script can be used on several documents, a single script may range over several documents to execute. The events on one document can be handled by event handlers from a different document in a different frame. Figure 9.5 shows a button in one frame that, when clicked, calls an event handler in the other frame to open an alert box.

The event specification used in this case is:

```
<INPUT TYPE="button" VALUE="run another window"s event handler" onClick="
top.frames[1].alerting()">
```

To find an event handler in another frame, we have to specify the path to the frame in which that event handler resides.

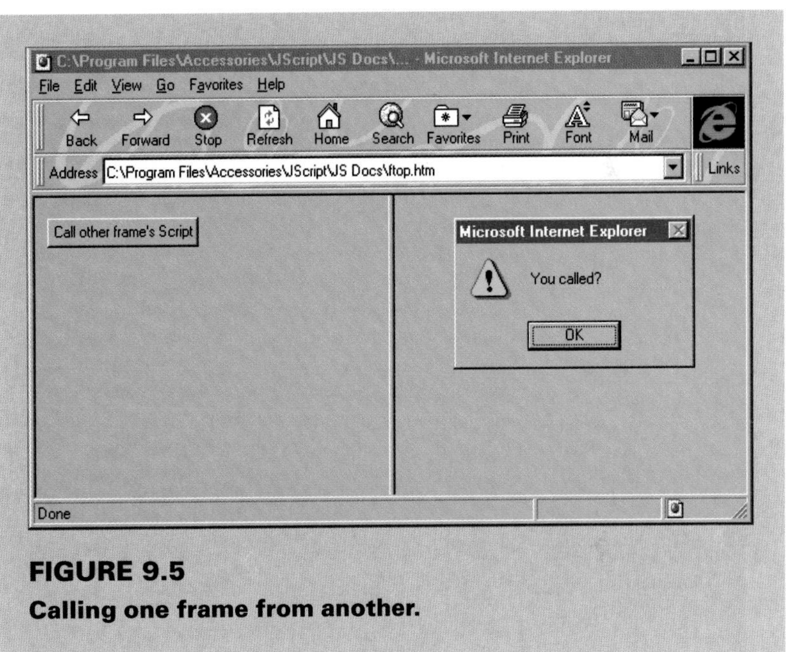


**FIGURE 9.5**
**Calling one frame from another.**

You may start to feel that the boundaries of what constitutes a single script are fluid. After all, we have seen that a single body of code can be called from several different documents, and we have seen that a single program may call event handlers from several different documents. This distributed environment is part of the object-oriented approach to programming. Good reusable objects can serve many situations, and good modular design allows objects to be drawn from wherever they are located, whenever they are needed.

To help us stay in control of this environment, let's take a detailed look at the control structures and operators JScript provides.

## Conditionals

Conditionals cover those situations in which the program flow must fork between one or more options. A conditional is a nonrepeating fork in the program, in contrast to a loop, which may repeat a branch of a program more than once.

**Name**: if

**Description**: Tests for a specified condition, and executes a list of statements if that condition returns a value of "true." The condition is contained within parentheses, (), and must contain an operation that returns a Boolean value. The execution list is contained with braces, {}, and can contain any legal JScript statements. If statements may be nested inside of other if statements.

**Usage**:

```
if (pword == password) {
   location = "protected.htm";
} //if statement with single statment execution list
if (login == lname) {
   if (pword == password) {
      document.write("You are now logged in.");
      top.frames[1].location = "protected.htm";
   }
} //nested if statements, multiple statement execution list.
```

**Name**: if... else

**Description**: Tests for a specified condition, executes one list of statements if that condition returns a value of "true," otherwise executes a different list of statements if that condition returns a value of "false." The condition is contained within parentheses, (), and must contain an operation that returns a Boolean value. The execution lists are contained within braces, {}, and can contain any legal JScript statements. If...else statements may be nested inside of other if statements.

**Usage**:

```
if (login == lname) {
   if (pword == password) {
      document.write("You are now logged in.");
      top.frames[1].location = "protected.htm";
   } else {
   msg = "Not a valid password for ";
   msg += lname;
   alert(msg);
} else {
alert("Not a valid user name");
```

```
}
//verifies login name or prints a warning; if login
//name is OK, verifies password or prints a warning.
```

**Name**: abbreviated if...else

**Description**: If the only purpose of an if...else statement is to select one of two values to assign to a variable, then you can use a sort of shorthand format:

```
variable = (condition) ? value 1 : value 2;
```

**Usage:**

```
if (yourchoice == door1) {
   prize = "lady";
} else {
   prize = "tiger";
}
//The command below is functionally the same as
//the command above.
prize = (yourchoice == door1) ? "lady" : "tiger";
```

**Name**: with

**Description**: Sets all object references within a list of statements to be relative to a specified object. The object specified must be contained within parentheses, (), and the statement list must be contained within braces, {}. If you have a series of statements that all apply to the same object, this can be a useful device to avoid retyping long object references.

**Usage**:

```
with (top.frames[2]) {
   open();
   write("This is the first line.<BR>");
   write("This is the second line.");
}
```

# Loops

Loops represent sections of a program that can be repeated more than once, depending on certain test conditions.

**Name**: for

**Description**: Executes a list of statements repeatedly, and modifies a loop counter by one iteration each time the list of statements is executed. The execution list must be contained within braces, {}. For loops can be nested one within another. Repetition continues while the loop counter satisfies a specified continuation condition.

The entire for loop specification must be contained within parentheses, (), and must contain three statements separated by semicolons, (;). The first statement sets the loop counter to an initial value. The second statement specifies a condition the loop counter must satisfy for continuation. The third statement specifies the value by which the loop counter will iterate each time through the loop.

**Usage**:

```
for (i = 1; i <= 10; i++) {
   document.write(msg[i]);
} //step through counter values by increasing one at a time.
for (i = 10; i >= 0; i-) {
   msg = (i == 0) ? "Blastoff!" : i;
   document.write(msg);
} //step through counter values by decreasing one at a time.
for (i = 2; i <= 128; i*2) {
   array1[i-1] = array2[i];
} //step through counter values by twos.
```

**Name**: while

**Description**: Repeatedly tests for a condition, and executes a body of statements if the condition returns a value of "true." This repetition will continue until the test condition returns a value of "false." The logic here is like an if statement that repeats so long as the test condition holds. The entire test condition must be contained within parentheses, (), and the execution list must be contained within braces, {}. While loops may be nested within while loops.

A for loop is, in fact, just a special case of a while loop, with some of the code automated. The first example under usage shows the for loop logic implemented as a while loop.

**Usage**:

```
i = 1;
while (i <= 10) {
    document.write(msg[i]);
    i++;
} //step through counter values by increasing one at a time.
i = 1;
while (db[i] != matchItem) {
    i++;
}
//Iterates through an array called db until a matching item is found.
```

**Name**: break

**Description**: Terminates the immediate for loop as if the terminating condition had been satisfied. The counter value remains whatever it was when the break condition occurred. If the for loop is nested within other loops, only the immediate for loop containing the break statement is terminated. The second while loop example above could easily be written as a for loop with a break statement; see below.

**Usage**:

```
for (i = 1; i <= db.length; i++) {
    if (db[i] == matchItem) {break}
}
```

**Name**: continue

**Description**: The continue statement is a limited form of the break statement. When the program encounters a "continue" within a for loop, it breaks immediately to the end of the loop without executing any of the statements in between, but then resumes normal execution on the next iteration.

**Usage**:

```
for (i = 1; i <= users.length; i++) {
   if (users[i] == "Mark") {continue}
      document.write("Greetings, " + users[i]);
} //Prints out a greeting to all users except Mark.
```

# Operations

Operations are the basic building blocks of JScript statements. Each statement typically must perform at least one operation of some kind. You can think of operations as the methods of the JScript object.

## Arithmetic Operators

JScript divides mathematical operations into two groups: more advanced operations are methods of the Math object, and basic arithmetic operations are just JScript operators.

**Names**: addition (+), subtraction (-), multiplication (*), and division (/)

**Description**: These operators work in the standard way: + returns a value that is the sum of two values, - returns a value that is the difference between two values, * returns a value that is the product of two values, and / returns a value that is the ratio of two values.

**Usage:**

```
val = 2 + 2; //val is 4.
val = 4 - 2; //val is 2.
val = 4*2; //val is 8.
val = 4/8; //val is .5.
```

**Name**: Modulo (%)

**Description**: Returns the remainder portion of a division operation expressed as an integer.

**Usage**:

```
val = 8 % 5; //val is 3.
val = 8 % 4; //val is Ø.
val = 8 % 3; //val is 2.
```

**Names**: Increment (++), Decrement(– –)

**Description**: Increases or decreases, respectively, the value of the value it is applied to by one. The increment/decrement mark can be placed on either side of the value in an expression; this affects the order in which operations are executed.

**Usage**:

```
val = 1;
val++; //val is now 2.
newval = ++val; //newval is 3 and val is 3.
newval = val++; //newval is 3 and val is 4.
val--; //val is now 3.
newval = --val; //newval is 2, val is 2.
newval = val--; //newval is 2, val is 1.
```

**Name**: negation (-)

**Description**: Changes the sign of the value it is applied to. Must be placed in front of that value.

**Usage**:

```
val = 1;
val = -val; //val is now -1.
val = -val; //val is now 1 again.
```

## Bitwise Operators

Bitwise operators operate on and return decimal, hexadecimal, or octal numbers, but convert their operands to binary (zeros and ones), perform the operation in binary, and then convert the resulting value into the numerical form of the original operands.

**Name**: Bitwise And (&)

**Description**: The operands are converted to 32-bit integers, and expressed as a series of bits. Each bit in the first operand is paired with the corresponding bit in the second operand. & returns 1 if both operands are 1, otherwise 0.

**Usage**:

```
val = 15 & 9; //val is 9 (1111 & 1001 = 1001)
```

**Name**: Bitwise or (|)

**Description**: The operands are converted to 32-bit integers, and expressed as a series of bits. Each bit in the first operand is paired with the corresponding bit in the second operand. | returns 1 if either operand is 1, otherwise 0.

**Usage:**

```
val = 15 | 9; //val is 15 (1111 | 1001 = 1111)
```

**Name**: Bitwise exclusive or (^)

**Description**: The operands are converted to 32-bit integers, and expressed as a series of bits. Each bit in the first operand is paired with the corresponding bit in the second operand. ^ returns 1 if only one operand is 1, otherwise 0.

**Usage**:

```
val = 15 ^ 9; //val is 6 (1111 ^ 1001 = 0110)
```

**Name**: Left Shift (<<)

**Description**: Takes two operands. The first is the value to be shifted, and the second specifies the number of bit positions by which the first operand is to be shifted to the left. Excess bits shifted off to the left are discarded. Zero bits are shifted in from the right.

**Usage**:

```
val = 9 << 2; val is 36 (1001 shifted two bits left is 100100)
```

**Name**: Right Shift (>>)

**Description**: Takes two operands. The first is the value to be shifted, and the second specifies the number of bit positions by which the first operand is to be shifted to the right. Excess bits shifted off to the right are discarded. Copies of the left-most bit are shifted in from the left.

**Usage:**

```
val = 9>>2; val is 2 (1001 shifted two bits right is 10)
```

## Boolean Operators

Boolean operators are very similar to bitwise operators. However, instead of operating on numbers converted to bits they operate on expressions that return a Boolean value. In effect, they are like bitwise operators operating on a pair of single bits, each of which is either 0 or 1.

**Name**: And (&&)

**Description**: Operates on two expressions. If both expressions return a value of "true," then the "and" operator returns a value of "true" for the whole. Otherwise it returns a value of "false."

**Usage**:

```
val = (1 < 2) && (2 < 3); //val is true.
val = (1 > 2) && (2 < 3); //val is false.
```

**Name**: Or (||)

**Description**: Operates on two expressions. If either expression returns a value of "true," then the "or" operator returns a value of "true" for the whole, otherwise it returns a value of "false."

**Usage**:

```
val = (1 < 2) || (2 < 3); //val is true.
val = (1 > 2) || (2 < 3); //val is true.
```

**Name**: Not (!)

**Description**: The logical "not" operator applies to a single operand and negates the value of the operand. If the operand is true, it returns a value of "false," and if the operand is false, then it returns a value of "true."

**Usage**:

```
val = !(1 < 2); //val is false
val = !(1 > 2); //val is true
```

## Comparison Operators

Comparison operators are essential to designing conditional statements and program loops. The test conditions that these control structures require will typically be based on a comparison operator. Beware of a very common programming error: confusing the assignment operator (=) with the equal operator (==). In other words, don't use the following statement form:

```
if (a = b) {
```

when what you really mean is:

```
if (a == b) {
```

**Names**: Equal (==), not equal (!=), greater than (>), greater than or equal to (>=), less than (<), less than or equal to (<=)

**Description**: A comparison operator compares its operands and returns a logical value based on whether or not the comparison is true. Operands may be either numerical values or string values. If they are string values, the orderings are as follows: lower case letters > upper case letters > numbers as strings, as in "a" > "A" > "0".

**Usage**:

```
val = ("abc" == "ABC"); //val is false.
val = ("abc != "ABC"); //val is true.
val = ("abc >= "ABC"); //val is true.
val = (10 > 1); //val is true.
val = (10 <= ((5*3)/2)); //val is false.
val = (1 < -(3*(2-8))); //val is true.
```

## String Operators

**Name**: Concatenate (+)

**Description**: Concatenates two string values together, returning another string value that is the union of the two operand strings, in the order in which those strings are specified.

**Usage**:

```
val = "cat";
val2 = "hat";
val = val + val2; //val is "cathat".
val += val2; //val is "cathathat". This is shorthand
//notation for val = val + val2.
val = "thing one " + "and thing two"; //val is "thing one and thing two".
```

Design Principles

A Simple Database Listing

Database Listing Based on User Input

Database with Keyword Queries

# Chapter 10
# Database Querying: Just JScript

Glitz and graphics aside, the Web is first and foremost a source of information. Think of the sites on the Web that you visit most often and the services you use most frequently on those sites, and you will realize that you use database queries of one form or another more than any other service on the Web. However, offering a database query by means of client-side scripting poses certain difficulties. After all, not only must the query script be included in the Web page, but the entire database must be included as well.

JScript's suitability as a database interface depends on the size of the database. To get some perspective on the problem, think about the size of images you are willing to include on a page. A Web page with a few navigational icons on it, one or two larger GIF images, and one JPEG image showing some sort of logo or banner would be considered quite understated in terms of graphics. Yet even a page like this could require 15k to 20k of image files to load. Plenty of sites burden the user with many times this in graphics, without regard to the majority of Web users connecting with 14,400- or 28,800-kbps modems. Good Web design requires some discretion, of course, and the most professional sites will seldom burden the user with more than 50k of files to load a single page. If you think in terms of database sizes rather than image sizes, you'll see that quite a range of data can be passed as part of your page without significantly affecting the time the page takes to load.

The database that we'll look at in this chapter is a small bibliography. The front page to this database program requires a parent document with two frames and an initial document for each frame to load. These three files total less than 7k. Although the bibliography in this example only includes 12 books, the bulk of the file's size is dedicated to the query script itself. Each database entry uses about 220 bytes; a database of 200 books would not increase the overall file sizes beyond about 50k.

## Design Principles

The Silicon Valley History Project is a bibliography of books that cover the history of companies and people in the computer industry, specifically books written for a general audience rather than a technical audience. Figure 10.1 shows the home page for the bibliography. In this chapter we will refine a series of scripts to make queries to this bibliography.

Ultimately we want users to be able to sort the bibliography by title, author, publisher, or publication year. We also want to allow a keyword search on these fields, including Boolean keyword combinations, and allow users to specify which fields they wish to include in the keyword search. We want to follow the design principles we have laid out in previous chapters, however, by keeping the design modular, and using an incremental approach. Our first script will implement only some of these capabilities, but will do so in a way that enables additional modules to be added for greater functionality later.

## A Simple Database Listing

The first script will take the database and simply write the entries out to a Web page in HTML format. Each entry in the bibliography has the following fields: title, author, publisher, publication year, and synopsis. These fields present certain design problems.

Even deciding on a standard way of representing titles raises questions. In an episode of a TV comedy, the boss turns to his secretary in exasperation after searching the filing cabinet for a memo sent to the staff:

"Oh, that would be filed under A," she replies.

The boss asks, "But why would you have filed the memo under A?"

To this she retorts, "Oh, I file most things under A. A memo, A letter, An expense report..."

Take this lesson to heart. "The" and "A" can wreak havoc with sorting routines based on alphabetical order. In our bibliography, any titles beginning with an article will have the title stored without the leading article.

Sorting problems also occur with the author field. If we simply have one field for author names, as in "Bertrand Russell" or "Immanuel Kant," then an alphabetical sort will not produce the expected results. We want to sort on last name, but the field begins with first name. The most flexible solution is to have two fields, one for the author's first name and one for the author's last name.

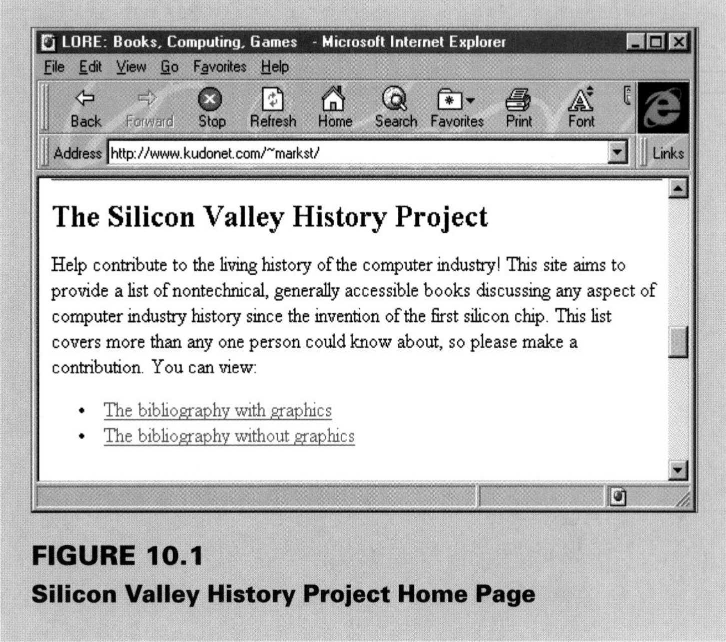


**FIGURE 10.1**
**Silicon Valley History Project Home Page**

The synopsis will be a short paragraph summarizing the book in question. Each of the other fields conforms to the structure of what is called a flat-file database: the number of fields in a given database record is fixed, and the maximum length of each field can also be fixed. The synopsis, however, could vary substantially in length, particularly if we look ahead to a future extension of this application in which users can submit comments and descriptions of their own for the books in the bibliography. Furthermore, we don't necessarily want to display the synopsis for each book right away. The synopses could clutter the look of the bibliography for users who just want the basic information first, and then want to see more detail on only the books of their choice. Finally, the number of characters in a synopsis can easily be several times the number of characters in the rest of a book's citation within the bibliography. Including the synopsis directly in the database, then, could make the file size of our database prohibitively large.

The problem is easily solved by making each synopsis a small HTML document of its own. Rather than including the whole synopsis in the database, only the file name of the synopsis need be included. Our database, then, will loosely resemble a conventional flat-file database.

Since the synopsis for any book will be a separate document that can optionally be viewed, it makes sense to display the database using two frames. One frame will list the entries in the bibliography; while blank initially, the other frame will display the synopsis for a book if the user clicks on the synopsis link for that book. The parent document, then, will be this:

```
<HTML>
<HEAD>
<TITLE>SV History Master Frame</TITLE>
</HEAD>
<FRAMESET COLS="65%, 35%">
   <FRAME SRC="svbib.htm" NAME="citation">
   <FRAME SRC="blank.htm" NAME="synopsis">
```

```
</FRAMESET>
<NOFRAME>
This page requires Netscape 2.0 or higher, or
Internet Explorer 3.0 or higher.
</NOFRAME>
</HTML>
```

Looking ahead to more-complex versions of this script, we know that we will need to store the database information in an array, as this will be the easiest data structure to manipulate. The data conforms to a table format: a number of entries—or rows—in the database, and a number of fields—or columns—for each entry. We have seen several different ways of using arrays to handle tabular data. In this case, we can easily make each field a property of the array. Thus the title of the first book would be stored as a value for *books[1].titl*; the last name of the author of the third book would be stored as a value for *books[3]authLName*; and so on.

This script will list the database's contents in alphabetical order by title. We could simply do the data entry in that order so that the database will not have to be sorted. However, this won't help us later when we want to sort by author or publisher. In the next chapter we will look at using CGI with JScript to add records to the database. At that point we would like to be able to add an entry to the database simply by appending to it, without having to worry about what order the records are in. So now, at the very beginning, we will make a routine for sorting the database into a particular order part of the script.

We now have an overall plan for the script. The script will be part of a two-frame window: one frame for displaying the bibliography, and one for displaying selected book synopses. The script will have to create a tablular array, and initialize the array with the database values. The array will then have to be sorted in alphabetical order by title, and the contents of the array written out to one frame in presentable HTML format. Figure 10.2 shows the output of the script.

Here is the full listing for the page "svbib.htm," which contains the script:

```
<HTML>
<HEAD>
<TITLE>Silicon Valley History: Bibliography</TITLE>
<BODY BGCOLOR=#FFFFFF>
<SCRIPT LANGUAGE="javascript">
<!-
//////////////////////////////
// variable declaration     //
```

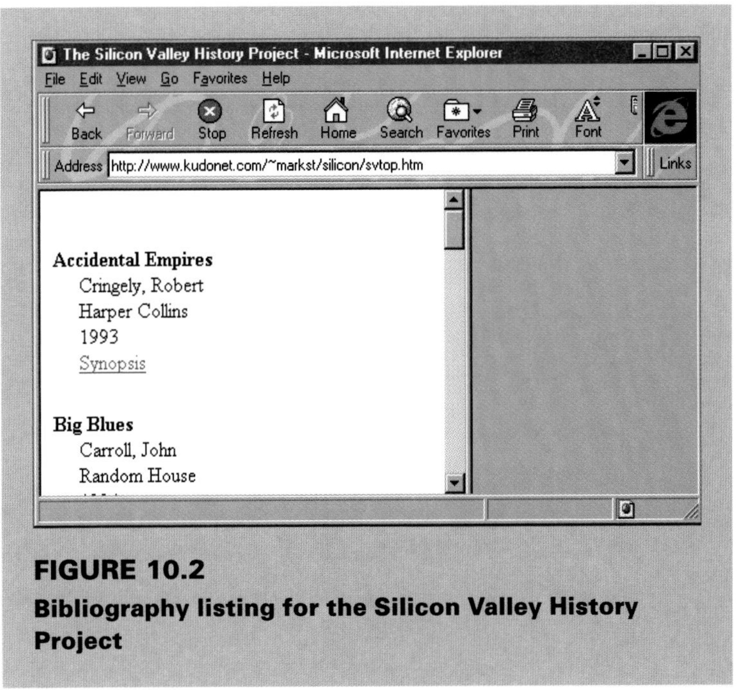


**FIGURE 10.2**
**Bibliography listing for the Silicon Valley History Project**

```
////////////////////////////////
var n; var m; var i; var j; var bkProperty
var titleOf; var authL; var authF; var pub; var yearOf; var synop;

////////////////////////////////
// function declaration     //
////////////////////////////////

//////////////////////////////////////////
// routine for sorting the database   //
// into order:                        //
// start with two arrays, one con-    //
// taining the database, books[], and //
// the other containing the order the //
// database is in initially, sortKey[]//
// values in sortKey will be swapped  //
// around based on comparing the cor- //
// responding elements of books[]     //
// until the values of sortKey reflect//
// the order in which items in        //
// books[] should be displayed.       //
```

```
////////////////////////////////////////
function sorting(bkProperty) {
var sorted = false;
var tempSwap;
while (sorted == false) {
   sorted = true;
   for (i = 1; i < books.length; i++) {
      if (books[sortKey[i]].titl > books[sortKey[i+1]].titl) {
         tempSwap = sortKey[i];
         sortKey[i] = sortKey[i+1];
         sortKey[i+1] = tempSwap;
         sorted = false;
      }
   }
}
}

//////////////////////////////
// generic array maker      //
//////////////////////////////
function MakeArray(n) {
   this.length = n;
   for (i = 1; i <= n; i++) {
      this[i] = 0;
   }
   return this;
}

//////////////////////////////
// making cols for 2D array //
//////////////////////////////
function bookFields(titleOf, authL, authF, pub, yearOf, synop) {
   this.titl = titleOf;
   this.authLName = authL;
   this.authFName = authF;
   this.publisher = pub;
   this.yr = yearOf;
   this.synopsis = synop;
```

```
}

function addbook(i, titl, authLName, authFName, publisher, yr, synopsis) {
   books[i].titl = titl;
   books[i].authLName = authLName;
   books[i].authFName = authFName;
   books[i].publisher = publisher;
   books[i].yr = yr;
   books[i].synopsis = synopsis;
}
}
////////////////////////////////
// making books as a 2D array //
// for bibliography database  //
// when # of books in database//
// changes, change # in two   //
// lines below. current val:12//
////////////////////////////////
books = new MakeArray(12);
for (i = 0; i <= 12; i++) {
   books[i] = new bookFields(0,0,0,0,0,0,0);
}

////////////////////////////////
// making sortKey as array for//
// sorting order of database  //
////////////////////////////////
sortKey = new MakeArray(books.length);
for (i = 1; i <= sortKey.length; i++) {
   sortKey[i] = i;
}

////////////////////////////////
// loading the database into  //
// the books array            //
////////////////////////////////
i = 1;
addbook(i, "Startup: A Silicon Valley Adventure Story",
```

```
            "Kaplan",
            "Jerry",
            "Houghton Mifflin",
            "1995",
            "starsili.htm"
           )
i++;
addbook(i, "Accidental Empires",
            "Cringely",
            "Robert",
            "Harper Collins",
            "1993",
            "acciempi.htm"
           )
i++;
addbook(i, "Insanely Great",
            "Levy",
            "Steven",
            "Viking",
            "1994",
            "insagrea.htm"
           )
i++;
addbook(i, "Macintosh Way",
            "Kawasaki",
            "Guy",
            "Scott, Foresman and Company",
            "1989",
            "maciway.htm"
           )
i++
addbook(i, "Hackers: Heroes of the Computer Revolution",
            "Levy",
            "Steven",
            "Doubleday",
            "1984",
            "hackhero.htm"
           )
```

```
i++
addbook(i, "Gates",
           "Manes",
           "Stephen",
           "Doubleday",
           "1993",
           "gates.htm"
          )

addbook(i, "Odyssey: Pepsi to Apple",
           "Sculley",
           "John",
           "Harper and Row",
           "1987",
           "odyspeps.htm"
          )
i++
addbook(i, "Fumbling the Future",
           "Smith",
           "Douglas",
           "William Morrow",
           "1988",
           "fumbfutu.htm"
          )
i++
addbook(i, "Microsoft Secrets",
           "Cusumano",
           "M",
           "MacMillan",
           "1995",
           "micrsecr.htm"
          )
i++
addbook(i, "Fugitive Game",
           "Littman",
           "Jonathan",
           "Little Brown",
           "1995",
```

```
                "fugigame.htm"
              )
i++
addbook(i, "Takedown",
              "Shimomura",
              "T",
              "Warner",
              "1995",
              "take.htm"
              )
i++
addbook(i, "Big Blues",
              "Carroll",
              "John",
              "Random House",
              "1994",
              "bigblue.htm"
              )
}//end of initializer

////////////////////////////////
// BEGIN MAIN PROGRAM         //
////////////////////////////////

//////////////////////////////////////
// First step: sort database into   //
// the desired order; the parameter //
// passed to the sorting function   //
// is the book field by which the   //
// database will be sorted.         //
// Second step: write out the data- //
// base as an HTML-formatted list.  //
//////////////////////////////////////
sorting("titl");
document.writeln("<DL>");
for (i = 1; i <= books.length; i++) {
   document.writeln("<P><DT><B>" + books[sortKey[i]].titl + "</B>");
   document.writeln("<DD>" + books[sortKey[i]].authLName + ", " +
```

```
books[sortKey[i]].authFName);
    document.writeln("<DD>" + books[sortKey[i]].publisher);
    document.writeln("<DD>" + books[sortKey[i]].yr);
    document.writeln('<DD><A HREF="');
    document.writeln(books[sortKey[i]].synopsis + '"
TARGET="synopsis">Synopsis</A>');
}
document.writeln("</DL>");

//->
</SCRIPT>
</BODY>
</HTML>
```

The HTML output is simple enough. The bibliography is displayed as a list, and each entry has a synopsis link that targets its output for the adjacent frame.

Initializing the database is more complicated, but follows the ideas discussed in Chapter 8 regarding two-dimensional arrays. In that case, we looked at an array where each row corresponded to a week of the year, and each row had a property for Monday, a property for Tuesday, and so on. Here we have a row for each book instead of each week, and our properties are title, author last name, and so on. The structure is still the same. First we create a simple one-dimensional array called "books[]". Then for each item in that area we create a property called "titl," a property called "authLName," a property called "authFName," a property called "publisher," a property called "yr," and a property called "synopsis." Once the array and its associated properties have been created, initializing the database is a simple matter of assigning values to each array element.

The "synopsis" property stores the URL of the document containing the synopsis. We need a naming scheme to follow for the file names of these documents. Since JScript has no file-writing capabilities of its own, this may not seem like an important decision. However, we again have an opportunity to plan ahead toward future variations of this program. Ideally, the scheme for naming each file should meet these requirements:

- It should have a reasonable assurance of producing a unique file name.
- It should not require user input to produce a file name.
- It should be able to derive the file name from the information about the book that is at hand.

The naming scheme followed is this one: ignoring articles and prepositions, use the first four letters of the first word in the title concatenated with the first four letters of the second word in the title. If a word has less than four letters, then use as many letters as the word has. Thus "Accidental Empires" would have the file name acciempi.htm, and "Takedown" would have the file name take.htm.

The only complex part of this program is the sorting function. None of the values of the books[] array are actually changed after the array is initialized with the database. Instead, sorting is done indirectly by means of the sortKey[] array. This array, like the books[] array, has 12 items. The values of the 12 items will determine the order of the bibliography.

Look at Table 10.1.The table shows in column one that if we want to list the bibliography items in order by title, we need to list the second item first, the twelfth item second, and so on. The sortKey[] array dictates initially, as shown in column two, that we list the first item first, the second item second, and so on. We need to change the values of sortKey[] to reflect the order in column one; this is shown in column three. We can then use the values of sortKey[] as our indices to the books[] array to list citations in the right order, as in:

```
document.writeln("<P><DT><B>" + books[sortKey[i]].titl + "</B>");
```

While this may seem indirect, it is also very efficient. If we change the values of the books[] array directly, each time we changed a book's place in the array we would have to change values for each of its six fields: title, author last name and

**TABLE 10.1 SORTING THE BIBLIOGRAPHY**

| books[i].titl: values for i to list entries in alphabetical order | sortKey[] initial values | sortKey values after sort |
|---|---|---|
| 2 | sortKey[1]=1 | sortKey[1]=2 |
| 12 | sortKey[2]=2 | sortKey[2]=12 |
| 10 | sortKey[3]=3 | sortKey[3]=10 |
| 8 | sortKey[4]=4 | sortKey[4]=8 |
| 6 | sortKey[5]=5 | sortKey[5]=6 |
| 5 | sortKey[6]=6 | sortKey[6]=5 |
| 3 | sortKey[7]=7 | sortKey[7]=3 |
| 5 | sortKey[8]=8 | sortKey[8]=5 |
| 9 | sortKey[9]=9 | sortKey[9]=9 |
| 7 | sortKey[10]=10 | sortKey[10]=7 |
| 1 | sortKey[11]=11 | sortKey[11]=1 |
| 11 | sortKey[12]=12 | sortKey[12]=11 |

first name, publisher, year, and synopsis URL. By using sortKey as a key to the order of books[] we only have to change one value; this portion of the program thus runs six times faster than the direct method.

One other feature of the sorting function should be noted. When the function is called from the main program:

```
sorting("titl");
```

we pass a parameter to the function, specifically the string corresponding to the property we want to use as the basis for the sort. Careful scrutiny of the function code will reveal, however, that this parameter is actually never used in the function. It is a placeholder for future enhancements to the program. In the next variation we want to be able to sort the database based on user input that specifies the field to sort by. Including this extraneous parameter now lets us know what needs to be added and where to make this enhancement possible.

## Database Listing Based on User Input

In order to accomodate user input, the overall layout of the frames will have to be changed. This next version of the script will permit only simple input: the user can specify which field to sort the database on, and initiate the sort by clicking a button. Further sorts can be requested by again clicking the button.

A new frame will be added across the top to contain user-input elements. Radio buttons will specify the sort fields, and a “submit” button will initiate the sort. What had been the right and left frames in the previous version will now become nested frames within the bottom frame. Our new parent document, then, will look like this:

```
<HTML>
<HEAD>
<TITLE>SV History Master Frame</TITLE>
</HEAD>
<FRAMESET ROWS="30%, 70%">
   <FRAME SRC="sort.htm" NAME="sort">
   <FRAME SRC="bottom.htm" NAME="bottom">
</FRAMESET>
<NOFRAME>
This page requires Netscape 2.0 or higher, or
Internet Explorer 3.0 or higher.
```

```
</NOFRAME>
</HTML>
```

This document requires another <FRAMESET> document, "bottom.htm," to be nested within it:

```
<HTML>
<HEAD></HEAD>
<FRAMESET COLS="65%, 35%">
   <FRAME SRC="blank.htm" NAME="citation">
   <FRAME SRC="blank.htm" NAME="synopsis">
</FRAMESET>
</HTML>
```

The opening window for these frames is shown in Figure 10.3. It shows the user input elements in the upper frame. The bottom left frame is initially blank, but will display the bibliography once a sort is initiated. The bottom right frame is initially blank, but will display synopsis requests from the bibliography listing.

The actual script will be moving to a new location: it will now be contained within the <HEAD></HEAD> tags of the "sort.htm" document. The script itself requires few alterations. What had been the main body of the program now becomes an event handler for an onClick event. This event handler will call the sorting function, and pass one of several sort options as a parameter to it. The sorting function will now require some mechanism for acting on this parameter. As a final modification, we will need to redirect output to a different frame rather than simply writing out the bibliography to the current frame.

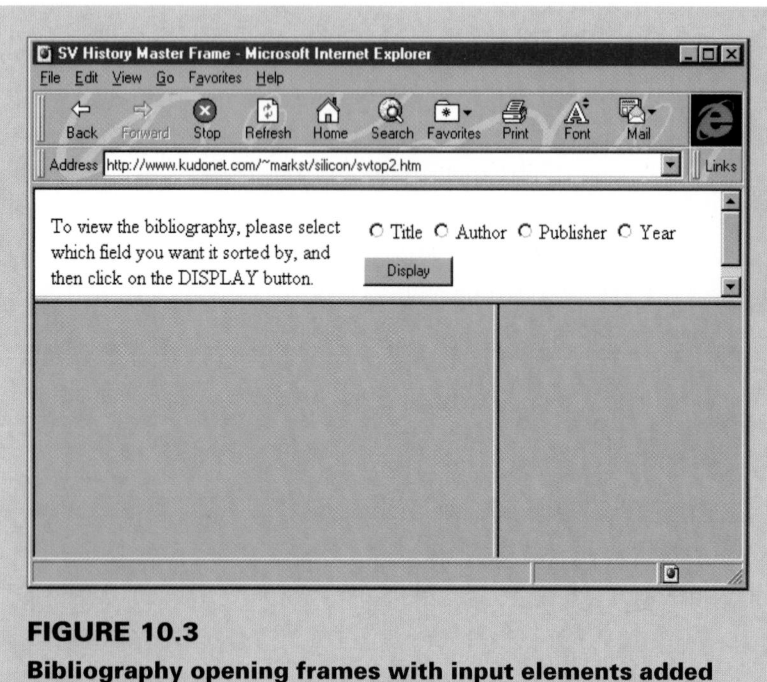


**FIGURE 10.3**
**Bibliography opening frames with input elements added**

These alterations can be implemented incrementally. As a first step, we can simply write the bibliography to the lower left frame instead of the upper frame in which the script resides. Since we are no longer targeting output to the current frame, the script can be moved into the <HEAD></HEAD> of the document, and triggered by an onLoad event. What had been the main body of the program will now be enclosed within a function called initializer(), which is the event handler for the onLoad event. Because we are writing to a different frame, the writeln statements need to be written as properties of that frame, not the current frame. This section of code, when revised, reads as follows:

```
with (top.frames[1].frames[0].document) {
writeln("<HTML><HEAD></HEAD><BODY BGCOLOR=#FFFFFF><DL>");
for (i = 1; i <= books.length; i++) {
   writeln("<P><DT><B>" + books[sortKey[i]].titl + "</B>");
   writeln("<DD>" + books[sortKey[i]].authLName + ", " +
books[sortKey[i]].authFName);
   writeln("<DD>" + books[sortKey[i]].publisher);
   writeln("<DD>" + books[sortKey[i]].yr);
   writeln('<DD><A HREF="');
   writeln(books[sortKey[i]].synopsis + '" TARGET="synopsis">Synopsis</A>');
}
writeln("</DL></HTML>");
close();
}
```

We use the “with” command to avoid repeating a long object reference for each statement. What we are writing now is a full HTML document, so we must add the <HTML></HTML> tags. We also need to close output at the end.

With these small changes, we have a new version of the script: one that leaves the upper frame in which the script resides empty, but that writes the bibliography to the lower frame. With two more changes, we can further advance this script's evolution. First, we will write an HTML form in the upper frame with the radio buttons for field selection and the submit button. Since we are adding this form, we have no reason to keep the sorting and writing out of the bibliography within the same event handler that initializes the bibliography. These tasks will be split into a separate function called writeBib(). This function will be made an event handler of the “onClick” event for the submit button. The added HTML is as follows:

```
<BODY BGCOLOR=#FFFFFF onLoad="initializer()">
<FORM><TABLE>
   <TR><TD ROWSPAN=2 WIDTH=250>
```

```
    To view the bibliography, please select which field you want it sorted by,
and then click on the DISPLAY button.
    </TD>
    <TD>
     <INPUT TYPE="radio" NAME="bkfield" VALUE="titl">Title
     <INPUT TYPE="radio" NAME="bkfield" VALUE="authLName">Author
     <INPUT TYPE="radio" NAME="bkfield" VALUE="publisher">Publisher
     <INPUT TYPE="radio" NAME="bkfield" VALUE="yr">Year
    </TD></TR>
    <TR><TD>
     <INPUT NAME="callsort" TYPE="button" VALUE="Display" onClick="writeBib()">
    </TD>
    </TR>
   </TABLE>
   </FORM>
</BODY>
</HTML>
```

We now have a complete script that triggers display of the bibliography based on user input: see Figure 10.4. For the last increment, we need to vary the sort routine based on that input.

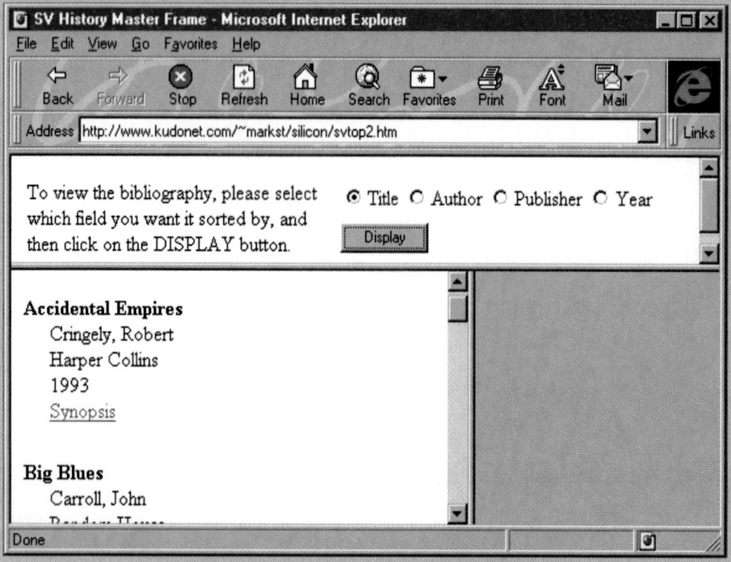

This requires two steps. First, the program needs to read which radio button was selected, and extract a value to pass to the sorting function based on that selection. Second, it needs to vary the sort based on this parameter. Reading the radio buttons provides a typical situation in which to use the "break" command

**FIGURE 10.4**
**Outputting the bibliography from form input**

discussed in the last chapter. We want to browse through the radio buttons until we find the one selected, and then break out of the loop to return that value:

```
for (i = 0; i < document.forms[0].bkfield.length; i++) {
   if (document.forms[0].bkfield[i].checked) { break }
}
sortChoice = document.forms[0].bkfield[i].value;
```

The value of sortChoice is then passed to sorting() as a parameter. In performing the sort, we need to select a property of the books[] array for comparison based on sortChoice. To do so, we add the following to the sorting function:

```
compare1 = eval("books[sortKey[i]]." + bkProperty);
compare2 = eval("books[sortKey[i+1]]." + bkProperty);
```

The function then compares the value of compare1 and compare2 to sort the values of sortKey. With these changes we have a new complete script, one that presents the bibliography in varying order depending on user input. Figure 10.5 shows the final output. Here is the code for the completed script:

```
<HTML>
<HEAD>
<TITLE>Silicon Valley History: Bibliography</TITLE>
```

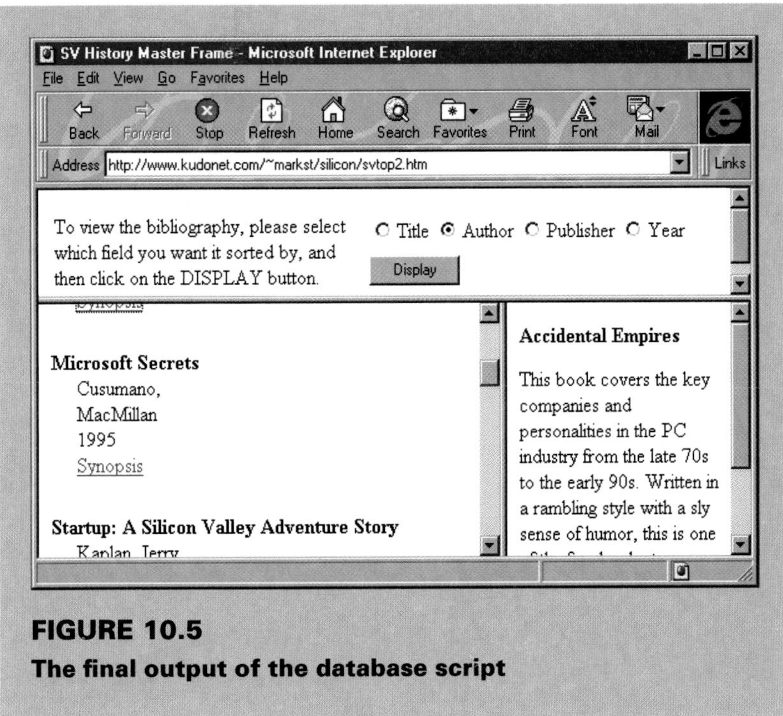


**FIGURE 10.5**
**The final output of the database script**

```
<SCRIPT LANGUAGE="javascript">
<!-
////////////////////////////////
// variable declaration       //
////////////////////////////////
var n; var m; var i; var j; var bkProperty; var sortChoice;
var titleOf; var authL; var authF; var pub; var yearOf; var synop;

////////////////////////////////
// function declaration       //
////////////////////////////////

///////////////////////////////////////
// sorts the books array based       //
// on one of four properties of      //
// that array; the choice of         //
// property is passed as parameter.//
///////////////////////////////////////
function sorting(bkProperty) {
var sorted = false;
var tempSwap;
var compare1; var compare2;
while (sorted == false) {
   sorted = true;
   for (i = 1; i < books.length; i++) {
      compare1 = eval("books[sortKey[i]]." + bkProperty);
      compare2 = eval("books[sortKey[i+1]]." + bkProperty);
      if (compare1 > compare2) {
         tempSwap = sortKey[i];
         sortKey[i] = sortKey[i+1];
         sortKey[i+1] = tempSwap;
         sorted = false;
      }
   }
}
}

////////////////////////////////
```

```
// generic array maker      //
//////////////////////////////
function MakeArray(n) {
   this.length = n;
   for (i = 1; i <= n; i++) {
      this[i] = 0;
   }
   return this;
}

//////////////////////////////
// making cols for 2D array //
//////////////////////////////
function bookFields(titleOf, authL, authF, pub, yearOf, synop) {
   this.titl = titleOf;
   this.authLName = authL;
   this.authFName = authF;
   this.publisher = pub;
   this.yr = yearOf;
   this.synopsis = synop;
}

function addbook(i, titl, authLName, authFName, publisher, yr, synopsis) {
   books[i].titl = titl;
   books[i].authLName = authLName;
   books[i].authFName = authFName;
   books[i].publisher = publisher;
   books[i].yr = yr;
   books[i].synopsis = synopsis;
}

function initializer() {
///////////////////////////////////
// run as an event handler from  //
// onLoad, this initializes the  //
// database by making books as a //
// 2D array for bibliography     //
// database. when # of books in  //
```

```
// database changes, change # in //
// lines below. current val:12   //
//////////////////////////////////
books = new MakeArray(12);
for (i = 0; i <= 12; i++) {
   books[i] = new bookFields(0,0,0,0,0,0,0);
}

//////////////////////////////
// making sortKey as array for//
// sorting order of database  //
//////////////////////////////
sortKey = new MakeArray(books.length);
for (i = 1; i <= sortKey.length; i++) {
   sortKey[i] = i;
}

//////////////////////////////
// loading the database into  //
// the books array            //
//////////////////////////////
i = 1;
addbook(i, "Startup: A Silicon Valley Adventure Story",
           "Kaplan",
           "Jerry",
           "Houghton Mifflin",
           "1995",
           "starsili.htm"
          )
i++;
addbook(i, "Accidental Empires",
           "Cringely",
           "Robert",
           "Harper Collins",
           "1993",
           "acciempi.htm"
          )
i++;
```

```
addbook(i, "Insanely Great",
          "Levy",
          "Steven",
          "Viking",
          "1994",
          "insagrea.htm"
         )
i++;
addbook(i, "Macintosh Way",
          "Kawasaki",
          "Guy",
          "Scott, Foresman and Company",
          "1989",
          "maciway.htm"
         )
i++
addbook(i, "Hackers: Heroes of the Computer Revolution",
          "Levy",
          "Steven",
          "Doubleday",
          "1984",
          "hackhero.htm"
         )
i++
 addbook(i, "Gates",
          "Manes",
          "Stephen",
          "Doubleday",
          "1993",
          "gates.htm"
         )

addbook(i, "Odyssey: Pepsi to Apple",
          "Sculley",
          "John",
          "Harper and Row",
          "1987",
          "odyspeps.htm"
```

```
          )
i++
addbook(i, "Fumbling the Future",
           "Smith",
           "Douglas",
           "William Morrow",
           "1988",
           "fumbfutu.htm"
          )
i++
addbook(i, "Microsoft Secrets",
           "Cusumano",
           " ",
           "MacMillan",
           "1995",
           "micrsecr.htm"
          )
i++
addbook(i, "Fugitive Game",
           "Littman",
           " ",
           "Little Brown",
           "1995",
           "fugigame.htm"
          )
i++
addbook(i, "Takedown",
           "Shimomura",
           " ",
           "Warner",
           "1995",
           "take.htm"
          )
i++
addbook(i, "Big Blues",
           "Carroll",
           "John",
           "Random House",
```

```
            "1994",
            "bigblue.htm"
           )
} //end of initializer

function writeBib() {
////////////////////////////////////////
// retrieve which field was selected //
// from the form, pass that field as //
// a parameter for sorting database, //
// then write out sorted database to //
// lower frame.                      //
////////////////////////////////////////
for (i = Ø; i < document.forms[Ø].bkfield.length; i++) {
   if (document.forms[Ø].bkfield[i].checked) { break }
}
sortChoice = document.forms[Ø].bkfield[i].value;
sorting(sortChoice);
with (top.frames[1].frames[Ø].document) {
writeln("<HTML><HEAD></HEAD><BODY BGCOLOR=#FFFFFF><DL>");
for (i = 1; i <= books.length; i++) {
   writeln("<P><DT><B>" + books[sortKey[i]].titl + "</B>");
   writeln("<DD>" + books[sortKey[i]].authLName + ", " +
books[sortKey[i]].authFName);
   writeln("<DD>" + books[sortKey[i]].publisher);
   writeln("<DD>" + books[sortKey[i]].yr);
   writeln('<DD><A HREF="');
   writeln(books[sortKey[i]].synopsis + '" TARGET="synopsis">Synopsis</A>');
}
writeln("</DL></HTML>");
close();
}
}//end writeBib
//->
</SCRIPT>
</HEAD>
```

```
<BODY BGCOLOR=#FFFFFF onLoad="initializer()">
<FORM><TABLE>
   <TR><TD ROWSPAN=2 WIDTH=250>
   To view the bibliography, please select which field you want it sorted by,
and then click on the DISPLAY button.
   </TD>
   <TD>
    <INPUT TYPE="radio" NAME="bkfield" VALUE="titl">Title
    <INPUT TYPE="radio" NAME="bkfield" VALUE="authLName">Author
    <INPUT TYPE="radio" NAME="bkfield" VALUE="publisher">Publisher
    <INPUT TYPE="radio" NAME="bkfield" VALUE="yr">Year
   </TD></TR>
   <TR><TD>
    <INPUT NAME="callsort" TYPE="button" VALUE="Display" onClick="writeBib()">
   </TD>
   </TR>
  </TABLE>
  </FORM>
</BODY>
</HTML>
```

## Database with Keyword Queries

The final version of this database program will let the user enter keywords to be used in searching for specific database entries. This keyword search will have these features:

- The user can enter either one keyword or two keywords.
- The user can select which Boolean operation will be performed with the two keywords, either AND or OR.
- The user can select which fields each keyword will apply to; this can be any combination of fields, or all.

This input form will be much more complex. It will require a larger frame to display all the elements. We can push the top frame down further, however, because our query should return one, or only a few bibliography entries. Thus the citation frame will need less space. Given the complexity of the form, it will make sense to add an online help section, as we did with the stopwatch program in Chapter 6. This can be displayed in the same frame that we have been using to display the synopsis.

This script takes a big leap forward in complexity. Planning out incremental development from the previous script will be a challenge. This script will go through three evolutions. At first we simply want to update the display, without changing any of the program functions. Next we want to add a single-keyword search. This will be implemented in two parts: by integrating new search functions into the program flow, and by linking those search functions to the database. Finally, we want to augment this to include two keywords with Boolean operations.

The new display demonstrates the importance of tables as a layout technique. The display will have checkboxes, radio buttons, text-entry fields, a selection list, a submit button, and a simple hyperlink. Every forms element except text area has been used (wait until next chapter), for a total of 17 forms elements. Getting any kind of layout control over this assortment would be impossible without tables.

The radio buttons will perform the same function as in the previous script: specifying which of four mutually exclusive fields will be used to sort the output. The checkboxes refer to the same four fields, but must be used inclusively to allow the user to indicate on which fields to perform the keyword search; the default should be “all.” Because the user must be permitted to select more than one field, radio buttons will not work. The selection box sets the Boolean method of the search, defaulting to “OR.” A radio button could have been used in this case as well, but a selection box is more compact and less visually distracting here. The text-input areas allow the keywords to be entered, and the submit button initiates the whole search. There is also a link to the help page. The resulting page is shown in Figure 10.6; the HTML for this page is shown below.

```
<BODY BGCOLOR=#FFFFFF onLoad="initializer()">
<FORM><TABLE>
<TR>
   <TD COLSPAN=3 ALIGN=CENTER WIDTH=300>Search For:</TD>
   <TD WIDTH=240 ALIGN=CENTER>Sort Results By:</TD>
</TR><TR>
   <TD WIDTH=120><INPUT TYPE=TEXT NAME="key1" SIZE=15></TD>
   <TD WIDTH=60><SELECT NAME="bool">
      <OPTION>OR
      <OPTION AND>AND
   </SELECT></TD>
   <TD WIDTH=120><INPUT TYPE=TEXT NAME="key2" SIZE=15></TD>
```

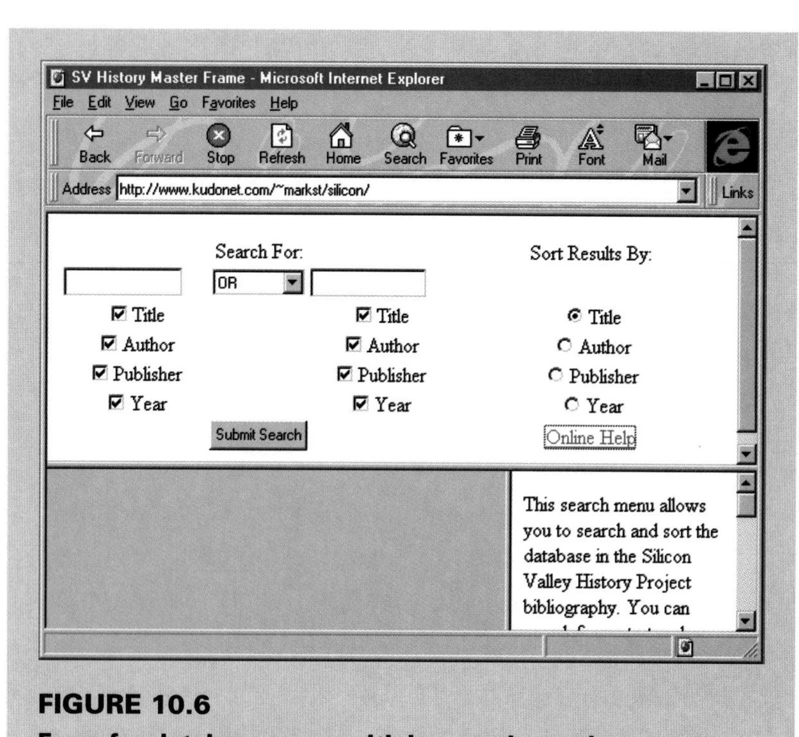


**FIGURE 10.6**
**Form for database query with keyword search**

```
    <TD WIDTH=240 ALIGN=CENTER></TD>
</TR><TR>
    <TD WIDTH=120 ALIGN=CENTER><INPUT TYPE="checkbox" NAME="chktitl"
VALUE="titl" CHECKED>Title</TD>
    <TD WIDTH=60></TD>
    <TD WIDTH=120 ALIGN=CENTER><INPUT TYPE="checkbox" NAME="chktitl2"
VALUE="titl" CHECKED>Title</TD>
    <TD WIDTH=240 ALIGN=CENTER><INPUT TYPE="radio" NAME="bkfield" VALUE="titl"
CHECKED>Title</TD>
</TR><TR>
    <TD WIDTH=120 ALIGN=CENTER><INPUT TYPE="checkbox" NAME="chkauthl"
VALUE="authLName" CHECKED>Author</TD>
    <TD WIDTH=60></TD>
    <TD WIDTH=120 ALIGN=CENTER><INPUT TYPE="checkbox" NAME="chkauthl2"
VALUE="authLName" CHECKED>Author</TD>
    <TD WIDTH=240 ALIGN=CENTER><INPUT TYPE="radio" NAME="bkfield"
VALUE="authLName">Author</TD>
</TR><TR>
    <TD WIDTH=120 ALIGN=CENTER><INPUT TYPE="checkbox" NAME="chkpub"
```

```
VALUE="publisher" CHECKED>Publisher</TD>
   <TD WIDTH=60></TD>
   <TD WIDTH=120 ALIGN=CENTER><INPUT TYPE="checkbox" NAME="chkpub2"
VALUE="publisher" CHECKED>Publisher</TD>
   <TD WIDTH=240 ALIGN=CENTER><INPUT TYPE="radio" NAME="bkfield" VALUE=
"publisher">Publisher</TD>
</TR><TR>
   <TD WIDTH=120 ALIGN=CENTER><INPUT TYPE="checkbox" NAME="chkyr" VALUE="yr"
CHECKED>Year</TD>
   <TD WIDTH=60></TD>
   <TD WIDTH=120 ALIGN=CENTER><INPUT TYPE="checkbox" NAME="chkyr2" VALUE="yr"
CHECKED>Year</TD>
   <TD WIDTH=240 ALIGN=CENTER><INPUT TYPE="radio" NAME="bkfield"
VALUE="yr">Year</TD>
</TR><TR>
   <TD COLSPAN=3 ALIGN=CENTER WIDTH=300><INPUT TYPE="BUTTON" NAME="search"
VALUE="Submit Search" onClick="StringCheck()"></TD>
   <TD ALIGN=CENTER WIDTH=240><A HREF="bibhelp.htm" TARGET="synopsis">Online
Help</A></TD>
</TR>
</TABLE>
</FORM>
</BODY>
</HTML>
```

The database array is still initialized from an onLoad() event; there is no reason to change that part of the program. Anticipating the need for processing the keywords entered by the user, a function named "stringCheck()" is given as the event handler for the onClick event now. This function has yet to be specified, but we can include a reference to it now just to check the appearance of the display. The width of table cells is specified explicitly. While the size and resolution of computer monitors varies, the lowest common denominator would be a resolution width of 640 pixels. Any display that can be kept under this width should be; this table is 600 pixels wide.

As shown in Figure 10.6, the one new feature implemented at this stage is the online help file. Since this is simply a matter of HTML coding, it is an easy feature to include at this point.

Implementing string comparisons can be challenging, particularly given the primitive state of JScript's methods for the string object. Fortunately, we have a ready-made tool in the form of the word comparison function presented in the last chapter. We will include that function almost verbatim, although at this stage it won't be tied to any input. We will make one small modification. In the last chapter, the function returned an alert box announcing the results of the comparison; now we want it to simply return a value of "true" or "false," depending on the results.

The database array also needs to be modified. In addition to its other properties, books[] will now have a property called "match" that will indicate whether that entry contains a match to a keyword or not. The modified array-creation code looks like this:

```
function bookFields(titleOf, authL, authF, pub, yearOf, synop, match) {
    this.titl = titleOf;
    this.authLName = authL;
    this.authFName = authF;
    this.publisher = pub;
    this.yr = yearOf;
    this.synopsis = synop;
    this.match = match;
}
```

At this point our program flows in this order: clicking on the button calls the stringCheck() function, which will process user input and then call other functions. The processing code hasn't been written yet, but we can still use this function as a shell to initiate other actions. It will call the SMatch() function, which compares words, and then call the writeBib() function, which prints the search results to the lower left frame. While we have included the SMatch code, we have yet to tie it to any words for matching.

Thus at this point stringCheck() and SMatch() are extraneous functions. We've included them in the program flow, but they don't do any work within the program. Still, this modified code will produce output. We can use it exactly as we used the last script, to select a field and print out the sorted bibliography based on that field. This is how incremental development works. The process is a little like designing a house: you may put a room in a house in the floor plan before you know exactly what will go in the room. Right now stringCheck() and SMatch() are empty rooms added to the house, but the structure of the house is still intact.

Now we want to allow a single-keyword search. The writeBib() function must be modified, but it requires only a simple change. Previously this function had begun the printout with these two lines:

```
for (i = 1; i <= books.length; i++) {
   writeln("<P><DT><B>" + books[sortKey[i]].titl + "</B>");
```

Now we need to make this "writeln" statement and the ones that follow conditional on the success of the keyword search. We don't want to display the whole bibliography; we will display only those citations whose match property has been set to true.

We also need to expand on the keyword-search function. A book title, after all, contains multiple words. The keyword "Macintosh" will return no matches if the program thinks that the title "Macintosh Way" is all one word. So we'll need a function to parse a title into individual words, and then we'll need to check each word. The following function will break down the title into separate strings based on where a space occurs:

```
function parsePhrase(phrase) {
var i; var j = 1; var searchWord = "";
for (i = 1; i <= 20; i++) {
   titleWords[i] = "";
}
for (i = 0; i < phrase.length; i++) {
   if (phrase.charAt(i) == " ") {
      titleWords[j] = searchWord;
      searchWord = "";
      j++;
   } else {
      searchWord += phrase.charAt(i);
   }
}
titleWords[j] = searchWord
return j;
}
```

Checking for a match at this point in the program, after we have already sorted the database, may seem inefficient. After all, what point is there to sorting citation records that will not even be displayed? However, this is the point where we can introduce this check with the least modification to existing code. At the price of some inefficiency, we get greater portability out of the code we have already written.

More importantly, the amount of processing required in this case should always be trivial. By far the most time-intensive task the client computer must perform is receiving the document containing the script over the Internet in the first place. This will require orders of magnitude more time than the actual processing of the script itself. If we restrict our database size to what can be transferred over the Internet in a reasonable length of time, then the length of time required to sort the resulting database will always be trivial by comparison.

Now we need to link our word-comparison functions to user input. The code below shows a keyword search on the title field:

```
function StringCheck() {
var k; var n;
keyOne = document.forms[0].key1.value;
for (i = 1; i <= books.length; i++) {
   books[i].match = false;
   if (document.forms[0].chktitl.checked) {
      k = parsePhrase(books[i].titl);
      for (n = 1; n <=  k; n++) {
         if (books[i].match == true) { continue }
         books[i].match = SMatch(keyOne, titleWords[n]);
      }
   }
}
}
```

We read input from the text input field for the first keyword, and assign it to keyOne. If the user has not entered a keyword, we'll use the wildcard character as a default. Then we simply need to pass keyOne and the title field of each entry to the SMatch function to see if they match. Once any match has been found in any field for an entry, there is no longer a need to check for a match for that entry.

This same code extends to the other fields that need to be checked. Note that if the user requests an author search, the authLName field must be checked, and then the authFName field must be checked as well.

With these modifications we now have a functioning keyword-search program for the database. Figure 10.7 shows the output of a keyword search. All that remains is to enable a second keyword to be combined in searches with the first keyword.

To determine whether one keyword OR another has been found requires little extra effort. After searching each field for the first keyword, we simply need to repeat the search with the second keyword in those entries whose match property is still false.

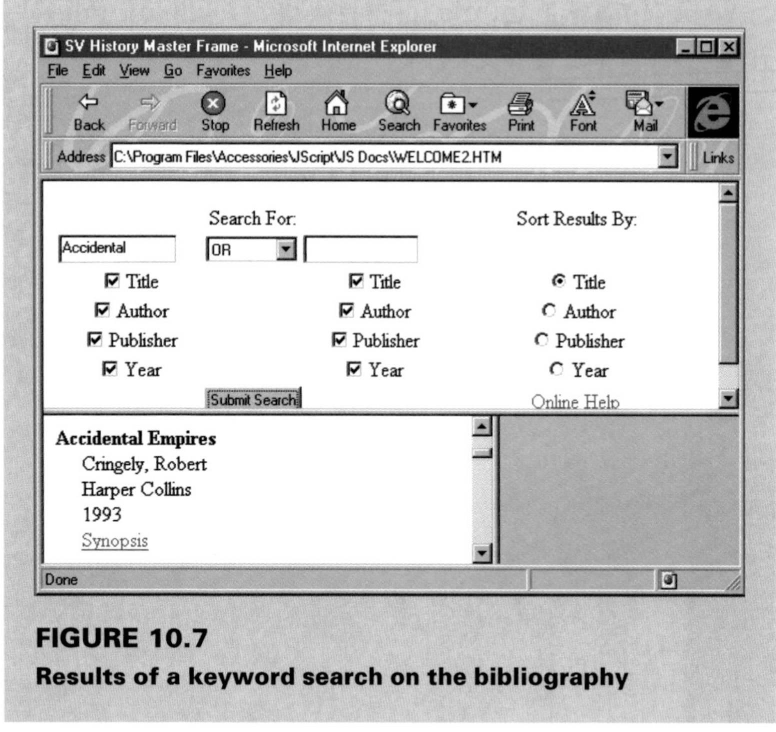


**FIGURE 10.7**

**Results of a keyword search on the bibliography**

Determining whether one keyword AND another has been found is more complex. The program must perform several tasks. First, it must restrict its search to only those entries where a match has been previously found, since any match must match both words. These entries must then have their match property reset to false, pending the results of the second keyword search. Only if the second keyword finds a match in the field should the match property be set to true.

Putting this all together, we get this code:

```
function StringCheck() {
var k; var n;
var j = document.forms[0].bool.selectedIndex;
var bl = document.forms[0].bool.options[j].text;
keyOne = document.forms[0].key1.value;
keyTwo = document.forms[0].key2.value;
keyOne = (keyOne == "") ? "*" : keyOne;
keyTwo = (keyTwo == "") ? "*" : keyTwo;
for (i = 1; i <= books.length; i++) {
   books[i].match = false;
   if (document.forms[0].chktitl.checked) {
      k = parsePhrase(books[i].titl);
      for (n = 1; n <=  k; n++) {
         if (books[i].match == true) { continue }
            books[i].match = SMatch(keyOne, titleWords[n]);
      }
   }
```

```
    if ((document.forms[0].chkauthl.checked) && (books[i].match != true)) {
        books[i].match = SMatch(keyOne, books[i].authLName);
    }
    if ((document.forms[0].chkauthl.checked) && (books[i].match != true)) {
        books[i].match = SMatch(keyOne, books[i].authFName);
    }
    if ((document.forms[0].chkpub.checked) && (books[i].match != true)) {
        books[i].match = SMatch(keyOne, books[i].publisher);
    }
    if ((document.forms[0].chkyr.checked) && (books[i].match != true)) {
        books[i].match = SMatch(keyOne, books[i].yr);
    }
}

for (i = 1; i <= books.length; i++) {
    if ((bl == "OR") && (books[i].match != true) && (document.forms[0].
chktitl.checked)) {
        k = parsePhrase(books[i].titl);
        for (n = 1; n <=  k; n++) {
            if (books[i].match == true) { continue }
            books[i].match = SMatch(keyTwo, titleWords[n]);
        }
    }
    if ((bl == "AND") && (books[i].match == true) && (document.forms[0].
chktitl2.checked)) {
        books[i].match = SMatch(keyTwo, books[i].titl);
    }
if (books[i].match == true) continue;
    if ((bl == "OR") && (books[i].match != true) &&
(document.forms[0].chkauthl2.checked)) {
        books[i].match = SMatch(keyTwo, books[i].authLName);
    }
    if ((bl == "AND") && (books[i].match == true) &&
(document.forms[0].chkauthl2.checked)) {
        books[i].match = SMatch(keyTwo, books[i].authLName);
    }
    if (books[i].match == true) continue;
    if ((bl == "OR") && (books[i].match != true) &&
```

```
(document.forms[0].chkauthl2.checked)) {
        books[i].match = SMatch(keyTwo, books[i].authFName);
    }
    if ((bl == "AND") && (books[i].match == true) &&
(document.forms[0].chkauthl2.checked)) {
        books[i].match = SMatch(keyTwo, books[i].authFName);
    }
    if (books[i].match == true) continue;
    if ((bl == "OR") && (books[i].match != true) &&
(document.forms[0].chkpub2.checked)) {
        books[i].match = SMatch(keyTwo, books[i].publisher);
    }
    if ((bl == "AND") && (books[i].match == true) &&
(document.forms[0].chkpub2.checked)) {
        books[i].match = SMatch(keyTwo, books[i].publisher);
    }
    if (books[i].match == true) continue;
    if ((bl == "OR") && (books[i].match != true) &&
(document.forms[0].chkyr2.checked)) {
        books[i].match = SMatch(keyTwo, books[i].yr);
    }
    if ((bl == "AND") && (books[i].match == true) &&
(document.forms[0].chkyr2.checked)) {
        books[i].match = SMatch(keyTwo, books[i].yr);
    }
}
writeBib();
}
```

These last modifications complete the script. We now have an online database that allows full keyword searches, including Boolean matches between two keywords. Figure 10.8 shows the results of a combined keyword search. The full code for the final script is given below.

```
<HTML>
<HEAD>
<TITLE>Silicon Valley History: Bibliography</TITLE>
<SCRIPT LANGUAGE="javascript">
<!-
```

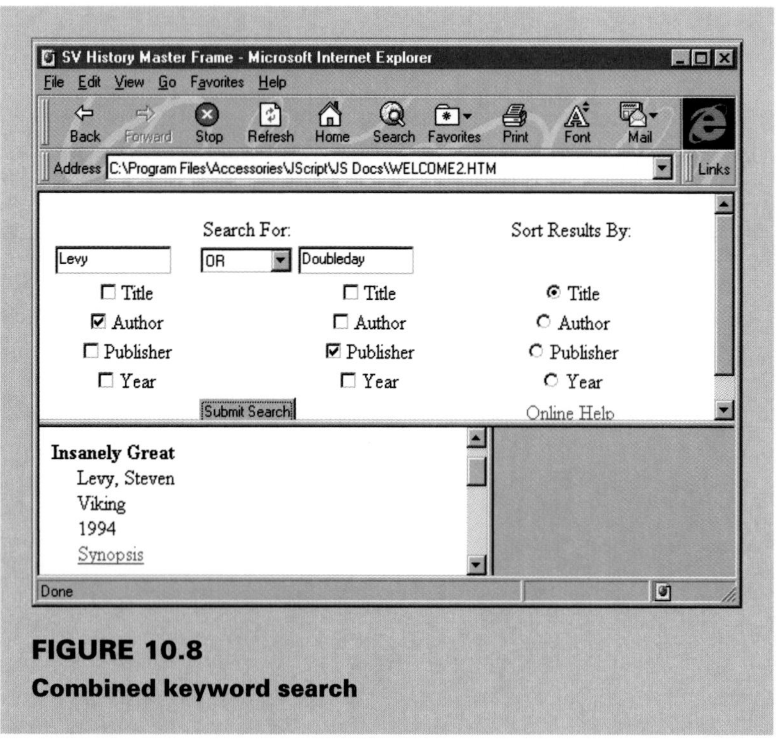


**FIGURE 10.8**
**Combined keyword search**

```
////////////////////////////////
// variable declaration       //
////////////////////////////////
var n; var m; var i; var j; var bkProperty; var sortChoice;
var titleOf; var authL; var authF; var pub; var yearOf;
var synop; var wildcard; var sTarget; var msg;
var len; var blen; var elen; var bstr; var estr; var wc;
var startChar; var endChar; var keyword; var keyOne; var keyTwo;

////////////////////////////////
// function declaration       //
////////////////////////////////

function sorting(bkProperty) {
var sorted = false;
var tempSwap;
var compare1; var compare2;
while (sorted == false) {
   sorted = true;
   for (i = 1; i < books.length; i++) {
```

```
      compare1 = eval("books[sortKey[i]]." + bkProperty);
      compare2 = eval("books[sortKey[i+1]]." + bkProperty);
      if (compare1 > compare2) {
         tempSwap = sortKey[i];
         sortKey[i] = sortKey[i+1];
         sortKey[i+1] = tempSwap;
         sorted = false;
      }
   }
}
}

function MakeArray(n) {
   this.length = n;
   for (i = 1; i <= n; i++) {
      this[i] = 0;
   }
   return this;
}

function bookFields(titleOf, authL, authF, pub, yearOf, synop, match) {
   this.titl = titleOf;
   this.authLName = authL;
   this.authFName = authF;
   this.publisher = pub;
   this.yr = yearOf;
   this.synopsis = synop;
   this.match = match;
}

function addbook(i, titl, authLName, authFName, publisher, yr, synopsis) {
   books[i].titl = titl;
   books[i].authLName = authLName;
   books[i].authFName = authFName;
   books[i].publisher = publisher;
   books[i].yr = yr;
   books[i].synopsis = synopsis;
}
```

```
function initializer() {
//////////////////////////////////////////////////////
//change 12 in the next two lines to whatever the //
//current number of items in the bibliography is  //
//////////////////////////////////////////////////////
books = new MakeArray(12);   //change 12
for (i = 0; i <= 12; i++) {  //change 12
   books[i] = new bookFields(0,0,0,0,0,0,0,0);
}

sortKey = new MakeArray(books.length);
for (i = 1; i <= sortKey.length; i++) {
   sortKey[i] = i;
}

titleWords = new MakeArray(20);
for (i = 1; i <= 20; i++) {
   titleWords[i] = "";
}

////////////////////////////////
// loading the database into  //
// the books array            //
////////////////////////////////
i = 1;
addbook(i, "Startup: A Silicon Valley Adventure Story",
           "Kaplan",
           "Jerry",
           "Houghton Mifflin",
           "1995",
           "starsili.htm"
          )
i++;
addbook(i, "Accidental Empires",
           "Cringely",
           "Robert",
           "Harper Collins",
```

```
            "1993",
            "acciempi.htm"
           )
i++;
addbook(i, "Insanely Great",
            "Levy",
            "Steven",
            "Viking",
            "1994",
            "insagrea.htm"
           )
i++;
addbook(i, "Macintosh Way",
            "Kawasaki",
            "Guy",
            "Scott, Foresman and Company",
            "1989",
            "maciway.htm"
           )
i++
addbook(i, "Hackers: Heroes of the Computer Revolution",
            "Levy",
            "Steven",
            "Doubleday",
            "1984",
            "hackhero.htm"
           )
i++
 addbook(i, "Gates",
            "Manes",
            "Stephen",
            "Doubleday",
            "1993",
            "gates.htm"
           )
i++
addbook(i, "Odyssey: Pepsi to Apple",
            "Sculley",
```

```
                "John",
                "Harper and Row",
                "1987",
                "odyspeps.htm"
               )
    i++
    addbook(i, "Fumbling the Future",
                "Smith",
                "Douglas",
                "William Morrow",
                "1988",
                "fumbfutu.htm"
               )
    i++
    addbook(i, "Microsoft Secrets",
                "Cusumano",
                "M",
                "Macmillan",
                "1995",
                "micrsecr.htm"
               )
    i++
    addbook(i, "Fugitive Game",
                "Littman",
                "Jonathan",
                "Little Brown",
                "1995",
                "fugigame.htm"
               )
    i++
    addbook(i, "Takedown",
                "Shimomura",
                "T",
                "Warner",
                "1995",
                "take.htm"
               )
    i++
```

```
addbook(i, "Big Blues",
           "Carroll",
           "John",
           "Random House",
           "1994",
           "bigblue.htm"
          )
}//end of initializer

function parsePhrase(phrase) {
var i; var j = 1; var searchWord = "";
for (i = 1; i <= 20; i++) {
   titleWords[i] = "";
}
for (i = 0; i < phrase.length; i++) {
   if (phrase.charAt(i) == " ") {
      titleWords[j] = searchWord;
      searchWord = "";
      j++;
   } else {
      searchWord += phrase.charAt(i);
   }
}
titleWords[j] = searchWord
return j;
}

function writeBib() {
for (i = 0; i < document.forms[0].bkfield.length; i++) {
   if (document.forms[0].bkfield[i].checked) { break }
}
sortChoice = document.forms[0].bkfield[i].value;
sorting(sortChoice);
with (top.frames[1].frames[0].document) {
writeln("<HTML><HEAD></HEAD><BODY BGCOLOR=#FFFFFF><DL>");
for (i = 1; i <= books.length; i++) {
   if (books[sortKey[i]].match == true) {
      writeln("<P><DT><B>" + books[sortKey[i]].titl + "</B>");
```

```
        writeln("<DD>" + books[sortKey[i]].authLName + ", " +
books[sortKey[i]].authFName);
        writeln("<DD>" + books[sortKey[i]].publisher);
        writeln("<DD>" + books[sortKey[i]].yr);
        writeln('<DD><A HREF="');
        writeln(books[sortKey[i]].synopsis + '" TARGET=synopsis>Synopsis</A>');
    }
}
writeln("</DL></HTML>");
close();
}
}//end writeBib

function charmatch(startChar, endChar, wc) {
var i; var j=0
var wcBuild
var targStartChar = (startChar == 0) ? 0 : sTarget.length - elen;
for (i = startChar; i <= endChar; i++) {
    if (wc.charAt(i) == "?") {
        wcBuild = wc. substring(0, i);
        wcBuild += sTarget.charAt(targStartChar + j);
        wcBuild += wc.substring(i+1, wc.length);
        wc = wcBuild;
    }
    j++;
}
return wc;
}

function StringCheck() {
var k; var n;
var j = document.forms[0].bool.selectedIndex;
var bl = document.forms[0].bool.options[j].text;
keyOne = document.forms[0].key1.value;
keyTwo = document.forms[0].key2.value;
keyOne = (keyOne == "") ? "*" : keyOne;
keyTwo = (keyTwo == "") ? "*" : keyTwo;
for (i = 1; i <= books.length; i++) {
```

```
   books[i].match = false;
   if (document.forms[Ø].chktitl.checked) {
      k = parsePhrase(books[i].titl);
      for (n = 1; n <=  k; n++) {
         if (books[i].match == true) { continue }
            books[i].match = SMatch(keyOne, titleWords[n]);
      }
   }
   if ((document.forms[Ø].chkauthl.checked) && (books[i].match != true)) {
      books[i].match = SMatch(keyOne, books[i].authLName);
   }
   if ((document.forms[Ø].chkauthl.checked) && (books[i].match != true)) {
      books[i].match = SMatch(keyOne, books[i].authFName);
   }
   if ((document.forms[Ø].chkpub.checked) && (books[i].match != true)) {
      books[i].match = SMatch(keyOne, books[i].publisher);
   }
   if ((document.forms[Ø].chkyr.checked) && (books[i].match != true)) {
      books[i].match = SMatch(keyOne, books[i].yr);
   }
}

for (i = 1; i <= books.length; i++) {
   if ((bl == "OR") && (books[i].match != true) && (document.forms[Ø].
chktitl.checked)) {
      k = parsePhrase(books[i].titl);
      for (n = 1; n <=  k; n++) {
         if (books[i].match == true) { continue }
         books[i].match = SMatch(keyTwo, titleWords[n]);
      }
   }
   if ((bl == "AND") && (books[i].match == true) && (document.forms[Ø].
chktitl2.checked)) {
      books[i].match = SMatch(keyTwo, books[i].titl);
   }
if (books[i].match == true) continue;
   if ((bl == "OR") && (books[i].match != true) &&
(document.forms[Ø].chkauthl2.checked)) {
```

```
        books[i].match = SMatch(keyTwo, books[i].authLName);
    }
    if ((bl == "AND") && (books[i].match == true) &&
(document.forms[0].chkauthl2.checked)) {
        books[i].match = SMatch(keyTwo, books[i].authLName);
    }
    if (books[i].match == true) continue;
    if ((bl == "OR") && (books[i].match != true) &&
(document.forms[0].chkauthl2.checked)) {
        books[i].match = SMatch(keyTwo, books[i].authFName);
    }
    if ((bl == "AND") && (books[i].match == true) &&
(document.forms[0].chkauthl2.checked)) {
        books[i].match = SMatch(keyTwo, books[i].authFName);
    }
    if (books[i].match == true) continue;
    if ((bl == "OR") && (books[i].match != true) &&
(document.forms[0].chkpub2.checked)) {
        books[i].match = SMatch(keyTwo, books[i].publisher);
    }
    if ((bl == "AND") && (books[i].match == true) &&
(document.forms[0].chkpub2.checked)) {
        books[i].match = SMatch(keyTwo, books[i].publisher);
    }
    if (books[i].match == true) continue;
    if ((bl == "OR") && (books[i].match != true) &&
(document.forms[0].chkyr2.checked)) {
        books[i].match = SMatch(keyTwo, books[i].yr);
    }
    if ((bl == "AND") && (books[i].match == true) &&
(document.forms[0].chkyr2.checked)) {
        books[i].match = SMatch(keyTwo, books[i].yr);
    }
}
writeBib();
}

function SMatch(n, m) {
```

```
keyword = n;
wildcard = keyword;
sTarget = m
var matching = false;
len = wildcard.length;
blen = wildcard.indexOf("*", 0);
elen = len - (blen+1);
if (blen == -1) {
   wildcard = charmatch(0, len, wildcard);
   matching = (wildcard == sTarget) ? true : false;
} else {
   wildcard = charmatch(0, blen, wildcard);
   wildcard = charmatch(blen+1, len, wildcard);
   bstr = wildcard.substring(0, blen);
   estr = wildcard.substring(blen+1, len);
   if (sTarget.substring(0,blen) == bstr) {
      if (sTarget.substring(sTarget.length-elen, sTarget.length) == estr) {
      matching = true;
      }
   }
}
return matching;
}
//->
</SCRIPT>
</HEAD>
<BODY BGCOLOR=#FFFFFF onLoad="initializer()">
<FORM><TABLE>
<TR>
   <TD COLSPAN=3 ALIGN=CENTER WIDTH=300>Search For:</TD>
   <TD WIDTH=240 ALIGN=CENTER>Sort Results By:</TD>
</TR><TR>
   <TD WIDTH=120><INPUT TYPE=TEXT NAME="key1" SIZE=15></TD>
   <TD WIDTH=60><SELECT NAME="bool">
      <OPTION>OR
      <OPTION AND>AND
   </SELECT></TD>
   <TD WIDTH=120><INPUT TYPE=TEXT NAME="key2" SIZE=15></TD>
```

```
   <TD WIDTH=240 ALIGN=CENTER></TD>
</TR><TR>
   <TD WIDTH=120 ALIGN=CENTER><INPUT TYPE="checkbox" NAME="chktitl"
VALUE="titl" CHECKED>Title</TD>
   <TD WIDTH=60></TD>
   <TD WIDTH=120 ALIGN=CENTER><INPUT TYPE="checkbox" NAME="chktitl2"
VALUE="titl" CHECKED>Title</TD>
   <TD WIDTH=240 ALIGN=CENTER><INPUT TYPE="radio" NAME="bkfield" VALUE="titl"
CHECKED>Title</TD>
</TR><TR>
   <TD WIDTH=120 ALIGN=CENTER><INPUT TYPE="checkbox" NAME="chkauthl"
VALUE="authLName" CHECKED>Author</TD>
   <TD WIDTH=60></TD>
   <TD WIDTH=120 ALIGN=CENTER><INPUT TYPE="checkbox" NAME="chkauthl2"
VALUE="authLName" CHECKED>Author</TD>
   <TD WIDTH=240 ALIGN=CENTER><INPUT TYPE="radio" NAME="bkfield"
VALUE="authLName">Author</TD>
</TR><TR>
   <TD WIDTH=120 ALIGN=CENTER><INPUT TYPE="checkbox" NAME="chkpub"
VALUE="publisher" CHECKED>Publisher</TD>
   <TD WIDTH=60></TD>
   <TD WIDTH=120 ALIGN=CENTER><INPUT TYPE="checkbox" NAME="chkpub2"
VALUE="publisher" CHECKED>Publisher</TD>
   <TD WIDTH=240 ALIGN=CENTER><INPUT TYPE="radio" NAME="bkfield" VALUE=
"publisher">Publisher</TD>
</TR><TR>
   <TD WIDTH=120 ALIGN=CENTER><INPUT TYPE="checkbox" NAME="chkyr" VALUE="yr"
CHECKED>Year</TD>
   <TD WIDTH=60></TD>
   <TD WIDTH=120 ALIGN=CENTER><INPUT TYPE="checkbox" NAME="chkyr2" VALUE="yr"
CHECKED>Year</TD>
   <TD WIDTH=240 ALIGN=CENTER><INPUT TYPE="radio" NAME="bkfield"
VALUE="yr">Year</TD>
</TR><TR>
   <TD COLSPAN=3 ALIGN=CENTER WIDTH=300><INPUT TYPE="BUTTON" NAME="search"
VALUE="Submit Search" onClick="StringCheck()"></TD>
   <TD ALIGN=CENTER WIDTH=240><A HREF="bibhelp.htm" TARGET="synopsis">Online
Help</A></TD>
```

```
</TR>
</TABLE>
</FORM>
</BODY>
</HTML>
```

In this chapter we have pushed JScript's data-processing capabilities to the limit. The results are impressive. We have seen that virtually any database query function you might want can be implemented in JScript, and we have seen that databases of reasonable size and complexity can be used while still maintaining nearly instantaneous response.

Yet the logic employed here is seldom complex or subtle. JScript provides excellent facilities for handling forms input, and for managing frames. Some tasks involving these devices may actually be simpler with JScript than they would be if we were forced to rely on HTML alone.

Nevertheless, the final script we have devised is complex, running several hundred lines in length. It does illustrate the importance of modular design and incremental development. Trying to write this entire script from scratch would be a challenge for even an experienced programmer. By borrowing from previous code, and by implementing features one at a time, we can keep the task manageable.

If you have followed the discussion up to this point, you can rightly feel a sense of accomplishment. JScript can be employed in countless ways to enhance your Web site with scripts much simpler than this one. If you understand this database program, JScript should no longer mystify you: you are ready to put the full power of client-side scripting to work.

The scripts we will examine in the remainder of this book will actually be quite a bit simpler than the scripts we have worked through in this chapter. JScript does have limitations, and in the next two chapters we will look at how you can combine JScript with other applications to move your scripts beyond those limitations.

# Filling Out and Validating an E-mail Form

# Chapter 11
# Maintaining a Database: JScript and CGI

JScript processes data extremely well. It has a rich set of methods for manipulating data, and its object-oriented structure allows quite complex data-handling functions to be constructed out of smaller modules. While features such as arrays and String object methods are primitive, these features possess no inherent limitations. The programmer who wants more sophisticated tools can construct them.

JScript reads and writes data extremely poorly—in fact, it does so not at all. JScript cannot open a file to read data from it, and it can neither modify existing files nor create new ones. This is not an inherent limitation of the language, but an artificial constraint built in for security reasons. Future versions of the language may not have the same limits. JScript can be deployed in other ActiveX environments besides the Web, and the same security concerns will not be present in all these environments. Even in a networked environment like the Web, some less-restrictive form of file access may be allowed.

At present, however, JScript's data-handling capabilities are restricted to what can be contained within the script itself. Extending these capabilities to the maintenance and modification features needed by a full database requires the help of a server-side application accessed through CGI. JScript makes an excellent partner to CGI applications. Pairing a server-side process with a client-side scripting language lets each handle the tasks for which it is best suited.

A server-side process can read a file and write to a file, serving the results to the client. Server-side processes can be very particular about the input they receive, and input must be validated to assure that the process will run as expected. Validation is the checkpoint that determines whether input conforms to expectations, and this checkpoint should be as close to the point of origin as possible. The situation is analogous to mailing a letter: verifying that the address is correct ahead of time is much more efficient than waiting for the letter to be sent all the way to its destination, only to discover at the journey's end that its address is incorrect. Likewise, it makes no sense to waste either Internet bandwidth or server-side processing effort on faulty input. Validation is a task for client-side scripting.

As we have seen in earlier chapters, servers do not maintain state well. What seems like a simple activity from the user's point of view, namely moving from one document to the next and carrying over information, is a complex activity for the server. It requires the help of a CGI application. Often these activities can be simplified by handling the documents with client-side scripting. With careful use of frames, you can move the user through a series of documents that are all managed by the same script.

In this chapter we will extend the database of Chapter 10 to incorporate these ideas. Specifically we want to add these features:

- Allow the user to enter a new book citation to the database that will be immediately added to the bibliography
- Allow the user to enter a synopsis for the new book entered that will be e-mailed to the Webmaster before being added
- Allow the user to append information to an existing synopsis that will be e-mailed to the Webmaster before being added

We will start with the last of these features. It will be the easiest to implement, and, as we are always striving for reusable code, it will provide a starting point for developing the other features.

## Filling Out and Validating an E-mail Form

The frame layout used for the Silicon Valley History Project bibliography in the last chapter requires little modification to add the applications listed above. In the upper frame, which is the main control-panel frame, a link needs to be added to a form for submitting a new book to the bibliography. When the search results from the bibliography are listed, a link within each citation needs to be included—not only to view the synopsis for that citation, but to append new information to the citation. When this link is followed, instead of displaying the synopsis in the lower right frame the program will display a form for appending to the synopsis. Figure 11.1 illustrates the modifications to the layout.

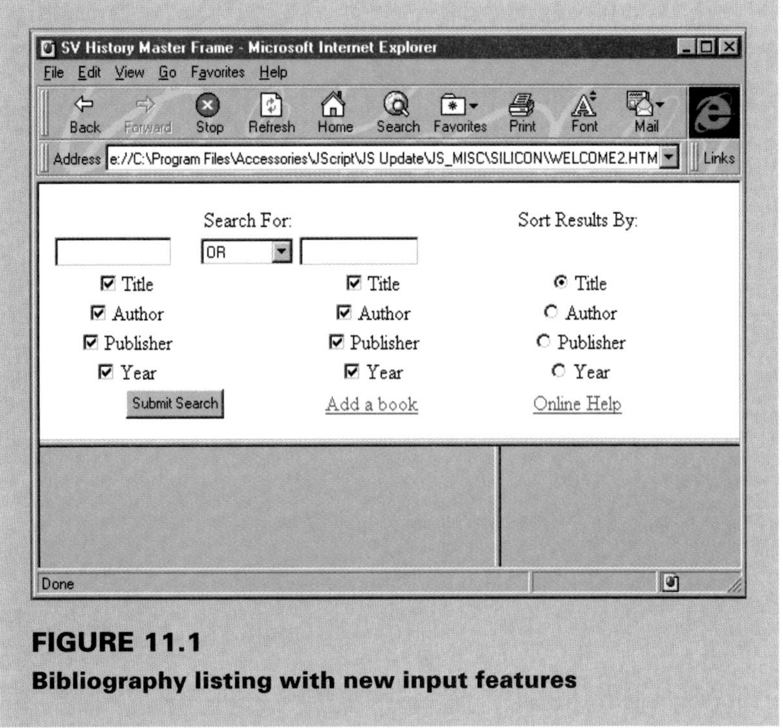


**FIGURE 11.1**
**Bibliography listing with new input features**

We will start by looking at this "synopsis append" feature. At first glance, little here seems to require the help of JScript. The form simply takes a block of text input by the user and submits it through CGI to the Perl program jsmail.cgi, which sends the content of the form as an e-mail message to the Webmaster. Here is the HTML code needed for the form:

```
<HTML>
<HEAD>
<TITLE>Synopsis Append</TITLE>
</HEAD>
<BODY BGCOLOR=#FFFFFF onLoad="top.putTitle()">
<FORM NAME="synsub" METHOD=POST ACTION="/cgi-bin/mail/jsmail.cgi">
<INPUT TYPE="BUTTON" NAME="SUBMIT" VALUE="Submit" onClick=" top.checkSub()">
<P>
<TEXTAREA NAME="Synopsis" ROWS=20 COLS=20>
</TEXTAREA>
</FORM>
</BODY>
</HTML>
```

This is not a particularly complex form that requires extensive validation. Since e-mail is a task that JScript cannot perform, the Perl script is required. If you're curious, here is the Perl script used to send e-mail:

```
#!/usr/bin/perl
#This script receives input from a form, and generates
#an email message containing the form data. Currently
#it takes PUT method input.
#
$mailto = "markst\@kudonet.com";          #change this variable to the
                                          #desired email destination.
print "Content-type: text/html\n\n";
open(MAIL, "|mail $mailto");
&parsing;
print MAIL "\n\n";
close MAIL;
#
#This subroutine parses name-value pairs for more readable content.
#
sub parsing {
read(STDIN, $in_put, $ENV{'CONTENT_LENGTH'});  #getting forms input
@form_data = split(/&/,$in_put);              #splitting into pairs
foreach $i (@form_data) {
  ($name, $value) = split(/=/,$i);            #splitting pairs
  $value =~ s/%(..)/pack("c",hex($1))/ge;     #turning hex into ASCII
  $value =~ s/\+/" "/ge;                      #turning + into space
  $value =~ s/;/\"."/ge;                      #turning ; into .
  print MAIL "\n$name = $value\n";
}
}
```

JScript can perform one invaluable task for us, however. How do we know which book this form submission is supposed to apply to? The problem here is the stateless nature of the Web. What we want to do is take information from one document—the bibliography listing—and use that information in another document: the form the user submits.

Using conventional CGI methods, we would have to make the bibliography listing itself into a form, submit it to the server, and have the server dynamically generate the "synposis append" form in response to this submission. The server could use information from the bibliography listing to construct the form, thus embedding information from the old document in the new document. This method is not very direct, and it does require the intervention of an additional server process, but it works.

With JScript we can approach the problem more directly. The challenge is to read information from one document and write that information out to another document in some way. JScript does have limitations. It can only read values from objects it recognizes within a document, and once a document has been loaded it can only write to a text-input field, a textarea input field, or a status bar. These limitations are acceptable, however.

The "synopsis append" form has a textarea input field, and this field is the logical place to write information, such as the title of the book the synopsis is for. The question is how to extract the correct title from the bibliography listing based on the link selected by the user.

A link is a JScript object. All we need is a place within that object to embed information about the title of the book to which the link belongs. This could be done in several ways, but one way is to include the book title as a search string in the URL the link points to. In the bibliography search script, then, the function writeBib() needs to be modified. When writing out the link that points to the "synopsis append" form, the title of the book must be written out as the search string, like this:

```
st = books[sortKey[i]].titl;
write('  <A HREF="synsub.htm?' + st + '" TARGET=synopsis');
write(' onClick="top.getTitle(this)">');
write("Add to synopsis</A>");
```

Thus when the user clicks on the link that says "Add to synopsis" for the book *Accidental Empires*, the URL for this link will be "synsub.htm?Accidental Empires" rather than just "synsub.htm".

We've also included a function, getTitle(), for retrieving this information when the user clicks on the link. The getTitle() function illustrates a convenient use of the "this" command. Recall that "this" always refers to the current object. Since the current object in this case is the link, getTitle(this) passes the entire Link object to the function. The function then has to do no more than read the value for the "search" property of this object and strip the "?" off the front of that value. This function is part of a script in the top document. Here is the listing for the whole script:

```
<SCRIPT LANGUAGE="javascript">
<!-
var synTitle; var syn;
```

```
function getTitle(linkname) {
synTitle = linkname.search;
synTitle = synTitle.substring(1, synTitle.length);
}

function putTitle() {
frames[1].frames[1].document.forms[0].Synopsis.value = synTitle;
}

function checkSub() {
with (frames[1].frames[1].document.forms[0]) {
   syn = Synopsis.value
   if (syn.length == 0) {
      alert("Please enter your\nsynopsis before submitting");
   } else {
      top. frames[1].frames[1].document.forms[0].submit();
   }
}
if (syn.length > 0) {
   frames[1].frames[1].location = "thanks.htm";
}
}


//->
</SCRIPT>
```

This script contains two other functions. One simply writes the title out to the textarea field, once the title has been retrieved by the getTitle() function. This function, putTitle(), is triggered by an onLoad event from the document "synsub.htm." This completes the transfer of information from one frame to another.

The other function performs the very limited validation used on this form. The checkSub() function simply checks the user's submission to make sure an empty textarea has not been submitted. If an empty textarea has been submitted, an alert box is displayed and no form is submitted; otherwise the form is submitted. Figures 11.2 and 11.3 show the results of invalid and valid submissions, respectively.

While we could have used a button of "SUBMIT" type on this form, whenever you are performing forms validation it is better to use a plain button and subsequently call the submit method. Aborting a submit event in the face of invalid input is much harder than initiating the submit method in the face of valid input.

Take a moment to trace the activity a typical user might engage in on these pages, and the steps needed by our scripts to keep pace. A user might come to the bibliography looking for books by a particular author, such as Robert Cringley. The user initiates a search for those citations, and gets the result, *Accidental Empires*. After perusing the synopsis for this book, one the user has read, the user might submit some additional comments about the book and move on to another Web site.

In response, we have served up one frameset document, and the documents to reside in each of two frames. One of these "child" documents itself sets two more frames. The other contains a script accepting user input, which is used to dynamically generate a new document for one of the other frames. That dynamically generated document in turn accepts further user input, which is sent for

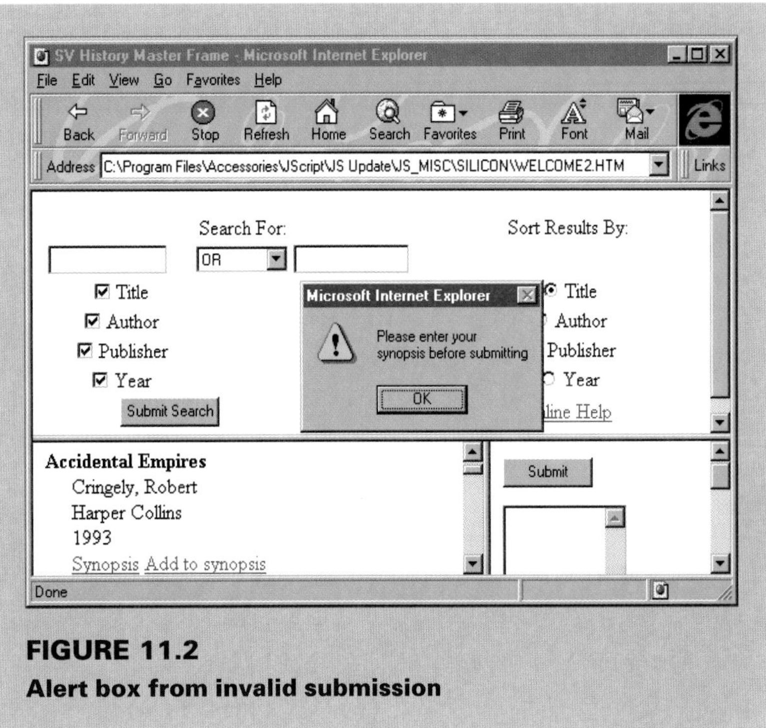


**FIGURE 11.2**
**Alert box from invalid submission**

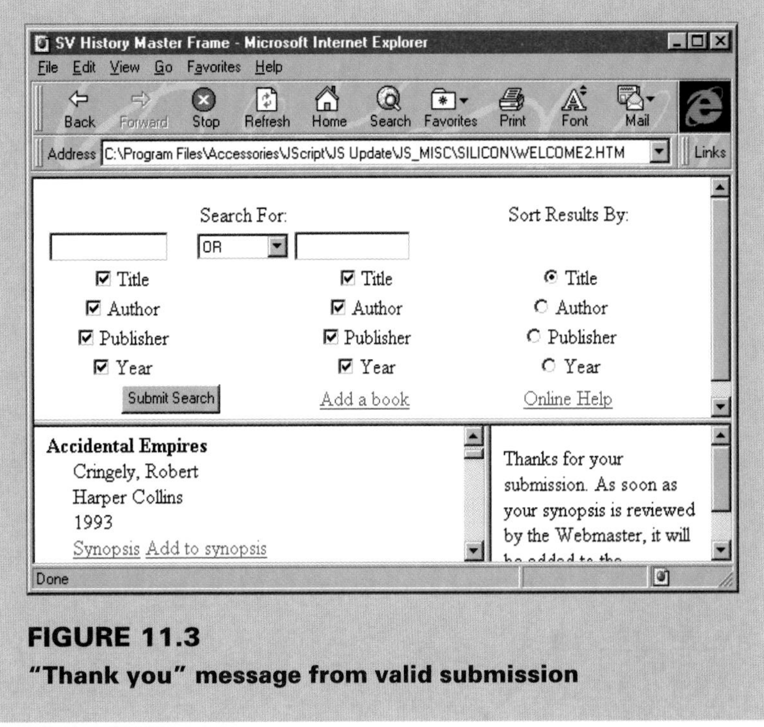


**FIGURE 11.3**
**"Thank you" message from valid submission**

processing to a script in the original top frameset document. This input also generates yet another document in the remaining frame. This document accepts output from the script in the original top frameset document, and also passes user input to that document for processing. If successfully processed, that input will then be sent on to the server, which will hand it off to a CGI application, leaving the user free to wander on.

Amidst this flurry of activity, the notion of the beginning and end of a script starts to lose meaning. In fact, the boundaries between one script and another begin to blur. We have used two different scripts in two different documents, but accepted calls to event handlers from three different documents, and indeed generated the possible event calls to one script dynamically from output of the other script. JScript can perform these feats because of its distributed nature, and that distributed nature is made possible by JScript's object-oriented approach. Well-designed objects, and their associated events and event handlers, will be modular and reasonably self-contained. As long as objects meet these design standards, this sort of distributed programming is not that difficult to script.

## Full Validation

The last step in our database program will be to provide a form for submitting a new book citation and a synopsis to go with that citation. Unlike the previous form submission, this one will require several validation steps.

We also face some design questions. This form will be fairly complex, and will require sufficient room on the screen. Yet we want to fit it consistently into the layout we have used so far, and we want a design that will enable us to reuse as much of the "synopsis append" programming that we did in the last section as possible.

The top frame is the only frame with space for a complicated form, so when the user clicks on "Add a book" from the main control panel, a new form will load in that frame. This means that once the user's submission is completed and validated, it can be displayed in the lower left frame. Since this is the space we have been using for citation displays, this will maintain consistency with the rest of the site. We can also then use the lower right frame for inputting a synopsis, just as we did in the previous example.

Our form needs to provide entry fields for title, author's last name, author's first name, publisher, and publication year; these correspond to the valid fields in the database. We'll also need a button to trigger form validation and submission. Once again we use tables to control the layout of form elements. Figure 11.4 shows the input form; the HTML for this page is listed below.

```
<BODY BGCOLOR=#FFFFFF>
<FORM METHOD=POST ACTION="/cgi-bin/silicon/jsadd.cgi">
<TABLE>

<TR>
<TD COLSPAN=2 WIDTH=300 ALIGN=LEFT>Title: <INPUT TYPE="TEXT"
NAME="title"></TD>
<TD WIDTH=120 ALIGN=RIGHT><INPUT TYPE="BUTTON" NAME="submit" VALUE="Submit
book" onClick="validator()"></TD>
</TR>

<TR>
<TD WIDTH=150 ALIGN=LEFT>Author's last name:
<INPUT TYPE="TEXT" NAME="lname"></TD>
<TD WIDTH=150 ALIGN=LEFT>Author's first name:
<INPUT TYPE="TEXT" NAME="fname"></TD>
<TD></TD>
```

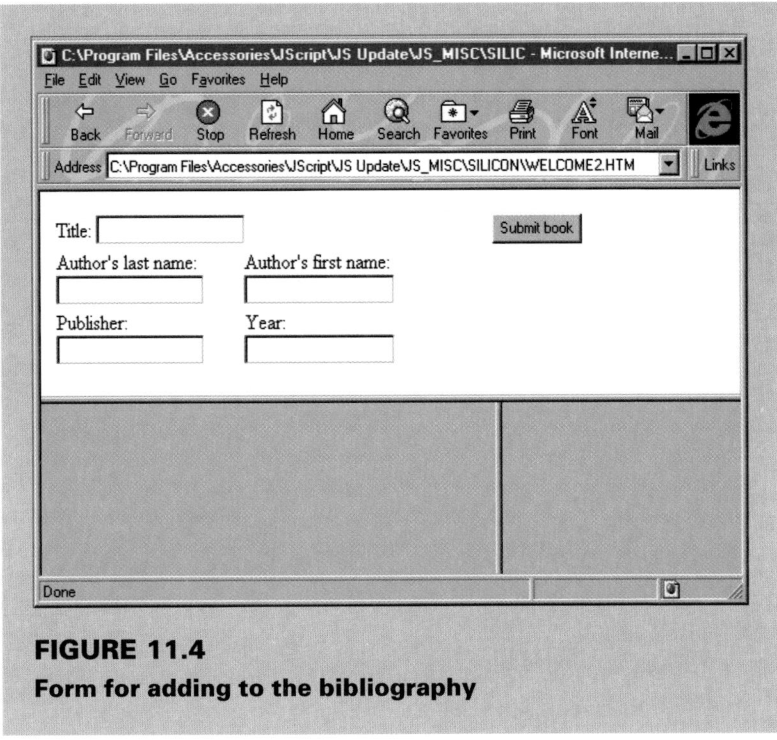


**FIGURE 11.4**
**Form for adding to the bibliography**

```
</TR>

<TR>
<TD WIDTH=150 ALIGN=LEFT>Publisher: <INPUT TYPE="TEXT" NAME="publisher"></TD>
<TD WIDTH=150 ALIGN=LEFT>Year: <INPUT TYPE="TEXT" NAME="year"></TD>
<TD></TD>
</TR>

</TABLE>
</FORM>
</BODY>
```

Input validation depends in part upon determining which input fields are essential, and must have some entry for a valid submission. For the bibliography, clearly the title of the book and the last name of the author are required. We will also choose to make publisher a required field, but not the author's first name and not the publication year. Part of our validation script must check to see that something has been entered for the three required fields. The procedure will be the same as in the last example: measure the length of the value for that field, with a length of 0 indicating no entry, and a length greater than 0 indicating some entry.

Some fields may have requirements that any data entered fit a certain form. Further validation will be required depending on what format the data has to fit. We have, then, four possibilities:

- The entry field must have some entry, and that entry must fit a particular format.
- The entry field must have some entry, but that entry need not fit any particular format.
- The entry field need not have an entry, but anything that is entered must fit a particular format.
- The entry field need not have an entry, nor does anything entered have to fit a particular format.

Neither the title nor publisher field can really have any format requirements. Book titles exhibit no common pattern: almost any string the user enters could conceivably be the title of an actual book. Publishers' names are almost as varied, offering no helpful hints for what format requirements should be.

The author's last name, on the other hand, does have certain restrictions. The only characters that occur in a name are letters of the alphabet, and in some cases—O'Malley, for example—an apostrophe. Any numbers would be out of place. Fortunately this is an easy condition to test for. In JScript strings can be compared using the "greater than" and "less than" operations, and the letters a-z and A-Z are ordered together at the beginning. To validate a name entered, we need to check each character to see that it is a letter of the alphabet. This is easily done using the following function:

```
function alpha(str) {
//checking to see if an entire string is alphabet
//characters only. Return true if it is, false
//otherwise.

var strvalid = 0;
for (i = 0; i < str.length; i++) {
   if ((str.charAt(i) <= "Z") || (str.charAt(i) == "'")) { strvalid++ }
}
strvalid = (strvalid > 0) ? false : true;
return strvalid;
}
```

The key to this function is the test to see if each character is less than or equal to "Z": only letters of the alphabet will pass this test.

Let's look at what we have so far for a validation function. We know that we are going to perform a series of tests on each input field. We want to submit the form only if all of the tests return valid input. Therefore, we need to keep track of the test results. To do so we will use the variable "valid" as a counter. We initialize it to 0, and perform the tests. If it still has a value of 0 when the tests are complete, we will know that all of the input is valid. We will know this because prior to each test, we will increment "valid" by one, and decrement it afterwards only if the test is passed. In other words, "valid" will count how many tests have been failed: if none have been failed, our input is valid.

```
function validator() {
////////////////////////////////////////////////////
//checking to see if all fields are valid. if  //
//valid = 0, then they are. So, for each field,//
//we increment valid if the field is not valid //
//and decrement valid if the field is valid.   //
```

```
///////////////////////////////////////////////////

var valid=0;
var validName;
var validYear;

valid++;
///////////////////////////////////////////////////
//title must have an entry, but the entry could//
//be any string of characters                 //
///////////////////////////////////////////////////
if (document.forms[0].title.value.length == 0) {
   warning("title");
} else {
   valid-;
valid++;
///////////////////////////////////////////////////
//author last name must have an entry, and only//
//alphabet characters are permitted            //
///////////////////////////////////////////////////
if (document.forms[0].lname.value. length == 0) {
   warning("author's last name");
} else {
   validName = alpha(document.forms[0].lname.value);
   if (validName == false) {
      warning("author's last name");
   } else {
      valid-;
   }
}
```

Thus far we have performed two tests. First, we have tested to see if the title entry has positive length. This is the only requirement for title, namely that there be one. For author's last name this same test is performed, because we must have some entry, but a second test is nested within the first. This is a function call to alpha() to verify that the name contains only letters of the alphabet. Figure 11.5 illustrates the results of entering invalid input for a field, in this case an author's last name.

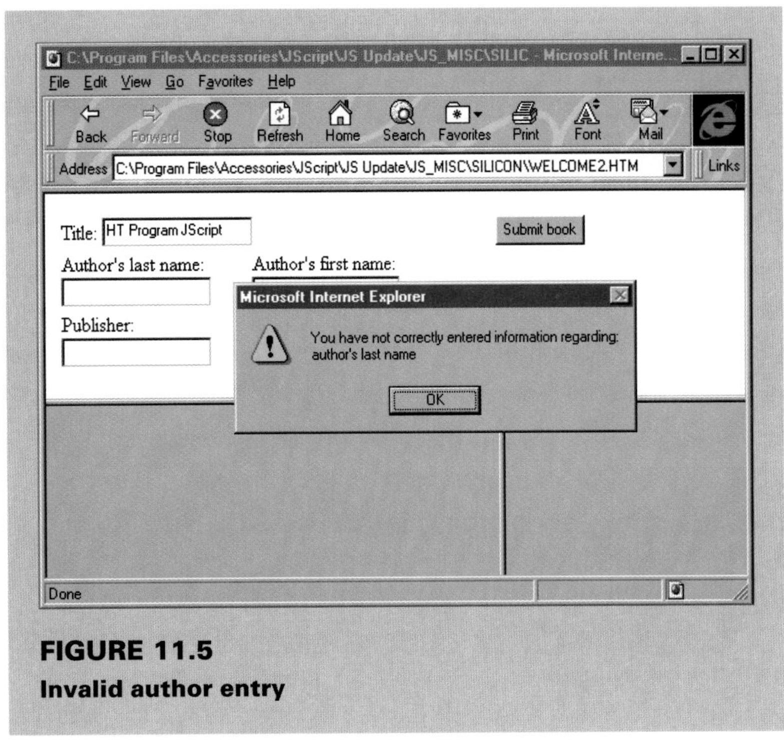


**FIGURE 11.5**
**Invalid author entry**

Author's first name represents a field where input is not required. Hence we need not do any test on the length of the input entry. However, whatever has been entered must conform to the same requirements as with Author's last name: it must be composed only of letters from the alphabet. The test will thus include only a call to the alpha() function.

Publisher, on the other hand, has the same requirements as title: there must be some entry, but it need not fit any particular format. Continuing our validation tests, then, we have:

```
valid++;
//////////////////////////////////////////////
//author first name need not have an entry,  //
//but if it has one, it must have only alpha-//
//bet characters.                            //
//////////////////////////////////////////////
validName = alpha(document.forms[Ø].fname.value);
if (validName == false) {
   warning("author's first name");
} else {
   valid–;
}
valid++;
//////////////////////////////////////////////
//publisher must have an entry, but the entry//
//could be any string of characters          //
//////////////////////////////////////////////
if (document.forms[Ø].publisher.value.length == Ø) {
   warning("publisher");
```

```
} else {
   valid–;
}
```

Surprisingly, the most difficult field to validate is publication year. Any two-digit number could be a valid publication year with an implied "19" in front: "89," for example, would imply a publication year of 1989. We could, of course, insist that the user enter the "19" as well, but that would be a poor design decision. JScript can make this adjustment easily enough on its own, so we shouldn't ask the user to do extra work for us.

Besides two-digit numbers, we can only accept zero-digit numbers—no entry at all—or four-digit numbers, but only if they begin with "19." The full validation test must therefore ask all these questions:

- Is it a number?
- Does it have zero digits?
- Does it have two digits?
- Does it have four digits?
- If it has four digits, are the first two "19"?

This leads to a rather complicated series of nested "if" statements:

```
valid++;
//////////////////////////////////////////////////
//publication year need not have an entry, but //
//if it has one, it must have either two digits//
//or four digits, and if it has four, the first//
//two must be "19".                            //
//////////////////////////////////////////////////
pyear = document.forms[0].year.value;
validYear = numb(pyear);
if (validYear == false) {
   ////////////////////
   //wasn't a number.//
   ////////////////////
   warning("publication year");
} else {
   if (((pyear.length != 2) && (pyear.length != 4)) && (pyear.length != 0)) {
```

```
            //////////////////////////////////
            //wasn't a 2 or 4 digit number.//
            //////////////////////////////////
            warning("publication year");
        } else {
            if ((pyear.length == 4) && (pyear.substring(Ø,2) != "19")) {
                //////////////////////////////////////////////////
                //wasn't a 4 digit number starting with "19".//
                //////////////////////////////////////////////////
                warning("publication year");
            } else {
                valid—;
            }
        }
    }
}
```

If all these conditions are met, then the new citation can be submitted, and we can move on to asking the user for a synopsis. The last lines of the validator() function contain a few subtleties:

```
if (valid == Ø) {
    if (pyear.length == Ø) {
        pyear = "unknown"
        document.forms[Ø].year.value = pyear;
    }
    if (pyear.length == 2) {
        pyear = "19" + pyear;
        document.forms[Ø].year.value = pyear;
    }
}
document.forms[Ø].submit();
msg="Thanks for your submission.\nAdd a synopsis?";
if (confirm(msg)) {
    synopURL = "synsub.htm?" + newTitle;
    top.frames[1].frames[1].location=synopURL;
}
with (top.frames[1].frames[Ø].document {
    writeln("<HTML><HEAD></HEAD><BODY BGCOLOR=#FFFFFF><DL>");
```

```
        writeln("<DT><B>" + newTitle + "</B>");
        writeln("<DD>" + newAuthL + ", " + newAuthF);
        writeln("<DD>" + newPub);
        writeln("<DD>" + pyear);
        writeln("</DL></BODY></HTML>");
    }
    document.location="http://www.kudonet.com/~markst/silicon/search.htm";
    }
    valid = 0;
    }
```

We do make some last-minute adjustments to publication year prior to form submission, adding the "19" if needed, and changing any blank entry to "unknown." Also, whenever we reach the end of the validator() function, "valid" must be reset to 0—otherwise the next time the function is called after the user corrects input, the validation process will start with the mistaken assumption that there are already errors.

A confirm dialog box is used to query the user on whether or not to add a synopsis: see Figure 11.6. This is not the only way to handle this step, but it serves a dual purpose here. Immediately before presenting this dialog box, the form data is submitted. Immediately after that, the top frame is reloaded with our main control panel, "search.html." The intervening dialog box assures that there will be some pause between these two events while the user responds to the dialog box, even if the pause is only a few seconds. Why is this important? The Perl script called by the form, "jsadd.cgi," not only sends an e-mail message to the Webmaster about the new submission, but it also immediately updates the

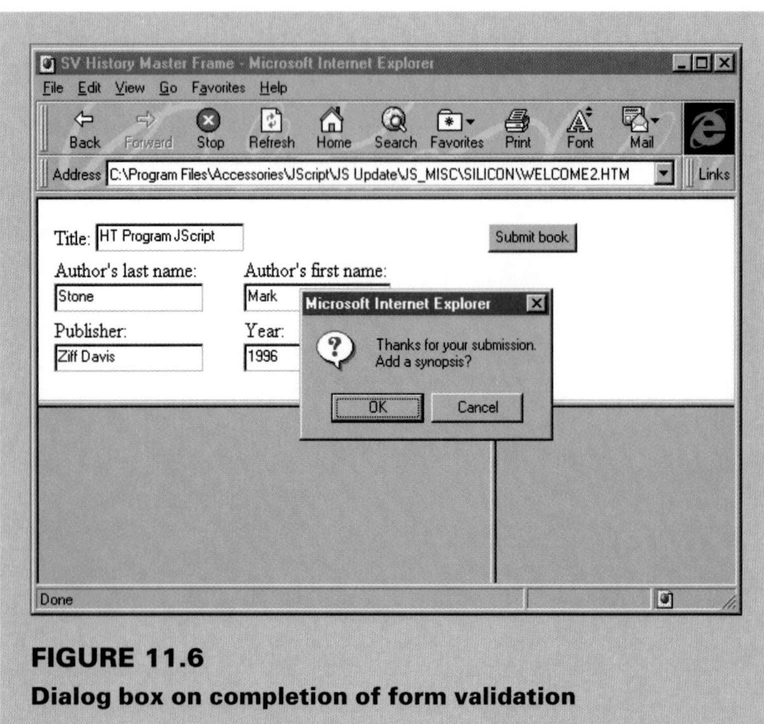


**FIGURE 11.6**
**Dialog box on completion of form validation**

database by adding the new citation to it. However, with JScript we do not have separate files for the database and the script that handle queries to it. The file "search.htm" is both our query program and the file that stores the database itself. In other words, the Perl script is going to modify the file that our JScript program is about to load into the current frame.

By inducing the user to pause at this point, and by specifying the file with its full URL, http://www.kudonet.com/~markst/silicon/search.html, we increase the chances that the file will have been updated by the time it is asked for again, and that the user's browser will reload the updated file rather than displaying a cached copy of it that does not contain the latest information. On the Internet there are no certainties. Depending on network traffic and routing choices made by machines along the path between browser and server, it is perfectly possible for the request to load "search.htm" to arrive at the server before the form data. If all goes smoothly, though, users should be able to immediately query a bibliography that already contains their submission.

Here, then, is our full forms submission and validation document:

```
<HTML><HEAD>
<SCRIPT LANGUAGE="javascript">
<!-
var msg; var str; var i; var num; var pyear;
var newTitle; var newAuthL; var newAuthF; var newPub;

function validator() {
//////////////////////////////////////////////////
//checking to see if all fields are valid. if  //
//valid = 0, then they are. So, for each field,//
//we increment valid if the field is not valid //
//and decrement valid if the field is valid.   //
//////////////////////////////////////////////////

var valid=0;
var validName;
var validYear;

valid++;
//////////////////////////////////////////////////
//title must have an entry, but the entry could//
//be any string of characters                  //
```

```
/////////////////////////////////////////////////
if (document.forms[0].title.value.length == 0) {
   warning("title");
} else {
   valid-;
   newTitle = document.forms[0].title.value;
}
valid++;
/////////////////////////////////////////////////
//author last name must have an entry, and only//
//alphabet characters are permitted            //
/////////////////////////////////////////////////
if (document.forms[0].lname.value.length == 0) {
   warning("author's last name");
} else {
   validName = alpha(document.forms[0].lname.value);
   if (validName == false) {
      warning("author's last name");
   } else {
      valid-;
      newAuthL = document.forms[0].lname.value;
   }
}
valid++;
///////////////////////////////////////////////
//author first name need not have an entry,  //
//but if it has one, it must have only alpha-//
//bet characters.                            //
///////////////////////////////////////////////
validName = alpha(document.forms[0].fname.value);
if (validName == false) {
   warning("author's first name");
} else {
   valid-;
   newAuthF = document.forms[0].fname.value;
}
valid++;
///////////////////////////////////////////////
```

```
//publisher must have an entry, but the entry//
//could be any string of characters          //
///////////////////////////////////////////////
if (document.forms[0].publisher.value.length == 0) {
   warning("publisher");
} else {
   valid-;
   newPub = document.forms[0].publisher. value;
}
valid++;
/////////////////////////////////////////////////
//publication year need not have an entry, but //
//if it has one, it must have either two digits//
//or four digits, and if it has four, the first//
//two must be "19".                            //
/////////////////////////////////////////////////
pyear = document.forms[0].year.value;
validYear = numb(pyear);
if (validYear == false) {
   ////////////////////
   //wasn't a number.//
   ////////////////////
   warning("publication year");
} else {
   if (((pyear.length != 2) && (pyear.length != 4)) && (pyear.length != 0)) {
      //////////////////////////////////
      //wasn't a 2 or 4 digit number.//
      //////////////////////////////////
      warning("publication year");
   } else {
      if ((pyear.length == 4) && (pyear.substring(0,2) != "19")) {
         ///////////////////////////////////////////////
         //wasn't a 4 digit number starting with "19".//
         ///////////////////////////////////////////////
         warning("publication year");
      } else {
         valid-;
      }
```

```
      }
   }
   }
   if (valid == Ø) {
      alert("OK!")
      if (pyear.length == Ø) {
         pyear = "unknown"
    document.forms[Ø].year.value = pyear;
      }
      if (pyear.length == 2) {
         pyear = "19" + pyear;
    document.forms[Ø].year.value = pyear;
      }
   }
   document.forms[Ø].submit();
   msg="Thanks for your submission.\nAdd a synopsis?";
   if (confirm(msg)) {
      synopURL = "synsub.htm?" + newTitle;
    top.frames[1].frames[1].location =synopURL;
   }
   with (top.frames[1].frames[Ø].document) {
      writeln("<HTML><HEAD></HEAD><BODY BGCOLOR=#FFFFFF><DL>");
      writeln("<DT><B>" + newTitle + "</B>");
      writeln("<DD>" + newAuthL + ", " + newAuthF);
      writeln("<DD>" + newPub);
      writeln("<DD>" + pyear);
      writeln("</DL></BODY></HTML>");
   }
   document.location="http://www.kudonet.com/~markst/silicon/search.htm";
   }
   valid = Ø;
   }

   function warning(msg) {
   msg = "You have not correctly entered information regarding:\n" + msg;
   alert(msg);
   }
```

```
function alpha(str) {
//checking to see if an entire string is alphabet
//characters only. Return true if it is, false
//otherwise.

var strvalid = 0;
for (i = 0; i < str.length; i++) {
   if ((str.charAt(i) < "Z") || (str.charAt(i) == "'")) { strvalid++ }
}
strvalid = (strvalid > 0) ? false : true;
return strvalid;
}

function numb(num) {
//checking to see if an entire string is digit
//characters only. Return true if it is, false
//otherwise.

var numvalid = 0; var j;
for (i = 0; i < num.length; i++) {
   j = parseInt(num.charAt(i));
   if (!((j <= 9) && (j >= 0))) { numvalid++ }
}
numvalid = (numvalid > 0) ? false : true;

return numvalid;
}

//->
</SCRIPT>
</HEAD>
<BODY BGCOLOR=#FFFFFF>

<FORM>
<TABLE>

<TR>
<TD COLSPAN=2 WIDTH=300 ALIGN=LEFT>Title: <INPUT TYPE="TEXT"
```

```
NAME="title"></TD>
<TD WIDTH=120 ALIGN=RIGHT><INPUT TYPE="BUTTON" NAME="submit" VALUE="Submit
book" onClick="validator()"></TD>
</TR>

<TR>
<TD WIDTH=150 ALIGN=LEFT>Author's last name:
<INPUT TYPE="TEXT" NAME="lname"></TD>
<TD WIDTH=150 ALIGN=LEFT>Author's first name:
<INPUT TYPE="TEXT" NAME="fname"></TD>
<TD></TD>
</TR>

<TR>
<TD WIDTH=150 ALIGN=LEFT>Publisher: <INPUT TYPE="TEXT" NAME="publisher"></TD>
<TD WIDTH=150 ALIGN=LEFT>Year: <INPUT TYPE="TEXT" NAME="year"></TD>
<TD></TD>
</TR>

</TABLE>
</FORM>
</BODY>
</HTML>
```

If you are interested, the Perl script that enables this is as follows:

```
#!/usr/bin/perl
#This script receives input from a form, and generates
#both an e-mail message of the form content, and a data
#file append of the form content, feeding back to the form
#submitter an opportunity to view the updated data file
#in HTML format.
#Currently it only takes GET method input.
#
$in_put = $ENV{'QUERY_STRING'};
$mailto = "markst\@kudonet.com";        #change this variable to the
                                        #desired email destination.
print "Content-type: text/html\n\n";
open(MAIL, "|mail $mailto");
```

```
&parsing;
print MAIL "\n\n";
close MAIL;
open(BIBLIO_IN, "../../silicon/search.htm");
open(BIBLIO_OUT, ">../../silicon/search.bak");
while (<BIBLIO_IN>) {
  if (/"end of initializer"/) {
    print BIBLIO_OUT $title;
    print BIBLIO_OUT $lname;
    print BIBLIO_OUT $fname;
    print BIBLIO_OUT $pub;
    print BIBLIO_OUT $year;
  }
  print BIBLIO_OUT $_;
}
close(BIBLIO_IN);
close(BIBLIO_OUT);
open(BIBLIO_IN, "../../silicon/search.bak");
open(BIBLIO_OUT, ">../../silicon/search.htm");
while (<BIBLIO_IN>) {
  print BIBLIO_OUT;
}
close(BIBLIO_IN);
close(BIBLIO_OUT);
#
#This subroutine parses name-value pairs for more readable content.
#
sub parsing {
@form_data = split(/&/,$in_put);   #splitting into pairs
foreach $i (@form_data) {
  ($name, $value) = split(/=/,$i); #splitting pairs
  $value =~ s/%(..)/pack("c",hex($1))/ge; #turning hex into ASCII
  $value =~ s/\+/" "/ge;           #turning + into space
  $value =~ s/;/\"."/ge;           #turning ; into .
  if ($name eq "title") {
    $title = "books[i].titl = \"" + $value + "\";\n";
  }
 if ($name eq "lname") {
```

```
        $lname = "books[i].authorLName = \"" + $value + "\";\n";
    }
  if ($name eq "fname") {
        $fname = "books[i].authorFName = \"" + $value + "\";\n";
    }
  if ($name eq "publisher") {
        $pub = "books[i].publisher = \"" + $value + "\";\n";
    }
  if ($name eq "year") {
        $year = "books[i].yr = \"" + $value + "\";\n";
    }
  print MAIL "\n$name = $value\n";
  }
  }
```

This Perl script plays on Perl's greatest strength, namely its impressive arsenal of tools for searching and manipulating strings. We know that the database portion of "search.htm" ends just before this line in the program:

```
}//end of initializer;
```

For Perl it is a simple matter to read the file until finding that line, and then to write out to a file the new entry that is now to precede this line. Because we know what format JScript will be expecting, we can ask Perl to write out the new lines in the form of JScript code as we need them.

Permitting this sort of user input is risky. An oversight in form validation could allow a submission that corrupts the file. Even a mild oversight could allow a database entry that, while not damaging the file, would introduce an error into the JScript query program. So you want to implement an example like this with great care.

Still, the example does demonstrate the power of combining JScript with CGI. JScript provides a way to provide immediate response to user queries, and a means for sustaining information across multiple frames or windows. This means that unlike conventional CGI applications, this combination won't leave your users idle as they wait for the server to receive query requests, run a CGI process, and return a reply. Nor will the server be overburdened by processes that can be more easily handled on the client side by JScript. With CGI, however, you have the means to make a permanent record based on user interactions. The combination of JScript and CGI can give you a Web site that is dynamic and constantly changing.

In the last two chapters we have looked at JScript examples under Internet Explorer that can just as easily serve as JavaScript examples under Netscape Navigator. Given the prevalance of Navigator and the diversity of the Web, designing with this kind of crossplatform compatibility in mind is important. Yet by restricting our applications to those that are compatible with Navigator, we limit the possibilities, and miss out on those features that distinguish JScript from JavaScript. In the next chapter we will conclude our survey of JScript applications by looking at the potential of JScript's distinctive ActiveX features.

Managing Frames: Giving Your Pages a Fluid Look

Performing the Calculations

Charting New Territory

Chapter 12

# Extending JScript with ActiveX

The 1996 NBA finals shaped up as a classic defensive struggle between two great defensive teams, the Chicago Bulls and the Seattle Supersonics. Yet this was supposed to be a season in which rules changes favored offense. So which was more important to success in the NBA: offense or defense? The answer to a question like this depends on establishing a correlation. Is scoring points more strongly correlated with winning, or is preventing your opponent from scoring points more strongly correlated with winning?

Computers provide marvelous tools for statistical analysis. Performing calculations on large tables of numbers is just the sort of task at which people tend to make errors, but at which computers excel. The application that really launched the PC revolution made businesses see the PC as a tool and not a toy: namely, the first spreadsheet program, Visicalc.

In today's world of graphical user interfaces, we expect computers to do more than just manage data, though. We expect them to help us visualize data. That's why Microsoft's core suite of office applications includes not just a spreadsheet (Excel) and a database (Access) but also a graphical presentation program, PowerPoint. That's why both Excel and Microsoft Works include chart and table functions as extensions of their spreadsheet capabilities, and that's why the Chart control is one of the first ActiveX controls Microsoft programmed beyond the basic HTML object controls.

The example presented in this chapter is simple enough. The program will permit the user to enter two columns of data, measure a correlation between them, and graph the results. The implications of this sort of JScript program are far-reaching, however. As with other programs, the most difficult part of this program to develop is the user interface; the actual calculations can be programmed in a few lines. So although this program stops at calculations of correlation, it could easily be extended to cover a range of statistical analyses.

Furthermore, while this program is demonstrated running within Internet Explorer, it is not an especially Web-centric application. This sort of program could be useful in a wide variety of situations, from the desktop to the Internet. In fact, this program could be set up to run on its own. Microsoft makes the JScript binary freely available for anyone to license, allowing scripts to be coupled with the binary to form standalone applications.

Development of this program also relies heavily on the ActiveX Control Pad. The Control Pad provides an easy mechanism for trying out different configurations of the Chart control to find one that looks right, and then performs HTML coding that would be quite difficult to do by hand.

These last two points demonstrate what makes Microsoft JScript a unique product, and not just a copy of JavaScript. A JScript application can run in any ActiveX host with a scripting interface, and Internet Explorer 3.0 is just one such host. JavaScript, on the other hand, is confined to the limitations of a Web browser. As we will see, JScript applications can also interact with ActiveX controls, expanding your ability to bring active content to your Web pages. So close down Netscape Navigator for awhile, and open up Internet Explorer. This is a chapter to show you how far you can go with that platform.

*You must be using a registered, final-release version of Internet Explorer 3.0 to view the Chart control used in this chapter. This and other ActiveX controls that extend the intrinsic HTML set are not included in the beta releases of Internet Explorer 3.0.*

## Managing Frames: Giving Your Pages a Fluid Look

Ironically, one of the program models that can be challenging to implement in JScript is the traditional linear program. When a Perl script runs from the command line in a terminal session, events unfold in a sequence of steps. The program prompts the user for input, the user responds, the program processes the input and asks for more, and so on. The user is led step by step from the beginning of the session to the end. In this model, there is no issue about displaying input and output. Perl simply updates the command line with new output, and expects the user to update the command line with new input. Even though the command line is just a single line, it can be continuously updated. As limited as the command line interface is, it does allow this kind of flow.

A window or frame in JScript does not behave this way. JScript expects an entire document to be written to a frame or window, and provides no way for document output to be modified by user input within that same document. You can use a text-input field or a textarea-input field as a window for displaying input and output much like a command line. However, this approach works only when that input and output can be confined to text and confined to command-line-style interactions. One major reason for programming in JScript in the first place is to get away from the limitations of simple text as an interface. But how do we reestablish the sense of program flow within a linear program?

The correlation program follows a linear model:

1 Query the user for the names and number of data items to be input.

2 Receive input data from the user.

3 Calculate and display the degree of correlation.

4 Graph the data that has been input.

What JScript can do is use information from one frame to dynamically generate another frame or window. The program presents a virtual slide-show. The user is directed from one frame or window to the next, step by step, with the information presented at each step conditional on the results of the previous step. If frames are designed and managed carefully, the program will flow from one step to the next in a manner that feels completely natural to the user.

A number of desktop applications allow graphics to be directly linked to data in order to help visualize data. This sort of effect has been difficult to achieve on a Web page, yet the correlation program leads to this striking result. Not only will we invoke the ActiveX Chart control with this program, but we will use JScript to dynamically set the parameters for the chart. While we will be using the chart specifically to illustrate the degree of correlation, this same program could be used to display any two columns of data as a pair of lines on a graph.

So what about defense versus offense in the NBA? We will limit our analysis to the four teams that made the conference finals in 1996: the Chicago Bulls, the Orlando Magic, the Seattle Supersonics, and the Utah Jazz. We want to look at how many points they scored and how many points they allowed, and see which more strongly correlates with how many games they won. Table 12.1 shows the data we'll be working with.

Our first steps will be querying the user for information about the data to be entered, and then setting up an input area based on that input. Figure 12.1 shows the opening frames for the program.

**TABLE 12.1 SCORING AND DEFENSE IN THE NBA**

| Team | Games Won | Points per Game Scored | Points per Game Allowed |
|---|---|---|---|
| Bulls | 72 | 105.2 | 92.9 |
| Magic | 60 | 104.5 | 99.0 |
| Supersonics | 64 | 104.5 | 96.7 |
| Jazz | 55 | 102.5 | 95.9 |

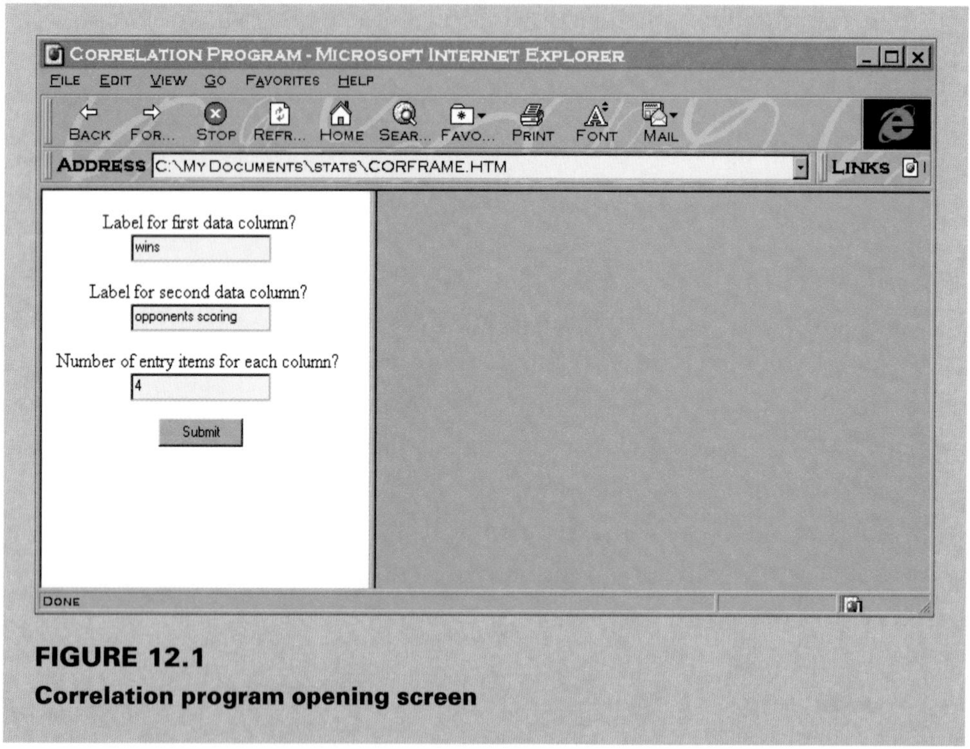


**FIGURE 12.1**
**Correlation program opening screen**

The HTML for the <FRAMESET> document is

```
<FRAMESET COLS="240, 400">
   <FRAME SRC="corrprog.htm" NAME="correlateProgram">
   <FRAME SRC="blank.htm" NAME="correlateData">
</FRAMESET>
</HTML>
```

The main script will reside in the <HEAD></HEAD> portion of this document, as both the "correlateProgram" frame and the "correlateData" frame will change during the course of the program. The width of the frames is also rigidly forced at 640 pixels, so that we will know exactly how many pixels we have to work with for data-entry fields later on.

Our initial form is in the document "corrprog.htm." The HTML for this document is

```
<HTML>
<HEAD>
<TITLE>Correlation Controls</TITLE>
</HEAD>
<BODY BGCOLOR=#FFFFFF>
<FORM>
<CENTER>
Label for first data column?
<BR><INPUT TYPE="TEXT" NAME="nOne">
<P>
Label for second data column?
<BR><INPUT TYPE="TEXT" NAME="nTwo">
<P>
Number of entry items for each column?
<BR><INPUT TYPE="TEXT" NAME="iNum">
<P>
<INPUT TYPE="BUTTON" VALUE="Submit" onClick="top.writeEntry()">
</CENTER>
</FORM>
</BODY>
</HTML>
```

This is a very simple form, but it will provide the data needed to generate the next frame in the program. This frame will be generated dynamically by the function writeEntry().

In this example, as shown in Figure 12.1, we enter "wins" and "opponents scoring" as the data fields to be entered, and we have four teams. This input will be read by the function writeEntry():

```
function writeEntry() {
var i; var j; var val = "";
//////////////////////////////////////////
// reading the values from forms input //
//////////////////////////////////////////
nameOne = frames[Ø].document.forms[Ø].nOne.value;
```

```
nameTwo = frames[0].document.forms[0].nTwo.value;
itemNum = frames[0].document.forms[0].iNum.value;
len = itemNum;
////////////////////////////////////////////
// writing out an HTML form to a frame //
////////////////////////////////////////////
with (frames[1].document) {
   writeln("<HTML><HEAD></HEAD><BODY BGCOLOR=#FFFFFF>");
   writeln("<FORM><TABLE>");
   writeln("<TR><TH WIDTH=200 ALIGN=CENTER>");
   writeln(nameOne + "</TH><TH WIDTH=200 ALIGN=CENTER>");
   writeln(nameTwo + "</TH></TR>");
   for (i = 1; i <= len; i++) {
      writeln("<TR>");
      for (j = 1; j <= 2; j++) {
         writeln("<TD WIDTH=200 ALIGN=CENTER>");
         writeln("<INPUT TYPE=TEXT VALUE=\"" + val + "\"></TD>");
      }
      writeln("</TR>");
   }
   writeln("</TABLE></FORM></BODY></HTML>");
}
frames[1].document.close();
//////////////////////////////////////////////////////
// loading a new document into the other frame //
//////////////////////////////////////////////////////
frames[0].location = "chartit.htm";
}
```

This function writes a new document into the “correlateData” frame. The document displays a table that has two columns, using the field names entered by the user as the head of each column, and in each column displaying a text-entry field for as many data records as the user indicated.

Figure 12.2 shows the results of processing the form input shown in Figure 12.1.

The function also replaces the document in the “correlateProgram” frame, removing “corrprog.htm” and instead loading “chartit.htm.” This is the slide-show effect: we start the user with one frame, direct the user’s attention to a new frame, and nudge the user along by removing the original frame and replacing it with yet another. The effect is to move the user through the steps in the right sequence, while retaining the event-driven feel of an object-oriented interface.

This is the HTML for "chartit.htm":

```
<HTML>
<HEAD>
<TITLE>Output Results</TITLE>
</HEAD>
<BODY BGCOLOR=#FFFFFF>
<FORM>
Please enter your data in the entry fields of the adjoining frame. When you
have finished, you may measure the correlation or chart the results.
<P>
<CENTER>
<INPUT TYPE="BUTTON" NAME="correlate" VALUE="Measure correlation"
onClick="top.correlate()">
<BR>
<INPUT TYPE="TEXT" NAME="Output">
<P>
<INPUT TYPE="BUTTON" NAME="chart" VALUE="Chart results" onClick=
```

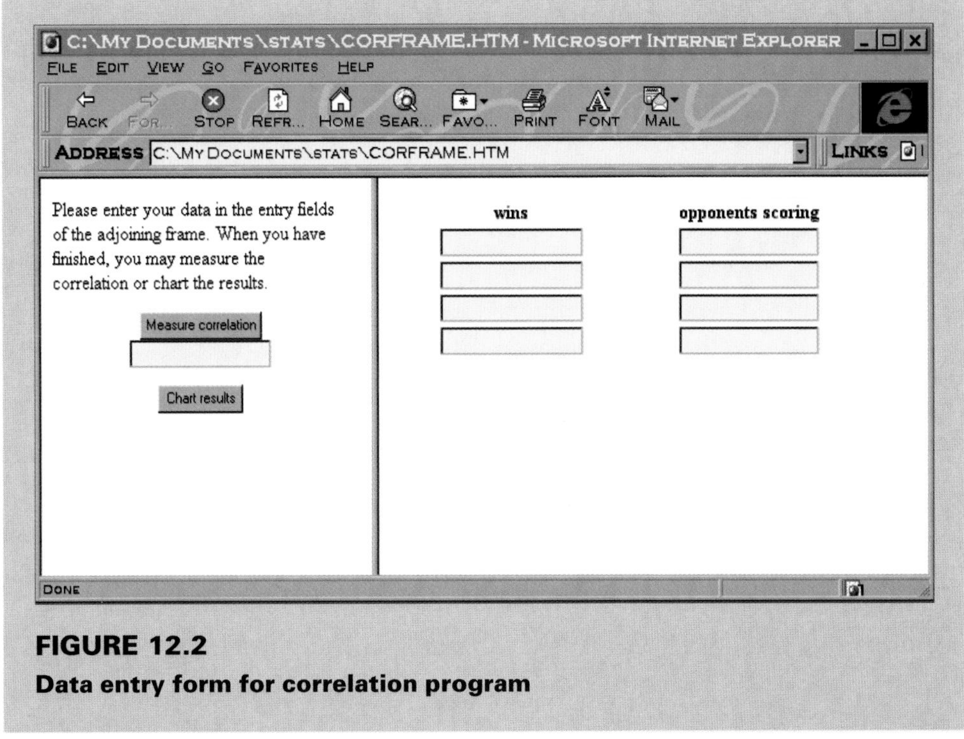


**FIGURE 12.2**
**Data entry form for correlation program**

```
"top.chartit()">
</CENTER>
</FORM>
</BODY>
</HTML>
```

## Performing the Calculations

The formula for measuring correlation is a bit complicated, but can be found in any standard statistics textbook. Suppose we have two columns of data, x and y. We will signify the average value for x, or the mean of x, by $\bar{x}$ and the average, or mean, of y by $\bar{y}$. Then the formula is this:

$$\text{correlation} = \frac{\Sigma(x_i - x)(y_i - y)}{\sqrt{\Sigma(x_i - \bar{x})^2}\ \sqrt{\Sigma(y_i - \bar{y})^2}}$$

If we graphed two columns of data using each as one axis for the graph, then we would have a perfect correlation if all of our data points fell on a diagonal line. The correlation would be positive on a rising diagonal, and negative on a descending diagonal. Roughly, the formula above measures the slope of the diagonal, and how far the data points vary from that diagonal.

Because this formula involves calculating three different sums over the entire body of data, it can be a tedious formula to calculate by hand. This is just the sort of task a computer can easily automate. In our correlation program, summation is handled with a "for" loop:

```
for (i = 1; i <= len; i++) {
   table[i].varOne = table[i].colOne - oneMean;
  table[i].varTwo = table[i].colTwo - twoMean;
   variance += table[i].varOne*table[i].varTwo;
   devOne += table[i].varOne*table[i].varOne;
   devTwo += table[i].varTwo*table[i].varTwo;
}
```

This loop iterates through an entire data table, which has four fields. It has two columns for data, called table[].colOne and table[].colTwo, and two columns for storing the variance of each data item from the mean for that data column, table[].varOne and table[].varTwo. Once the summations have been performed, the correlation can be calculated and displayed in just two steps:

```
corr = variance/(Math.sqrt(devOne)*Math.sqrt(devTwo));
frames[0].document.forms[0].Output.value = "Correlation = " + corr;
```

To make the whole calculation work, we just need to initialize the table[] array by gathering data from user input and reading it into the array. These steps are broken out into a separate function, gatherData(). In order to chart the data, we will also need to read user input into the same array. Since two separate functions need to perform the same task, good modular design dictates that we make a separate function out of that task:

```
function gatherData() {
var i = 0;
var j;
table = new MakeArray(len);
for (i = 1; i <= len; i++) {
   table[i] = new columns(0,0,0,0);
}
for (i = 1; i <= len; i++) {
   table[i].colOne = 0;
   table[i].colTwo = 0;
   table[i].varOne = 0;
   table[i].varTwo = 0;
}
for (i = 1; i <= len; i++) {
   with (frames[1].document.forms[0]) {
      table[i].colOne = parseFloat(elements[2*(i-1)].value);
      table[i].colTwo = parseFloat(elements[(2*(i-1))+1].value);
   }
}
}

function columns(c1, c2, v1, v2) {
   this.colOne = c1;
   this.colTwo = c2;
   this.varOne = v1;
   this.varTwo = v2;
}
```

```
function MakeArray(n) {
this.length = n;
for (i = 1; i  <=n; i++) {
   this[i] = 0;
}
return this;
}
```

This code should look very familiar by now. We create a one-dimensional array that we want to use as a two-dimensional table, and so we use a function to add properties to the array, one property for each field of data in our table. Then we simply iterate through each text-input field in the frame, and read in the input from the user.

Figure 12.3 shows the results of entering the NBA data for number of wins and opponents' points allowed. Correlation will produce a number between 0 and 1 or, in the case of negative correlation, between 0 and -1. A result of 1 or -1 would indicate a perfect correlation.

As we would expect, charting the numbers for allowing points and wins results in a strong negative correlation, to a degree of about -0.65. The fewer points a

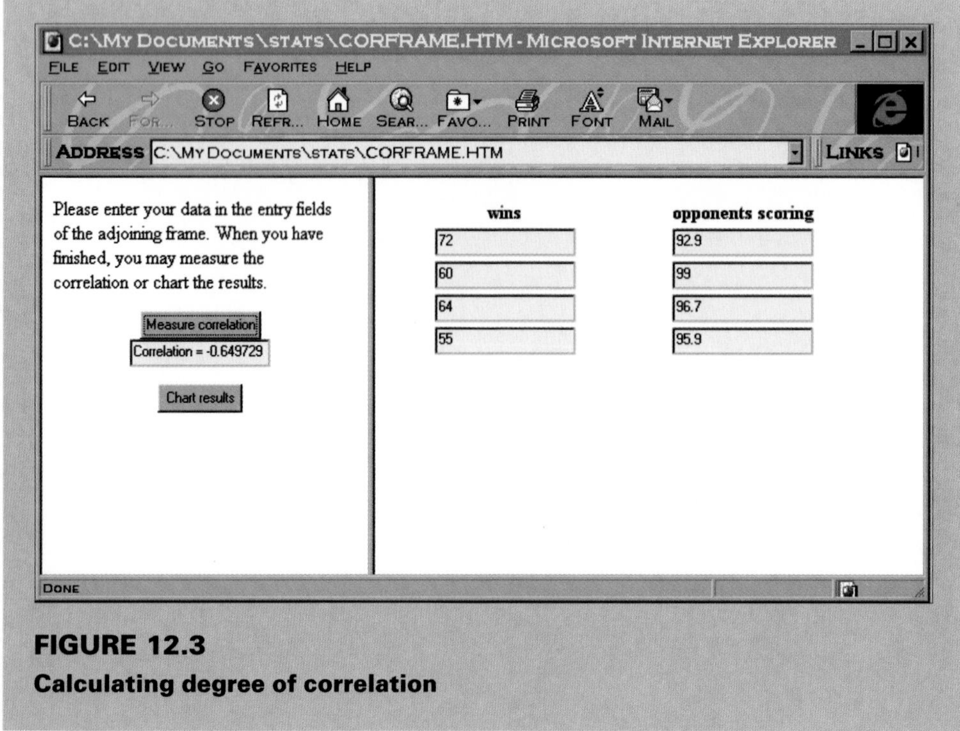


**FIGURE 12.3**
**Calculating degree of correlation**

team allows, the more likely it is to win. When we enter the data for number of wins per points scored, though, the result is surprising: an even higher degree of correlation, roughly 0.88. So for these four teams, at least, offense correlated with winning more than defense did. Well, as they say, offense wins games, but defense wins championships.

The full program listing for producing this result is given below.

```
function correlate() {
var oneSum = 0; var twoSum = 0; var oneMean; var twoMean;
var i; var j; var variance = 0;
var devOne = 0; var devTwo = 0;
gatherData()
//////////////////////////////////
// first we calculate the means //
//////////////////////////////////
for  (i  = 1; i <= len; i++) {
   oneSum += table[i].colOne;
   twoSum += table[i].colTwo;
}
oneMean = oneSum/len;
twoMean = twoSum/len;
///////////////////////////////////////////
// now we calculate the sum of variances //
// and deviations.                       //
///////////////////////////////////////////
for (i = 1; i <= len; i++) {
 table[i].varOne = table[i].colOne - oneMean;
 table[i].varTwo = table[i].colTwo - twoMean;
   variance += table[i].varOne* table[i].varTwo;
   devOne += table[i].varOne * table[i].varOne;
   devTwo += table[i].varTwo* table[i].varTwo;
}
///////////////////////////////////////////////////
// finally we calculate the degree of correlation //
///////////////////////////////////////////////////
corr = variance/(Math.sqrt(devOne)* Math.sqrt(devTwo));
frames[0].document.forms[0].Output.value = "Correlation = " + corr;
}
```

```
function gatherData() {
var i = 0;
var j;
////////////////////////////////////////////////
// first, initialize a 2D array to hold that //
// data and input the data into the array.   //
////////////////////////////////////////////////
table = new MakeArray(len);
for (i = 1; i <= len; i++) {
   table[i] = new columns(0,0,0,0);
}
for (i = 1; i <= len; i++) {
   table[i].colOne = 0;
   table[i].colTwo = 0;
   table[i].varOne = 0;
   table[i].varTwo = 0;
}
for (i = 1; i <= len; i++) {
   with (frames[1].document.forms[0]) {
   table[i].colOne = parseFloat(elements[2*(i-1)].value);
   table[i].colTwo = parseFloat(elements[(2*(i-1))+1].value);
   }
}
}
function columns(c1, c2, v1, v2) {
   this.colOne = c1;
   this.colTwo = c2;
   this.varOne = v1;
   this.varTwo = v2;
}

function MakeArray(n) {
this.length = n;
for (i = 1; i  <=n; i++) {
   this[i] = 0;
}
return this;
}
```

# Charting New Territory

ActiveX controls like the Chart control can be included within a Web page using the <OBJECT> tag. Giving a complete specification for an ActiveX control is complex. Each control must have a CLASSID specified as an attribute, can take an ID attribute that functions like the NAME attribute in a conventional HTML tag, and takes other attributes to specify the control's size and location within the document.

None of these features determine how an ActiveX control will behave. The control's behavior is determined by a list of parameters specified by <PARAM> tags placed between the <OBJECT></OBJECT> tags. While the attributes of the <OBJECT> tag are fairly uniform from control to control, the parameters are unique to each control.

All of these ActiveX control features threaten to become unmanageable for the programmer. To keep the task manageable, we need to keep JScript's object-oriented approach in mind, and we need to enlist some help. Because an ActiveX control is an object, we need to program it differently from how we program other objects. Because it is a complex object, we need some object-management help in the form of the ActiveX Control Pad.

Suppose that we have a conventional HTML forms object that we want to use in a document, and we want to make the behavior of the forms object conditional on prior results of the program. Typically, we would create a function to write the HTML for the object into a document, and pass as parameters to the function any variables on which the object's configuration will depend.

This is exactly how the data-input columns were created in the correlation program. We don't know ahead of time how the user will want to label these, and we don't know how many data items will be needed in each column. By writing the HTML form out from a function, we can get user input on these unknowns, and pass this information on to condition the function's output on the basis of user input.

Utilizing an ActiveX control is not so very different. Each ActiveX control has a default behavior, just as each HTML object has a default behavior. Some features of an ActiveX control can be changed by setting parameters, just as some features of an HTML object can be changed. If these changes will depend on user input, we can follow the same procedure we would follow with a conventional HTML object. We will make a function that writes the ActiveX Control tags to a document, and pass to that function any variables on which the output should depend.

The hardest part of this process is understanding the default behavior of ActiveX controls. This step in the process is greatly simplified by using the ActiveX Control Pad. Opening up the Control Pad automatically loads a blank HTML document. If we then select "Insert ActiveX Control" as an option, a window opens up showing

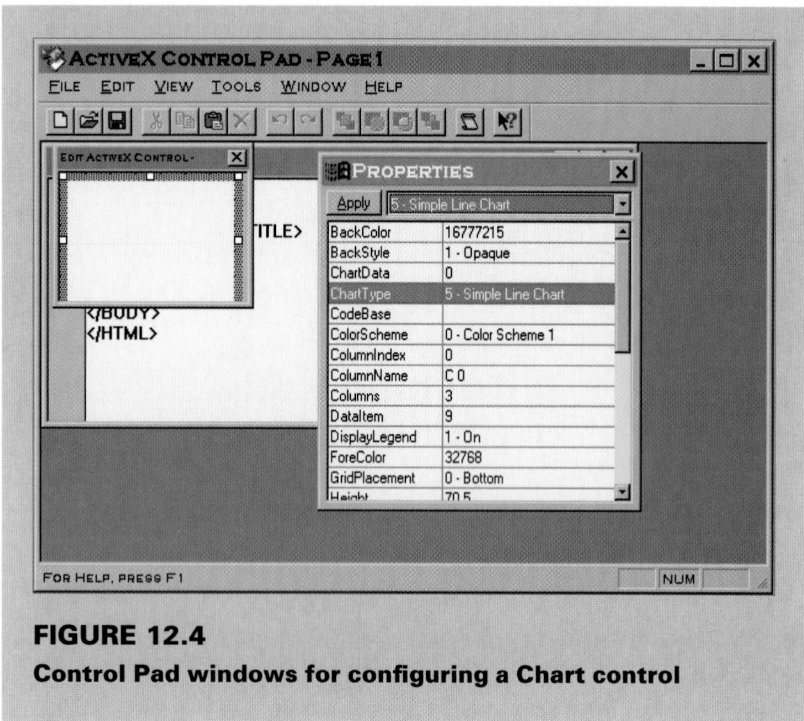


**FIGURE 12.4**

**Control Pad windows for configuring a Chart control**

a full list of ActiveX controls installed on that computer. If we select one — in our case, the Chart control — then two further windows open up: see Figure 12.4. One window shows the size and position of the control within the HTML document; this window corresponds to the attributes that can be set within the <OBJECT> tag. Setting the attributes is simply a matter of clicking and dragging to get the size and location that you want. The second window shows a list of parameters and their current values; this window corresponds to the attributes that can be set for a <PARAM> tag between the <OBJECT></OBJECT> tags. Clicking on any parameter displays its value in the menu bar at the top of the window, and clicking on the menu bar displays a pop-up menu of possible values for that attribute. Figure 12.4 shows that the Chart control allows many different kinds of charts and graphs to be displayed. Each is simply a different parameter value of the Chart control.

By simply pointing, clicking, and dragging, you can easily set a size and location for a control, and try out different parameter values to find those that suit your purposes. Once you're done, the Control Pad automatically generates the corresponding HTML code and inserts it into the current document.

For the correlation program, we know that we want a simple line chart, that it should chart two lines, and that it needs to be large enough to be easily readable. After tinkering with the settings a bit, we get the chart shown in Figure 12.5, which has roughly the characteristics we are looking for.

Here is the HTML code that the ActiveX Control Pad automatically generates for the display shown in Figure 12.5:

```
<HTML>
<HEAD>
<TITLE>New Page</TITLE>
```

```
</HEAD>
<BODY>

<OBJECT ID="iechart1" WIDTH=480 HEIGHT=280
 CLASSID="CLSID:FC25B780-75BE-11CF-8B01-444553540000">
    <PARAM NAME="_ExtentX" VALUE="12700">
    <PARAM NAME="_ExtentY" VALUE="7408">
    <PARAM NAME="Rows" VALUE="4">
    <PARAM NAME="Columns" VALUE="2">
    <PARAM NAME="ChartType" VALUE="5">
    <PARAM NAME="Data[0][0]" VALUE="9">
    <PARAM NAME="Data[0][1]" VALUE="10">
    <PARAM NAME="Data[1][0]" VALUE="7">
    <PARAM NAME="Data[1][1]" VALUE="11">
    <PARAM NAME="Data[2][0]" VALUE="6">
    <PARAM NAME="Data[2][1]" VALUE="12">
    <PARAM NAME="Data[3][0]" VALUE="11">
    <PARAM NAME="Data[3][1]" VALUE="13">
    <PARAM NAME="HorizontalAxis" VALUE="0">
```

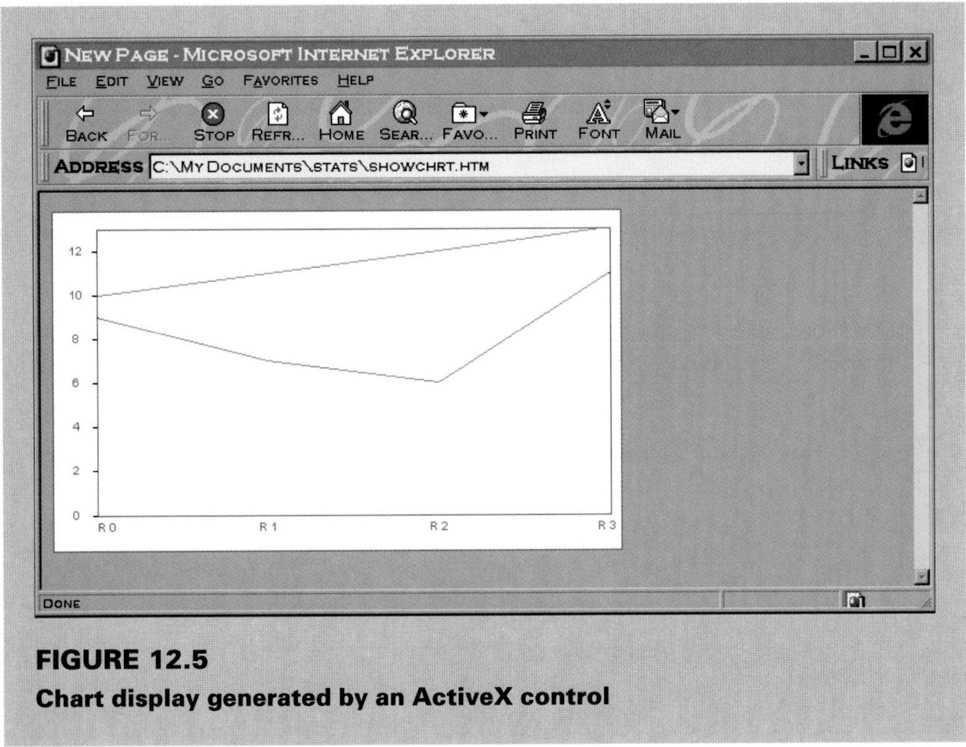


**FIGURE 12.5**
**Chart display generated by an ActiveX control**

```
    <PARAM NAME="VerticalAxis" VALUE="0">
    <PARAM NAME="hgridStyle" VALUE="0">
    <PARAM NAME="vgridStyle" VALUE="0">
    <PARAM NAME="ColorScheme" VALUE="0">
    <PARAM NAME="BackStyle" VALUE="1">
    <PARAM NAME="Scale" VALUE="100">
    <PARAM NAME="DisplayLegend" VALUE="0">
    <PARAM NAME="BackColor" VALUE="16777215">
    <PARAM NAME="ForeColor" VALUE="32768">
</OBJECT>

</BODY>
</HTML>
```

This is not the sort of HTML code you would want to compose by hand. For the correlation program, we will need a function that generates this sort of HTML code dynamically. Fortunately, the ActiveX Control Pad has given us an excellent blueprint for a first draft.

We know from the Control Pad that Chart Type 5 is a simple line chart. For this type of chart, the number of columns corresponds to the number of lines that will be drawn on the chart, so we want this value to be 2. The number of rows will be variable, depending on user input, so the line that now says

```
<PARAM NAME="Rows" VALUE="4">
```

will need to have "4" replaced with the value of a variable taken from prior input in the program. Looking back at our earlier code, we can see that, in fact, this is the "len" variable.

The actual data points on the graph are set by lines like the following:

```
<PARAM NAME="Data[0][0]" VALUE="9">
<PARAM NAME="Data[0][1]" VALUE="10">
```

These lines say that column 0 has the value (0,9) on the graph, and that column 1 has the value (0,10) on the graph. In other words, the first line starts at data point (0,9) and the second line starts at data point (0,10). These pairs of lines will have to have their values set by variables taken from user input. For the correlation program we would replace "9" with table[1].colOne and we would replace "10" with table[1].colTwo. The number of pairs of such lines that we need will also be variable; again, this should correspond to the "len" variable.

We now have a plan for the chartit() function. The function will consist of a series of writeln() statements, which will write out HTML code that is mostly identical to the HTML the ActiveX Control Pad provided above. It will differ in two respects. First, the number of rows will be set by the "len" variable. Second, the data parameters will be set by the values of the table[] array, and the number of pairs of data-parameter statements will be equal to the value of "len." This output can most easily be generated using a "for" loop.

Figure 12.6 displays the dynamically generated chart, charting points scored per game against number of wins. The complete code for the chartit() function is given below.

```
function chartit() {
var newWin = window.open("","");
newWin.document.open();
with (newWin.document) {
writeln("<HTML><HEAD><TITLE>Data Chart</TITLE></HEAD><BODY>");
writeln("<OBJECT ID=\"iechart1\" WIDTH=480 HEIGHT=280");
writeln(" CLASSID=\"CLSID:FC25B780-75BE-11CF-8B01-444553540000\">");
writeln("    <PARAM NAME=\"_ExtentX\" VALUE=\"12700\">");
writeln("    <PARAM NAME=\"_ExtentY\" VALUE=\"7408\">");
```

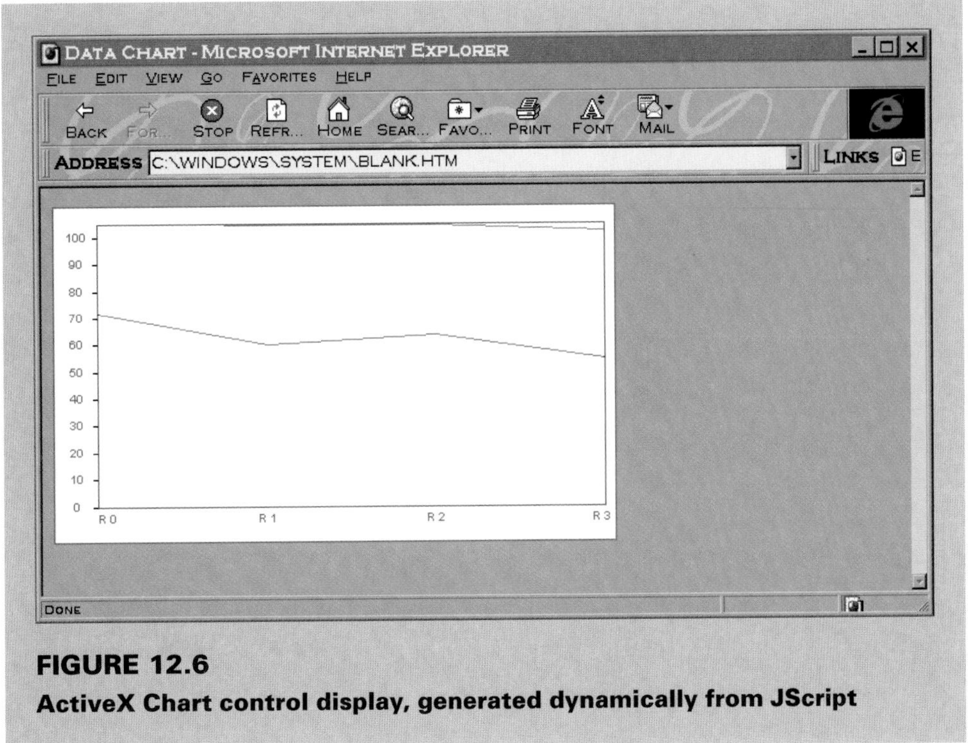


**FIGURE 12.6**
**ActiveX Chart control display, generated dynamically from JScript**

```
writeln("    <PARAM NAME=\"Rows\" VALUE=\"" + len + "\">");
writeln("    <PARAM NAME=\"Columns\" VALUE=\"2\">");
writeln("    <PARAM NAME=\"ChartType\" VALUE=\"5\">");
for (i = 0; i < len; i++) {
   write("    <PARAM NAME=\"Data[" + (i));
   write("][0]\" VALUE=\"");
   writeln(table[i+1].colOne + "\">");
   write("    <PARAM NAME=\"Data[" + (i));
   write("][1]\" VALUE=\"");
   writeln(table[i+1].colTwo + "\">");
}
writeln("   <PARAM NAME=\"HorizontalAxis\" VALUE=\"0\">");
writeln("   <PARAM NAME=\"VerticalAxis\" VALUE=\"0\">");
writeln("    <PARAM NAME=\"hgridStyle\" VALUE=\"0\">");
 writeln("   <PARAM NAME=\"vgridStyle\" VALUE=\"0\">");
writeln("    <PARAM NAME=\"ColorScheme\" VALUE=\"0\">");
writeln("    <PARAM NAME=\"BackStyle\" VALUE=\"1\">");
writeln("    <PARAM NAME=\"Scale\" VALUE=\"100\">");
writeln("    <PARAM NAME=\"DisplayLegend\" VALUE=\"0\">");
writeln("    <PARAM NAME=\"BackColor\" VALUE=\"16777215\">");
writeln("    <PARAM NAME=\"ForeColor\" VALUE=\"32768\">");
writeln("</OBJECT></BODY></HTML>");
}
newWin.document.close();
}
```

What we have demonstrated here could be done with any ActiveX control. ActiveX controls really are just an extension of HTML, and like any other HTML elements their parameters can be set dynamically by JScript. The reverse is also true: some ActiveX controls will have events defined for them, and those events can call JScript event handlers.

While ActiveX Web-page designs presently exclude most Netscape Navigator users, these designs provide powerful enhancements to your Web pages. You will see a close affinity between the ActiveX controls available now and the OLE objects you have encountered in traditional Microsoft applications. This is no accident. Because ActiveX is an extension of OLE, Microsoft will be able to rapidly port the OLE library of objects to ActiveX.

Microsoft's greatest asset is the pool of objects it can draw into ActiveX. The capabilities for active content, real-time response, animation, and interaction that right now are only a gleam in the eyes of Java developers are already being deployed by Microsoft. With JScript, you can extend the reach of your Web designs to include this ActiveX technology.

## Chapter 13

# The Future of JScript

Ironically, the state of scripting languages for the Web today resembles the state of HTML a year ago. At that time HTML had a standards body, but one that was hard-pressed to keep up with changes. Driven by the rapid pace of development at Netscape, browser technology brought new tags and features to HTML before final agreement on standards could be reached. The resulting diversity of HTML implementations created a dilemma for Web developers. Should they develop for the lowest common denominator, appealing to the broadest market base, or should they use the latest tags and features to make the most compelling site, even if it was one not everyone could view?

Today the HTML standards situation has largely resolved itself. Netscape Navigator 3.0 and Microsoft Internet Explorer 3.0 conform, for the most part, to the HTML 3.2 draft standard, and both support the most prevalent feature not included in that draft, namely, frames. Navigator and Internet Explorer at present account for roughly 90 percent of the browser market. While small discrepancies and experiments in implementation will no doubt continue, Web designers have a solid standard they can conform to that will reach the vast majority of Web users. This common denominator should make it possible, if crossplatform compatibility is the goal, to work around any differences.

With scripting languages, designers face new challenges. First of all, learning a scripting language is a necessity, not an option, for serious Web designers. We have seen clear demonstrations in this book of what even relatively simple scripts can bring to a Web page. Sites that lack this kind of active content will soon be considered obsolete. Learning a scripting language is part of the challenge of keeping pace with changes on the Web.

But which scripting language should a Web designer learn? Netscape has JavaScript; Microsoft has JScript and VBScript, and will probably add Perl and TCL; Apple will use OpenDoc to bring the next version of HyperCard to the Web; Sun is working on a scripting language to interface with Java, which may well turn out to be TCL. Licensing agreements may broaden the range of options supported by these and other vendors. All of these languages have some features in common. All are either object-oriented, or have been extended to include object-oriented features. Each is built on an object technology that its sponsoring company would like to make the Web standard.

For Microsoft, that object technology is ActiveX. For Netscape, the technology is ONE. These are both technologies that are on the market now. For Apple, the technology is OpenDoc; for Sun it will be Java Beans. These are technologies that are still under development, but should see full release in the very near future. The winner in the scripting-language competition will depend in large part on the winner in the competition between these underlying object technologies.

While media attention tends to focus on competition between Microsoft and Netscape, this view misses the larger picture. Microsoft has already shown that it can match Netscape's JavaScript with JScript. More importantly, what Microsoft, Apple, and Sun all have in common are object technologies that embrace much more than the Web and a particular Web browser. Each of their respective technologies provides the basis for building an operating system and its attendant applications. Given Apple's much diminished role in the Internet market, the most serious competition is between Microsoft and Sun.

Sun now finds itself to be the target of a strategy it once employed with great success. Ten years ago it was Sun that showed how a smaller machine—the workstation—could do the work of a much larger minicomputer or mainframe machine. Sun solidified its position in the market by making key pieces of its technology into open standards, encouraging other vendors to develop for those standards so they would gain industry-wide acceptance. Ten years later, it's Microsoft's turn to show that a smaller machine—the personal computer—can do the work of a larger machine, the workstation. Furthermore, Microsoft has announced plans to make ActiveX an open standard, which should encourage other vendors to develop ActiveX controls and win this technology wider acceptance.

Microsoft will most likely succeed in its endeavor. Sun's strategy was radical for its time, but has proven to be effective. And Microsoft has two important advantages over Sun. When Sun entered the workstation market, it was an upstart company; Microsoft, on the other hand, is already an industry leader. Sun also began its battle for the workstation market against an established leader, Apollo. Yet Microsoft has no one to dethrone in the contest for Web-object technology—this is a wide-open market.

Most importantly, Microsoft has taken a stand that is more cooperative than competitive. In the face of a successful technology from another company,

Microsoft's approach has been to accept and assimilate. Thus ActiveX does not directly compete with Java, but instead supports Java applets running in Internet Explorer. Similarly, Internet Explorer 3.0 incorporates JavaScript, in the form of JScript, alongside VBScript as a scripting interface for Internet Explorer.

HTML evolved from a common root. Thus even when extensions to HTML were implemented that not all browsers supported, it was always possible to go back to the root and design for the least common denominator. Scripting languages have evolved independently, rather than from a common root, so there is no least common denominator. The best strategy a Web developer can follow is to design for the most common denominator.

Clearly the most common denominator is JScript. Well-designed JScript should run successfully on both Netscape Navigator and Internet Explorer, covering the vast majority of the present browser market. The same claim could be made for JavaScript; JScript is, after all, an open implementation of JavaScript. Yet JScript's support for ActiveX controls, as we have seen in the previous chapter, already gives JScript a broader application domain than JavaScript. That domain will broaden even further in the future.

The ActiveX Scripting Interface can support any scripting language implemented to conform to that interface. Thus the choice to learn JScript is an open choice, not a limiting choice. JScript can serve as an introduction to scripting for ActiveX, preparing the programmer to learn other scripting languages for the ActiveX interface if need be. A programmer who has worked with several JScript programs involving ActiveX controls, like the correlation program from the previous chapter, has a familiarity with ActiveX that will make the transition to VBScript much easier. A programmer who has only worked with JavaScript will find VBScript to be a much less familiar environment.

JScript also has fewer limits, because it is a true object-based language. A scripting language like Perl may have object-oriented features added on, but they are not essential to the structure of the language. While JScript is not a full-featured language—it lacks classes and inheritance, for example—the features it does have are genuinely object-oriented. Because the Web is inherently interactive and event-driven, an object-oriented approach fits most naturally with the structure of the Web.

JScript's most exciting prospects lie outside the confines of the Web browser. Microsoft is moving toward a more seamless integration with the desktop and the Internet. Part of this will come about through a gradual convergence of Windows 95 and Internet Explorer. Under Internet Explorer 4.0, for example, the Internet will show up as just another branch on your computer's directory tree. Adding bookmarks in Explorer will look the same within the directory structure as adding files to a folder.

As the Windows 95 desktop becomes more fully integrated with ActiveX, and as more applications become network-aware through ActiveX, the number of ActiveX hosts with scripting interfaces will proliferate. Today, mastering a client-side scripting language is a Web-development skill; tomorrow, mastering JScript could be an applications-development skill as well.

All of this comes full circle with Microsoft's own Web server, the Internet Information Server (IIS). Many Web servers are replacing or supplementing the conventional CGI method of handling server-side processes with an API (Applications Programming Interface). An API filter looks at incoming document requests, and can be configured to recognize requests for certain types of documents, such as .exe files, as requests to execute a program. The filter then executes the program before the request reaches the server. To the user, the result looks like a conventional CGI process. However, the execution time will be faster and the server load will be lower than with conventional CGI calls. This efficiency comes about because the filter does not have to wait for the server to pass a request to it, and because the filter runs the program as part of the Web-server process already in memory, rather than spawning an entirely new process, as CGI must do.

The IIS includes an ActiveX Internet Server Application Programming Interface (ISAPI) filter. Because this filter is an API, it increases the efficiency of the IIS over that of the IIS using conventional CGI. Because the IIS is an ActiveX host, in principle it can support a scripting interface. When Microsoft releases a new version of the IIS at the end of 1996 or in early 1997, it should include an ActiveX Scripting Interface.

At that point JScript can become a complete Web-programming language. Not only will it continue to be used for client-side scripting, but JScript will also be able to function as a server-side scripting language as well. You will be able to write Web documents with links to .js files that are JScript programs on a server, and have the ISAPI filter run those scripts in response to requests.

This would transform the applications we looked at in Chapter 11. These applications would still require two sets of scripts, one running on the client side and one running on the server. But if the server used was the IIS, then both sets of scripts could be written in JScript.

The idea of a professional Web designer or site manager seemed far-fetched two years ago. Today Web professionals are an established part of the Internet community. Many of these designers and content providers are not schooled in traditional programming languages. Yet the need to have some mastery of programming has never been greater for the Web developer. Competence with HTML is yesterday's news; scripting languages are the Web technology of today. Microsoft has a long tradition of providing tools and resources to make programming more accessible. JScript is a remarkable contribution to that tradition. It is as close to a standard for client-side scripting languages as the Web has right now, and it opens the door to ActiveX scripting on the Web and beyond.

# Appendix A
# JScript Command Reference

This appendix contains a full listing of the commands used in JScript. Detailed explanations of these commands and their usage can be found in Chapters 7, 8, and 9. A brief summary of the more useful commands and their usage can be found in Appendix B.

## Objects

JScript's main hierarchy of objects includes Window, Frame, History, Navigator, Location, Document, Link, Anchor, Form, and Element.

### Window Object

**Contains:**

Properties: name, parent, opener, self, top, defaultStatus, status, frames, history, navigator, location, document

Methods: alert, confirm, prompt, open, close, setTimeout, clearTimeout, navigate

Events: onLoad, onUnload

### Frame Object

**Contains:**

Properties: name, parent, opener, self, top, defaultStatus, status, frames, history, navigator, location, document

Methods: alert, confirm, prompt, open, close, setTimeout, clearTimeout, navigate

Events: onLoad, onUnload

## History Object

**Contains:**

Properties: length

Methods: back, forward, go

## Navigator Object

**Contains:**

Properties: appCodeName, appName, appVersion, userAgent

## Location Object

**Contains:**

Properties: href, protocol, host, hostname, port, pathname, search, hash

## Document Object

**Contains:**

Properties: bgColor, fgColor, linkColor, aLinkColor, vLinkColor, location, lastModified, title, referrer, links, anchors, forms

Methods: write, writeLn, open, close, clear

## Link Object

**Contains:**

Properties: href, protocol, host, hostname, port, pathname, search, hash

Events: onMouseOver, onClick

## Anchor Object

**Contains:**

Properties: name

### Form Object

**Contains:**

Properties: action, encoding, method, target, elements

Methods: submit

Events: onSubmit

### Element Object

**Contains:**

Properties: form, name, value, defaultValue, checked, defaultChecked, length, options, selectedIndex

Events: onClick, onFocus, onBlur, onChange, onSelect

## Data Structures

JScript's basic data structure is the untyped variable. Using JScript's object structure in conjunction with variables, it is possible to define array variable types. JScript also has several specialized objects for manipulating data, including the Math, String, and Date objects.

### Variables

Variables are not typed. Variables must be declared prior to use. Variables can be, but are not required to be, initialized at the time of declaration. So either of the following declaration forms is valid:

```
var abc;
var abc = "def";
```

## Reserved Words

Variables may not be reserved words. Here is the full list of JScript and JavaScript reserved words:

| | | | | |
|---|---|---|---|---|
| abstract | do | if | package | throw |
| Boolean | double | implements | private | throws |
| break | else | import | protected | transient |
| byte | extends | in | public | true |
| case | false | instanceof | return | try |
| catch | final | int | short | var |
| char | finally | interface | static | void |
| class | float | long | super | while |
| const | for | native | switch | with |
| continue | function | new | synchronized | |
| default | goto | null | this | |

## Arrays

This is the standard array-making function for a one-dimensional array:

```
function MakeArray(n) {
//can be used for making arrays of length n,
//starting with 1 as first array element.
this.length = n;
   for (var i = 1; i <= n; i++) {
      this[i] = Ø;
   }
   return this
}
```

```
Array-making functions for two-dimensional array:

function MakeTable(rows, cols) {
   var i;
   this.length = cols;
   for (i = 1; i <= cols; i++) {
      this[rows] = new MakeArray(cols);
```

```
    }
    return this[rows];
}

for (i = 1; i <= rows; i++) {
    tableNew = new MakeTable(i,cols);
}
```

## Special ASCII Characters

Some ASCII characters occurring inside quotes may need to be prefaced with an escape sequence to be read properly. Table A.1 shows valid JScript escape sequences.

## Numbers

JScript permits operations with either base 10, base 8 (octal), or base 16 (hexadecimal) numbers. Octal integers are preceded by a "0."

```
00, 01, 02, 03, 04, 05, 06, 07
```

Hexadecimal numbers are preceded by "0X" or "0x":

```
0X0, 0X1, 0X2, 0X3, 0X4, 0X5, 0X6, 0X7, 0X8, 0X9, 0XA, 0XB, 0XC, 0XD,
0XE, 0XF
```

The A-F values here can also be in lowercase form.

**TABLE A.1 ESCAPE SEQUENCE INTERPRETATIONS**

| Escape Sequence | Interpretation |
|---|---|
| \' | indicates a single quote |
| \" | indicates a double quote |
| \b | indicates a backspace |
| \f | indicates a form feed |
| \n | indicates a new line character |
| \r | indicates a carriage return |
| \t | indicates a tab character |
| \\ | indicates a backslash |

## The String Object

**Contains:**

Properties: length

Methods: toLowerCase(), toUpperCase(), big(), small(), sub(), sup(), blink(), bold(), fixed(), italics(), fontcolor(RGB), fontsize(num), anchor("Name"), link(URL), indexOf(searchString, index), lastIndexOf(searchString, index), CharAt(index), substring(index1, index2)

The Math Object

**Contains:**

Properties: E, LN2, LN10, LOG2E, LOG10E, PI, SQRT1_2, SQRT2

Methods: abs(val), ceil(val), floor(val), max(val1, val2), min(val1, val2), random(), round(val), acos(val), asin(val), atan(val), cos(val), sin(val), tan(val), log(val), exp(val), pow(val1, val2), sqrt(val)

Table A.2 lists the properties of the Math Object, the constant that each property represents, and the value that each property represents that constant with.

**TABLE A.2 PROPERTIES OF THE MATH OBJECT**

| Property | Constant | Value |
|---|---|---|
| Math.E | e, natural log base | 2.718281828459045 |
| Math.LN2 | natural log of 2 | .6931471805599453 |
| Math.LN10 | natural log of 10 | 2.302585092994046 |
| Math.LOG2E | log base 2 of e | 1.4426950408889634 |
| Math.LOG10E | log base 10 of e | .4342944819032518 |
| Math.PI | pi | 3.141592653589793 |
| Math.SQRT1_2 | 1 over square root of 2 | .7071067811865476 |
| Math.SQRT2 | square root of 2 | 1.4142135623730951 |

## The Date Object

**Contains:**

Methods: getDate(), getDay(), getHours(), getMinutes(), getMonth(), getSeconds(), getTime(), getTimezoneOffset(), getYear(), setDate(val), setHours(val), setMinutes(val), setMonth(val), setSeconds(val), setTime(val), setYear(val), parse(), toGMTString(), toLocaleString(), UTC()

# Control Structures

JScript uses the same control structures common to most other high level languages: conditional statements that are some variation on the "if" statement, and loops that can be either "for" or "while" loops.

## Conditionals

**Name**: if

**Description**: Tests for a specified condition, and executes a list of statements if that condition returns a value of "true." The condition is contained within parentheses, (), and must contain an operation that returns a Boolean value. The execution list is contained within braces, {}, and can contain any legal JScript statements.

**Name**: if... else

**Description**: Tests for a specified condition, executes one list of statements if that condition returns a value of "true." Otherwise executes a different list of statements if that condition returns a value of "false." The condition is contained within parentheses, (), and must contain an operation that returns a Boolean value. The execution lists are contained within braces, {}, and can contain any legal JScript statements.

**Name**: abbreviated if...else

**Description**: If the only purpose of an if...else statement is to select one of two values to assign to a variable, then you can use a shorthand format:

variable = (condition) ? value 1 : value 2;

**Name**: with

**Description**: Sets all object references within a list of statements to be relative to a specified object. The object specified must be contained within parentheses, (), and the statement list must be contained within braces, {}.

## Loops

**Name**: for

**Description**: Executes a list of statements repeatedly, and modifies a loop counter by one iteration each time the list of statements is executed. The execution list must be contained within braces, {}. The entire for loop specification must be contained within parentheses, (), and must contain three statements separated by semicolons, (;). The first statement sets the loop counter to an initial value. The second statement specifies a condition the loop counter must satisfy for continuation. The third statement specifies the value by which the loop counter will iterate each time through the loop.

**Name**: while

**Description**: Repeatedly tests for a condition, and executes a body of statements if the condition returns a value of "true." This repetition will continue until the test condition returns a value of false.

**Name**: break

**Description**: Terminates the immediate for loop as if the terminating condition had been satisfied. The counter value remains whatever it was when the break condition occurred.

**Name**: continue

**Description**: The continue statement is a limited form of the break statement. When the program encounters a "continue" within a for loop, it breaks immediately to the end of the loop without executing any of the statements in between, but then resumes normal execution on the next iteration.

# Operations

In addition to the methods of various JScript objects, JScript has a number of built-in operators: arithmetic, bitwise, boolean, comparison, and string operators.

## Arithmetic Operators

**Contains:** addition (+), subtraction (-), multiplication (*), division (/), Modulo (%), Increment (++), Decrement (––), negation (-)

### Bitwise Operators

**Contains:** Bitwise And (&), Bitwise or (|), Bitwise exclusive or (^), Left Shift (<<), Right Shift (>>)

### Boolean Operators

**Contains:** And (&&), Or (||), Not (!)

### Comparison Operators

**Contains:** Equal (==), not equal (!=), greater than (>), greater than or equal to (>=), less than (<), less than or equal to (<=)

### String Operators

**Contains**: Concatenate (+)

## Known Issues Between JScript and JavaScript

Microsoft based its implementation of JavaScript on the version of JavaScript available with Netscape Navigator 2.0, sometimes referred to as JavaScript 1.0. Netscape's current version, 1.1, has some differences with the earlier version and with Microsoft's implementation. In addition, there are some small discrepancies between JScript and Javascript 1.0. These issues will likely change with the next release of Internet Explorer, which should be in late 1996 or early 1997. These issues will also change if Netscape makes JavaScript an open implementation, as they have indicated that they may do.

### Case Sensitivity

JScript's documentation from Microsoft's Scripting Object Model indicates that JScript, unlike VBScript, is case-sensitive about variable names. Thus Abc should be a different variable name than ABC. This would conform to JavaScript's usage, which is also case-sensitive.

But in practice JScript's behavior differs from the documentation. As implemented currently, JScript, like VBScript, ignores case for variable names. This need not cause any problems, provided you use variable names that do not depend on case for uniqueness.

## History Object

Netscape Navigator and Internet Explorer number items on the History list differently. Navigator uses a relative numbering scheme, so that the current URL is always history[0], URLs forward of that are indexed by positive numbers, and URLs back from that are indexed by negative numbers.

Internet Explorer uses an absolute numbering scheme, so that the first URL on the list is history[0], the second is history[1], etc.

## Form Elements Array

At present form elements in Internet Explorer can be accessed only by name, not by array index number. This is a known bug and should be corrected in the next release of Internet Explorer.

## Cookies

Netscape Navigator permits up to 20 cookies to be accessed by JavaScript. Internet Explorer permits only one cookie to be accessed by JScript.

## Date Last Modified

Internet Explorer always returns the current date and time for date last modified. This is a known bug and should be corrected in the next release of Internet Explorer.

## Referrer

Internet Explorer always returns the current URL for the referrer property. This is a known bug and should be corrected in the next release of Internet Explorer.

## Navigator 2 to Navigator 3 Changes

When Microsoft developed JScript, the only browser model it had to work with was Netscape Navigator 2.0. Netscape made some changes between version 2.0 to version 3.0 of Navigator, and added some new objects to the JavaScript object model. None of these changes or objects are present in Internet Explorer 3.0.

# Appendix B
# JScript Quick Reference

This appendix is intended to provide a quick overview of the most-used features of JScript. If you have a simple question, check here first, and then in Appendix A. More-involved reference questions can probably be answered in chapters 7, 8, and 9.

## Outline of the Object Hierarchy

```
Window
top.frames[]
     .history
     .navigator
     .location
     .document.link
          .anchor
          .link
          .forms[].elements[]
```

## Arrays

Standard array-making function for one-dimensional array:

```
function MakeArray(n) {
//can be used for making arrays of length n,
//starting with 1 as first array element.
this.length = n;
   for (var i = 1; i <= n; i++) {
      this[i] = Ø;
   }
   return this
}
```

Array-making functions for two-dimensional array:

```
function MakeTable(rows, cols) {
   var i;
   this.length = cols;
   for (i = 1; i <= cols; i++) {
      this[rows] = new MakeArray(cols);
   }
   return this[rows];
}

for (i = 1; i <= rows; i++) {
   tableNew = new MakeTable(i,cols);
}
```

## The String Object

Useful string-manipulation methods:

**Name**: indexOf(searchString, index)

**Description**: Attempts to match a search string to the target string as a substring of the target string. If a match is found, this method returns the index of the character in the target string that begins the first match.

**Name**: lastIndexOf(searchString, index)

**Description**: This method is identical to the previous method, except that the search scans from the end of the target string to the beginning looking for a match.

**Name**: charAt(index)

**Description**: Finds the character at the indexed point in the target string, and returns that character.

**Name**: substring(index1, index2)

**Description**: Returns a substring of the target string. The substring begins with the character in the target string at index1, and ends with the character in the target string just before index2.

# The Date Object

A new Date object can be created with:

```
val = new Date();
```

Some of the common methods applied to a Date object include:

```
getDate() //gets the day of the month as an integer.
getDay() //gets the day of the week as an integer.
//Sunday = Ø;
getHours() //gets the current of 24 hours.
getMinutes() //gets the current minute.
getMonth() //gets the current month as an integer.
//January = Ø.
getSeconds() //gets the current number of seconds.
```

# Control Structures

If statement:

```
if (condition) {
   statement 1;
   statement 2;
   statement 3;
   .
   .
   .
   statement n.
}
```

If... else statement:

```
if (condition) {
   statement 1;
   statement 2;
   statement 3;
   .
   .
   .
   statement n;
```

```
} else {
   alternate statement 1;
   alternate statement 2;
   alternate statement 3;
   .
   .
   .
   statement n;
}
```

Abbreviated if...else

```
variable = (condition) ? value 1 : value 2;
```

For loop:

```
for (variable = start; variable test condition; variable iteration) {
   statement 1;
   statement 2;
   statement 3;
   .
   .
   .
   statement n;
}
```

While loop:

```
while (condition) {
   statement 1;
   statement 2;
   statement 3;
   .
   .
   .
   statement n;
}
```

# Operations

+, -, *, /: arithmetic operations.

==, !=, <=, >=, <, >: Boolean operations.

# Appendix C
# ActiveX Resources

ActiveX is a rapidly changing technology. The best resources for keeping pace with ActiveX will be on line. The following is a list of the most important ActiveX links on the World Wide Web, together with some brief descriptions.

## Microsoft ActiveX Resources

**http://www.microsoft.com/activex** is the home page for ActiveX on the Microsoft Web site, and links to most of the other ActiveX pages can be found from here.

**http://www.microsoft.com/workshop/author/cpad** is the home page for the ActiveX Control Pad. Including ActiveX controls on your Web page can be an ordeal without the Control Pad. These pages describe it, provide a tutorial in using it, and provide a link for downloading the Control Pad.

**http://www.microsoft.com/intdev** is the home page for the Microsoft Site Builder Workshop. Since ActiveX is the technology Microsoft is using to build Internet awareness into its applications and operating systems, this area of their Web site is almost entirely devoted to ActiveX.

**http://www.microsoft.com/intdev/sdk** is the place to find out about the ActiveX SDK (Software Development Kit), for those who want to really get under the hood of the technology and who aren't afraid to dabble in C++ code. These pages describe the kit and provide documentation to using it.

**http://www.microsoft.com/msdownload/activex.htm** is for the really bold; those of you who want to download the ActiveX SDK can do so from this page.

## Other ActiveX Resources

**ACTIVEX.COM — The Way to Find ActiveX Controls on the Internet**

Located at http://www.activex.com, this site is managed by CINET. It provides a comprehensive list of companies working on ActiveX technology, with links to samples of ActiveX pages. Links to some downloadable samples are also provided.

**ActiveX Journal for HTML Writers**

Located at http://www.folkarts.com/journals/activex, this is a subscription based Web site. Subscription rates vary depending on the level of resources you want access to, but start at about $50 per year. This is a good site for news and information on current ActiveX developments.

**NCompass Labs Inc.**

Located at http://www.ncompasslabs.com. NCompass provides the ActiveX plug-in for Netscape Navigator. Although Navigator 3.0 will run under Windows 3.1 and support JavaScript, the ActiveX plug-in requires that Navigator run under Windows 95 or Windows NT 4.0.

**The W3 Consortium: Draft Specification for Inserting Objects into HTML**

Located at http://www.w3.org/pub/WWW/TR/WD-object.html. Microsoft is working hard to have the <OBJECT> tag made part of the official HTML specification. Microsoft's intention is to make ActiveX an open standard that is overseen by an independent standards body. Getting the <OBJECT> tag accepted as part of the HTML standard would be a big step in that direction that would benefit the Internet community at large. In the mean time, this draft provides the best source of information regarding Internet Explorer 3.0's use of the <OBJECT> tag.

## Appendix D

# What's on the CD-ROM?

The CD-ROM included with this book should provide you with all of the basic development tools needed to learn how to bring JScript's active content to your Web pages. On the CD-ROM you will find:

- **Scripts.** All of the scripts developed in this book are included on the CD-ROM. You will find them organized in directories by chapter, and each directory should contain all of the files needed to run that script. These scripts can also be viewed in action on the Web site for this book, at http://www.kudonet.com/~markst/jscript. This site should have the most current versions of these scripts and corrections for any bugs that have been found.
- **Internet Explorer.** The CD-ROM includes Internet Explorer 3.0, the final release of the 32-bit version. This will run on either Windows 95 or Windows NT. This browser is an ActiveX host and fully supports JScript; you can test all the scripts you write using this browser. Internet Explorer 3.0 for Windows 3.1 is only just now in beta release, and so is not included on the CD-ROM. You can download it from the Microsoft Web site at http://www.microsoft.com.
- **ActiveX Control Pad and HTML Layout Control.** In Chapter 2 and Chapter 12 we saw that Windows 95 offers the prospect of extending JScript's reach with ActiveX controls. Programming ActiveX controls is no easy task, however, and the best way to develop code for using ActiveX controls is with the help of Microsoft's ActiveX Control Pad.
- **Internet Information Server.** Microsoft's Internet Information Server (IIS) is a powerful and full-featured Internet hosting application. At 500MB for a full installation, its features are too numerous to list here. Anyone interested in experimenting with combined client-side scripting and server-side processing as illustrated in Chapter 11 will find the server useful. The server will be even more useful when Microsoft has finished extending JScript to be a server side scripting language as well.

# Index

## C

# D



# E

## F



## G



## H

# I



# J



# K

## L



## M



## N

# O



# P



# Q

## R



## S

## T



## U



## V



## W

## ■ END-USER LICENSE AGREEMENT

**READ THIS AGREEMENT CAREFULLY BEFORE BUYING THIS BOOK. BY BUYING THE BOOK AND USING THE PROGRAM LISTINGS, CD-ROM, AND PROGRAMS REFERRED TO BELOW, YOU ACCEPT THE TERMS OF THIS AGREEMENT.**

The program listings included in this book and the programs included on the CD-ROM contained in the package on the opposite page ("CD-ROM") are proprietary products of Macmillan Computer Publishing USA and/or third party suppliers ("Suppliers"). The program listings and programs are hereinafter collectively referred to as the "Programs." Macmillan Computer Publishing USA and the Suppliers retain ownership of the CD-ROM and copyright to the Programs, as their respective interests may appear. The Programs and the copy of the CD-ROM provided are licensed (not sold) to you under the conditions set forth herein.

License. You may use the CD-ROM on any compatible computer, provided that the CD-ROM is used on only one computer and by one user at a time.

Restrictions. You may not commercially distribute the CD-ROM or the Programs or otherwise reproduce, publish, or distribute or otherwise use the CD-ROM or the Programs in any manner that may infringe any copyright or other proprietary right of Macmillan Computer Publishing USA, the Suppliers, or any other party or assign, sublicense, or otherwise transfer the CD-ROM or this agreement to any other party unless such party agrees to accept the terms and conditions of this agreement. This license and your right to use the CD-ROM and the Programs automatically terminates if you fail to comply with any provision of this agreement.

**U.S. GOVERNMENT RESTRICTED RIGHTS.** The CD-ROM and the programs are provided with **RESTRICTED RIGHTS**. Use, duplication, or disclosure by the Government is subject to restrictions as set forth in subparagraph (c)(1)(ii) of the Rights in Technical Data and Computer Software Clause at DFARS (48 CFR 252.277-7013). The Proprietor of the compilation of the Programs and the CD-ROM is Macmillan Computer Publishing USA, 5903 Christie Avenue, Emeryville, CA 94608.

Limited Warranty. Macmillan Computer Publishing USA warrants the physical CD-ROM to be free of defects in materials and workmanship under normal use for a period of 30 days from the purchase date. If Macmillan Computer Publishing USA receives written notification within the warranty period of defects in materials or workmanship in the physical CD-ROM, and such notification is determined by Macmillan Computer Publishing USA to be correct, Macmillan Computer Publishing USA will, at its option, replace the defective CD-ROM or refund a prorata portion of the purchase price of the book. **THESE ARE YOUR SOLE REMEDIES FOR ANY BREACH OF WARRANTY**.

**EXCEPT AS SPECIFICALLY PROVIDED ABOVE, THE CD-ROM AND THE PROGRAMS ARE PROVIDED "AS IS" WITHOUT ANY WARRANTY OF ANY KIND. NEITHER MACMILLAN COMPUTER PUBLISHING USA NOR THE SUPPLIERS MAKE ANY WARRANTY OF ANY KIND AS TO THE ACCURACY OR COMPLETENESS OF THE CD-ROM OR THE PROGRAMS OR THE RESULTS TO BE OBTAINED FROM USING THE CD-ROM OR THE PROGRAMS AND NEITHER MACMILLAN COMPUTER PUBLISHING USA NOR THE SUPPLIERS SHALL BE RESPONSIBLE FOR ANY CLAIMS ATTRIBUTABLE TO ERRORS, OMISSIONS, OR OTHER INACCURACIES IN THE CD-ROM OR THE PROGRAMS. THE ENTIRE RISK AS TO THE RESULTS AND PERFORMANCE OF THE CD-ROM AND THE PROGRAMS IS ASSUMED BY THE USER. FURTHER, NEITHER MACMILLAN COMPUTER PUBLISHING USA NOR THE SUPPLIERS MAKE ANY REPRESENTATIONS OR WARRANTIES, EITHER EXPRESS OR IMPLIED, WITH RESPECT TO THE CD-ROM OR THE PROGRAMS, INCLUDING BUT NOT LIMITED TO, THE QUALITY, PERFORMANCE, MERCHANTABILITY, OR FITNESS FOR A PARTICULAR PURPOSE OF THE CD-ROM OR THE PROGRAMS. IN NO EVENT SHALL MACMILLAN COMPUTER PUBLISHING USA OR THE SUPPLIERS BE LIABLE FOR DIRECT, INDIRECT, SPECIAL, INCIDENTAL, OR CONSEQUENTIAL DAMAGES ARISING OUT THE USE OF OR INABILITY TO USE THE CD-ROM OR THE PROGRAMS OR FOR ANY LOSS OR DAMAGE OF ANY NATURE CAUSED TO ANY PERSON OR PROPERTY AS A RESULT OF THE USE OF THE CD-ROM OR THE PROGRAMS, EVEN IF MACMILLAN COMPUTER PUBLISHING USA OR THE SUPPLIERS HAVE BEEN SPECIFICALLY ADVISED OF THE POSSIBILITY OF SUCH DAMAGES. NEITHER MACMILLAN COMPUTER PUBLISHING USA NOR THE SUPPLIERS ARE RESPONSIBLE FOR ANY COSTS INCLUDING, BUT NOT LIMITED TO, THOSE INCURRED AS A RESULT OF LOST PROFITS OR REVENUE, LOSS OF USE OF THE CD-ROM OR THE PROGRAMS, LOSS OF DATA, THE COSTS OF RECOVERING SOFTWARE OR DATA, OR THIRD-PARTY CLAIMS. IN NO EVENT WILL MACMILLAN COMPUTER PUBLISHING USA'S OR THE SUPPLIERS' LIABILITY FOR ANY DAMAGES TO YOU OR ANY OTHER PARTY EVER EXCEED THE PRICE OF THIS BOOK. NO SALES PERSON OR OTHER REPRESENTATIVE OF ANY PARTY INVOLVED IN THE DISTRIBUTION OF THE CD-ROM IS AUTHORIZED TO MAKE ANY MODIFICATIONS OR ADDITIONS TO THIS LIMITED WARRANTY.**

**MACMILLAN COMPUTER PUBLISHING USA'S LICENSOR(S) MAKES NO WARRANTIES, EXPRESS OR IMPLIED, INCLUDING WITHOUT LIMITATION THE IMPLIED WARRANTIES OF MERCHANTABILITY AND FITNESS FOR A PARTICULAR PURPOSE, REGARDING THE SOFTWARE. MACMILLAN COMPUTER PUBLISHING USA'S LICENSOR(S) DOES NOT WARRANT, GUARANTEE OR MAKE ANY REPRESENTATIONS REGARDING THE USE OR THE RESULTS OF THE USE OF THE SOFTWARE IN TERMS OF ITS CORRECTNESS, ACCURACY, RELIABILITY, CURRENTNESS OR OTHERWISE. THE ENTIRE RISK AS TO THE RESULTS AND PERFORMANCE OF THE SOFTWARE IS ASSUMED BY YOU. THE EXCLUSION OF IMPLIED WARRANTIES IS NOT PERMITTED BY SOME JURISDICTIONS. THE ABOVE EXCLUSION MAY NOT APPLY TO YOU.**

**IN NO EVENT WILL MACMILLAN COMPUTER PUBLISHING USA'S LICENSOR(S), AND THEIR DIRECTORS, OFFICERS, EMPLOYEES OR AGENTS (COLLECTIVELY MACMILLAN COMPUTER PUBLISHING USA'S LICENSOR) BE LIABLE TO YOU FOR ANY CONSEQUENTIAL, INCIDENTAL OR INDIRECT DAMAGES (INCLUDING DAMAGES FOR LOSS OF BUSINESS PROFITS, BUSINESS INTERRUPTION, LOSS OF BUSINESS INFORMATION, AND THE LIKE) ARISING OUT OF THE USE OR INABILITY TO USE THE SOFTWARE EVEN IF MACMILLAN COMPUTER PUBLISHING USA'S LICENSOR HAS BEEN ADVISED OF THE POSSIBILITY OF SUCH DAMAGES. BECAUSE SOME JURISDICTIONS DO NOT ALLOW THE EXCLUSION OR LIMITATION OF LIABILITY FOR CONSEQUENTIAL OR INCIDENTAL DAMAGES, THE ABOVE LIMITATIONS MAY NOT APPLY TO YOU.**

Some states do not allow the exclusion or limitation of implied warranties or limitation of liability for incidental or consequential damages, so the above limitation or exclusion may not apply to you.

General. Macmillan Computer Publishing USA and the Suppliers retain all rights not expressly granted. Nothing in this license constitutes a waiver of the rights of Macmillan Computer Publishing USA or the Suppliers under the U.S. Copyright Act or any other Federal or State Law, international treaty, or foreign law.